Spiritual Enterprise

By the same author

American Spirit: Visions of a New Corporate Culture

Barbarians to Bureaucrats: Corporate Life Cycle Strategies

Behavior Management: The New Science of Managing People at Work

Competing in the New Capitalism: How Individuals, Teams and Companies are Creating the New Currency of Wealth

From Management to Leadership

Lawrence M. Miller is editor and co-founder of the *Journal of Organizational Behavior Management*

Spiritual Enterprise

Building Your Business in the Spirit of Service

Lessons in
Moral Leadership and Management
from the
Teachings of the Bahá'í Faith

by
Lawrence M. Miller

George Ronald
Oxford

George Ronald, *Publisher*
Oxford
www.grbooks.com

A catalogue record for this book is available from the British Library

ISBN 978-0-85398-507-5

Printed and bound in Great Britain
by Biddles Ltd, King's Lynn Norfolk

Contents

Acknowledgments

More than 20 years ago the National Spiritual Assembly of the United States asked me to participate on a national committee to explore how the Bahá'í community could address the needs and interests of business people. As far as I can recall we did not accomplish anything in particular. However, we began a process of dialogue in the United States on this subject and that dialogue has continued to this day and been an encouragement to many. I want to acknowledge the encouragement and reinforcement that this institution and other Bahá'í institutions have provided to furthering this dialogue.

I also want to acknowledge the continued promotion of this similar dialogue that has been provided by the European Bahá'í Business Forum (EBBF). George Starcher, in particular, has not only worked tirelessly to develop this forum but has provided personal encouragement and very useful feedback on an early manuscript of this book. Wendi Momen, both a member of the EBBF Governing Board and the editor of this book at George Ronald, Publisher, has been extremely helpful and encouraging.

In addition, Chris Gilbert, David House and Farsheed Ferdowsi all provided helpful feedback and encouragement. Finally, and as usual, my wife Carole was my first editor and support.

Preface

Religion will play an increasing role in our personal and public lives. Religion is on the march in both the East and the West. Religious influence is pushing the traditional boundaries that have separated commercial institutions and practices of faith, while managers and business owners are seeking the unity of their spiritual and business lives.

Extending the boundaries of religious influence is causing anxiety as leaders of government and business are increasingly forthright in expressing the need for principles of religion as a guide to personal behavior and public policies. The pendulum has swung from a time when religion guided all of our affairs, to a time when religion and faith were presumed to be an illegitimate topic for consideration in public institutions. It is now swinging back to a time when we are seeking an integration of personal faith and public life. Only 20 or 30 years ago it was an assumed yet essential rule in western countries that you never discussed religion in a business meeting or in front of a business audience. It was considered an inappropriate invasion of personal space. But times have changed. Increasingly executives, and particularly owners of privately held companies, are refusing to conform to a dividing line between this private and public space. Many executives are willing to publicly state that the purpose of their business life is to serve their God or their faith. Many employees and managers are refusing to engage in practices that they feel are a violation of their personal religious principles. And managers are seeking guidance in the books of their faiths to find answers regarding matters of organization, human resource policies and relationships with customers and suppliers.

The anxiety about the role of religion is caused by a cognitive dissonance. The dissonance is a result of the apparent evidence of a contradiction between religious faith and material progress. Many have come to view the role of religion as one that inhibits rational thinking and scientific and economic progress. We see the most devotedly religious societies in the Middle East, where their interpretation of Islam condemns women to subservient roles and produces an educational system where more time is consumed memorizing Qur'ánic verses than learning math and science. And in the United States local school boards have been consumed by debates over creationism, intelligent design and evolution. Church leaders have decided to impose their expertise on the subjects of evolution, global warming and genetics over scientists trained in those fields, and we wonder whether our schools may be heading on a downward slope of rejecting rationalism in favor of faith-based theories. There is good evidence that a high degree of religiosity is incompatible with economic progress. No Middle Eastern Islamic country appears in the top 50 countries filing patents, while Mongolia appears with 56 patents per million people and South Korea, second on the list of patents per capita after Japan, has 779 per million residents.[1] Economic growth is strongest in the least religious countries such as China, Finland and South Korea, while most of the Latin American and the Middle Eastern countries are at the bottom of the list. No wonder we have a sense of unease as we struggle both to return to a foundation of moral principles yet preserve a culture of equality, pluralism and economic and scientific progress. We are left with a conundrum: is religion good for business? How can I apply my religious values in my workplace without offending others? Is there an inevitable contradiction between economic progress and religion? Is there a necessary contradiction between science and religion?

However, this is not a book of questions. I believe that there are good answers to these questions. I believe that religion – not in all of its forms and expressions but the essence of religion – does not contradict what is good for the progress of business, the economy or science. On the contrary, moral standards not subject to the whims of intellectual fads, the trustworthiness that comes from submission to God, and a world view that places business in the role of contributing to the unfolding of God's plan all have the tendency to enable and enrich our business lives. I believe that religion must conform to the laws of science because truth must, inevitably, be one unified whole, not a chaos of contradictions. I believe that true religion is not what any human being may decide to preach from a pulpit but is found in the essential teaching and the spirit of Jesus, Moses, Buddha, Krishna and the other great religious teachers. That essence is most often corrupted by man's desire to make God conform to his own prejudices and material desires. For this reason religion must, from time to time, be renewed and we must struggle through manmade dogmas to find the purity of God's own teachings.

I also believe that there is no necessary contradiction between the pursuits of material progress, whether in the form of a nation's economy or personal wealth, and the teachings of religion. In fact, it is the great challenge of one's personal spiritual struggle to remain centered in spiritual reality while pursuing success in business. Both material and spiritual strength emerge from this struggle.

In writing a book such as this it is essential that my personal views are honestly stated for what they are: beliefs, derived from my religious faith. If I were a perfect writer and this a perfect book it might, perhaps, represent equally and without bias the views of all religions. While I respect all religions I cannot claim to represent their views with equal clarity or conviction. I am a member of the Bahá'í Faith and I believe the founder, Bahá'u'lláh, and the writings of the other central figures and institutions of this Faith represent a renewal of religion for the modern world.[2] Their teachings speak directly to the issues of economics and enterprise in a way no previous religion has. There is direct guidance on profit sharing, decision-making processes and the role of management and labor. Bahá'u'lláh, living in relatively recent times of the 19th century, was able to address those issues that now face our global economy. These teachings, therefore, are my primary source of guidance and inspiration.

The promise of the Bahá'í Faith is the re-creation of civilization, a new order of life on this planet in which spiritual principles will permeate every aspect of the life of the followers of this Faith and will animate the revitalization of all institutions from the family to those of global governance. The institutions of commerce as well as organizations of government and education will all gradually be guided by new principles and methods that will be in harmony with the animating spirit of this new civilization. Precisely how this will come about is not defined by the writings of the Bahá'í Faith. The principles are laid out with absolute clarity and it remains for the followers of the Faith to engage in the struggle to find the best ways to realize them in their daily life.

This application of spiritual principles will come about through an extensive period of trial and error and it will be encouraged and fueled by dialogue and the exchange of experiences by those engaged in this exploration. No one, at this early stage, can define the best compensation system, given the Bahá'í principle of abolishing the extremes of wealth and poverty, for example, but we can seek to apply this principle in our organizations. No one can with certainty say how the principle of consultation will best be applied in the management of employees in a factory or of software engineers working from distant locations on the Internet, or in the management of learning between students and professors. Yet we can all use our best judgment and seek the application of this critical principle. We will advance through meditation, application, experimentation and dialogue.

The purpose of this book is to advance this dialogue. It is not the purpose of this book to present the one best way to do anything.

The world is torn between the addictive pull of material progress and the longing of the soul for the Kingdom of God on earth. As the armies of McDonald's, Disney and Toyota march forward, the forces of traditional religion call for *jihad* against the apparent demonic force of materialism eating at the roots of traditional cultures. The world will not stay as it is. Cultures will change. The great question facing the people of the planet is whether these two forces – the progress of technology and wealth and the renewal of spiritual community, both possessing potential for good – can be united in a harmonious symphony appealing to people of all cultures.

It is hoped this book will make some small contribution to that process.

Part One

New Principles of Management for a New Age

Some time ago I found myself in Malaysia at a mountaintop resort where I was leading a strategy retreat with my client, the UMW Corporation. As an American consultant I was struck by the realities of global integration while sitting with the senior managers of this Malaysian company that assembles and markets Japanese Toyota cars and Komatsu heavy equipment. The primary strategic issue for this company was responding to the challenge of the removal of trade barriers among Southeast Asian nations, the formation of the Asian Free Trade Association (AFTA) and the new role it will have to play on this more united stage. The managers are half Chinese and half Malay by ethnic background. We were eating dinner in a Korean restaurant while the music pouring too loudly from the stereo was 'The House of the Rising Sun' sung by the British group The Animals. Communication was not a problem because English is the common language of business in Southeast Asia and we easily swapped data files from my laptop to theirs in the common Windows format. The client managers were all familiar with the up and down trends of reengineering and total quality management and were all well versed in the Toyota Production System, the globally accepted benchmark of effective manufacturing process. My Malaysian affiliate consultants were able to share my firm's Lotus Notes database and instantly communicate with my network of consultants in the US and Latin America to receive help solving a problem and access case studies, surveys, agendas and other documents that are the tools of the consulting trade.

This is the reality of global integration and similar scenes are being repeated thousands of times every day. In the scene described above, a relatively normal occurrence, national borders matter little; language barriers have been obliterated; large and small companies operate as one seamless process; information technology links sources of knowledge and experience in a global mind network; and the speed of change is highly compressed. A common business culture is emerging, an integrated global economy is a fact and English is the accepted universal auxiliary language of commerce. While a world economy is a long promoted principle of the Bahá'í Faith, there is no need for its further promotion – only its recognition. Although not complete in breadth or depth of integration, and its implications not yet understood by political leaders, its momentum and acceptance is tantamount to its accomplishment. While there are more than three times the number of nation states today since the founding of the United Nations (191 members versus 51 at its founding) and it appears that there is an emergence of nationalism, there is a paradoxical dominance of globalism. The electronic currency of VISA and American Express care no more for the artificial boundaries of nation states than do acid rain or global warming. The Internet and the massive distribution of every kind of information know no national limitations. Capital moves from individuals to global mutual funds to corporations and back in seconds through fiber optic cable and satellite transmission with no concern for local currencies, translated by computers within a few milliseconds, an operation unnoticed among the thousands of operations handled by any one computer in one second. These are the integrating mechanisms rushing forward to unite the world while governments run behind waving their flags in confusion, pretending to have influence. It matters not whether there are one hundred or one thousand nations.

We now are confronted with a difficulty. These integrating mechanisms of global economy and culture require integrating principles. The advancement of technology without a corresponding advancement in human values and behavior can have disastrous consequences. The human race must learn to manage itself towards higher principles if we are to use our new material power for the good of humankind.

The planet is a whole-system. The planet's economic, environmental and human systems are all sub-systems of the whole. In order to bring order to complex systems one must either impose iron-fisted rule or one must create willingness, a desire, to adhere to common principles that will then allow self-organization around those principles. In order to motivate the mass of humankind those principles cannot simply come from the imagination of some writer or philosopher; they must be derived from some divine source of authority. Those principles have been enunciated by the Bahá'í Faith. I also believe that the models developed by business enterprises – always quick to adopt better ways – can be a stimulus to the adoption of common principles.

The Meaning of 'Spiritual'

We would all like to work within an organization that is guided by spiritual principles and contributes to the development of our own spiritual qualities. I believe that we would all like to work within an organization that does not tear us in different directions, asking us to behave in ways we feel contradict our beliefs or which create internal dissonance between our ideals and required behavior. Within a spiritual enterprise there would be a harmony between our moral or spiritual self and the norms of the organization. Rather than the subtle anxiety created by dissonance between our higher spiritual selves and the demands of the material world, we would experience an energizing harmony like that between two perfectly tuned instruments. The absence of dissonance conserves energy. Harmony creates energy. A spiritual enterprise would, therefore, be energizing and contribute to the development of the capacities of its members.

What does it mean to be *spiritual*? Can an organization possess qualities of the human spirit? These are questions that do not lend themselves to simple answers. I have pondered the definition of the word 'spiritual' for many years without reaching a point of certainty in my own understanding. I think this word has somewhat different meanings for each individual based on each one's background and experience and the degree to which he or she has actually considered the question. I cannot say that I know the one right definition of this word. I do, however, have a number of thoughts about what the word 'spiritual' means and implies.

The first understanding of spiritual comes from a contrast with the material world and with the self. It is easy to understand the material world that we can touch, count, measure and control. As business people we make a product that is made out of material stuff. We know what it costs and how much we charge for it. It is easy to get our hands around. That which is spiritual is the opposite of that. You cannot touch it, measure it, count it and you can't define the process of how you make it, yet it exists. It exists as an attraction of the heart. Does love exist? Does motivating purpose exist? Do some people act for the sole reason to conform to a value or principle despite the personal sacrifice that may entail? Of course they do. You may say, but wait; these are merely emotions or ideas within the mind. To which I say, fine. They are certainly emotions and ideas, yet to the degree to which they are motivated by a view outside of oneself, a perspective gained through meditation, prayer or reflection, they represent a spiritual perspective.

True spirituality is selfless, rather than self-centered. The purpose of prayer or meditation is to attain a perspective beyond oneself, as if detached and looking down on oneself from a higher point of view, able to see oneself in relation to the larger world but with an interest that is beyond the whims of personal desires. To acquire a spiritual perspective is to acquire a perspective other than one determined by habits, conditioning or influences of human persuasion.

Those who practice meditation seek to heighten their spiritual awareness by attaining a peaceful, reflective or meditative state. There is no doubt that this is beneficial. However, there is a different quality to the pursuit of a spiritual state through the vehicle of a religion. All religions say 'rely on God' and 'obey God's teachings'. Prayer, as presented by the major religions, offers not only the quality of meditation but also the quality of reflection on specific principles enunciated by their founders. The purpose is to elevate perspective in a particular direction. That direction is towards the qualities of the soul or the qualities of God. Mercy, justice, compassion and other words are used to describe the many qualities of God. I believe the very purpose of the appearance of a Jesus, Moses or Muhammad in our lives is to make us aware of the qualities of God and thereby give us a spiritual goal to pursue, a demonstration of God's qualities in human form so we may seek to imitate these in our own life. These are the qualities of the soul; these are the spiritual qualities we seek to attain through prayer and meditation. It is the very purpose of all the writings of all the religions to define the characteristics of the soul or the spiritual life.

The attempt to define that which is spiritual is one of those endeavors the benefit of which is in the journey rather than in its end. It is a journey without an end. But by asking the questions, by seeking the meaning of the spiritual life, the muscle is exercised and the capacities are developed. I think the same is true for the concept of spiritual enterprise. We cannot know a final definition and that knowledge, if we found it, would be an illusion. What we can do is engage in the journey, exercise the muscle and thereby enhance our sense of the spiritual and gradually bring our organizations into nearer proximity to those spiritual qualities.

The definition of the spiritual may be very similar to the attempt to define the soul. Of that desire, the founder of the Bahá'í Faith has said the following:

> Wert thou to ponder in thine heart, from now until the end that hath no end, and with all the concentrated intelligence and understanding which the greatest minds have attained in the past or will attain in the future, this divinely ordained and subtle Reality, this sign of the revelation of the All-Abiding, All-Glorious God, thou wilt fail to comprehend its mystery or to appraise its virtue. Having recognized thy powerlessness to attain to an adequate understanding of that Reality which abideth within thee, thou wilt readily admit the futility of such efforts as may be attempted by thee, or by any of the created things, to fathom the mystery of the Living God, the Day Star of unfading glory, the Ancient of everlasting days. This confession of helplessness which mature contemplation must eventually impel every mind to make is in itself the acme of human understanding, and marketh the culmination of man's development.[1]

Therefore the task is to struggle with each principle and with its application to each system of each organization. In other words, a principle such as trustworthiness or honesty is rather easy to understand at the outset but its application to organizational systems is not necessarily simple. In compensation systems, does it mean complete transparency so that every employee knows what everyone earns and thereby can have trust in the system? Does it mean that all information is shared regarding all decisions made by an executive team? Does it mean that all employees have a responsibility to simply trust their managers? I don't think it means any of these things. The application is not so simple. But this is the struggle in which we must now engage.

Competition, Cooperation and Choice

Many who see the deficiencies of our current economic systems decry the evils of competition in the workplace and the economy. Some say that the future economic system, if it is to reflect spiritual virtues, must be based on cooperation and not on competition. Academics, heavily influenced by Marxist and other related ideologies, frequently condemn the competitive nature of the western economic systems. Unfortunately, the only alternative to a competitive system ever devised is the state controlled system, which produced greater poverty, little innovation and poor quality products and services, as well as the constriction of human rights and freedoms. If we are to have a system in which private individuals have the choice to start a business – the very mechanism of innovation and wealth creation – competition is the inevitable and necessary result. It is the nature and regulation of that competition on which we should focus.

I would ask the reader to consider the diverse nature of competition. The discussion about competition versus cooperation is often at such a general level as to be almost meaningless. Both competition and cooperation come in extremely broad and diverse forms and each has different consequences at different times. Consider the difference between two friends who get together after work to play tennis and two armies meeting on a battlefield. The two friends compete fiercely on the tennis court, exerting themselves mightily, and then laugh, shake hands and walk off the court promising to reverse the outcome in the next match. This voluntary competition is enjoyed by both and increases their skill and friendship. Two armies meeting on the battlefield results in consequences that are of an entirely different nature. The understanding of competition is entirely different and the two cannot be discussed rationally as one.

I would also ask the reader to consider the nature of choice. A college selection committee considers applicants and makes a series of choices as to who they will admit. We assume the college, within certain boundaries, has the freedom to make this choice. Similarly, the student has made a choice regarding the colleges he or she wishes to attend. In both cases choice is necessarily accompanied by competition. One cannot exist without the other. Colleges compete to attract the best students by designing attractive programs, an attractive campus and publicizing the accomplishments of their faculty and students. And on the other side, students compete by making themselves attractive to the college. In both cases the college and the student seek some form and degree of excellence in order to be chosen by the other.

Imagine a system in which the college had no choice. For example, colleges had to admit all those students who lived within their county or province – no choice, no competition. And students could not choose. They had to apply to that one college in their county or province. In which set of arrangements would the best education be achieved? In other words, would the advancement of society as a whole through the development of human capacity be best served by the choice–competition model or the no choice–no competition model? There is no doubt in this writer's mind that society is far better served by the competition and freedom to choose that causes both students and colleges to make themselves attractive to the other.

The competition in business is precisely the same. If competition is to be eliminated then choice must end. In each town there will be only one restaurant, one car sold, one home builder, one grocery store, etc. This is the only way to end competition. The moment you are able to choose between two restaurants, two cars you may buy, etc., you have introduced the system of free enterprise and free competition.

Competition and cooperation are often discussed as if one necessarily diminishes the other. In other words, cooperation is only achieved at the expense of competition and vice versa. In fact, there is often high competition and high cooperation, as well as the reverse.

Most sports are team sports. Baseball, football and basketball are all highly cooperative as well as competitive. Cooperation, trusting relationships, are essential to every sport. When we go to the basketball game we are focused on the competition between the two teams. It is likely that we do not notice the cooperative behavior, even though it is critical both within the teams as well as between them. Within each team, each player is trained in a role that is supportive of other players. The point guard's primary function in basketball is to pass the ball to someone else who will score and to set up plays that create opportunities for his teammates. We measure 'assists' for each player each game. Each player has a role, not only to make an individual contribution but to behave in a way that does more than simply add to his own statistics. If a player is overly focused on his own numbers he is likely to become an unpopular player and other members of the team will react in a way that will lessen his own opportunities to score. Therefore cooperation is in the player's own self-interest.

But while we see the cooperative behavior within the team, we may miss that the entire performance requires extreme cooperation between the teams. They agree on the rules and those rules define the cooperation. They agree to give up the ball and hand it to the other team immediately after they score, presumably to give the other team an equal chance. They agree on the boundaries and agree to abide by the judgments of the referee. They even agree to switch sides at half time, just in case one end of the court has an advantage. Cooperation is so common in sports that we barely notice. After every significant victory of an American football team the star quarterback is interviewed and, without fail, the first thing out of his mouth is his credit to the offensive line, without which he couldn't have done it! While he is no doubt sincere, he is also acting out of self-interest. He knows he would be buried out there without the dedicated support of his linemen.

Of course, some sports are individual sports – tennis, golf, swimming, auto racing. However, even in those sports there is a team of supporting actors around the golf or tennis pro. The success of these athletes, much like in the team sports, depends on his or her ability to create cooperation and trust.

It is clear from the example of sports that a high degree of competition does not dictate a low degree of cooperation. Both competition and cooperation may be simultaneously high or low. The interplay of competition and cooperation is similar in business.

How one views competition and cooperation depends to a large degree on whether one makes zero-sum or non-zero-sum assumptions. Non-zero-sum behavior is easily seen in the example of our basketball players. Imagine that there was a fixed amount, a zero-sum, of credit – applause, appreciation or respect afforded to a basketball team. Let's call that amount of credit 100 units. If the star center performs so well that his amount of credit goes up from 20 units to 30 units, the ten unit gain must come from the other players. In this zero-sum competition, the other players are diminished by his success. In other words, this transaction is a win–lose transaction because it is zero-sum – the sum of credit remains the same. It is not hard to imagine the type of behavior this transaction would create within the team. They would compete to the detriment of each other and reduce the probability of the team's victory.

The fact is that credit, or respect, is highly elastic. It is not a fixed or zero-sum. In other words, if the team performs extremely well, they win the NBA championship and the amount of credit expands greatly. If they lose, the amount of credit shrinks. Therefore the real game is a win–win game in which the amount of credit is non-zero-sum or highly elastic. Owing to the realities of this basketball economy (the earning and payoff in appreciation, applause, etc.), the sport generates highly cooperative behavior among the players on a team. The goal of the players is to increase the amount of total credit available to all team members because they know that their amount of credit will increase as a result. Our ability to see that the economy – of the sport in this case but also the larger economy – is non-zero-sum leads us to develop and reward cooperative, trust-based, relationships. Non-zero-sum games lead to unity; zero-sum games lead to disunity. The biggest sport of all is the sport of business and it is also a non-zero-sum game. Wealth is elastic.

Businesses compete with each other while at the same time they cooperate. Within every industry there is cooperation among competitors. Oil companies, car companies, software or computer companies engage in a variety of legal forms of cooperation. They cooperate by agreeing on technical standards that allow the interchangeable use of their products, common safety requirements and language that may be understood by the consumer. Every industry, every profession, has an 'association'. There are associations within the oil industry, semi-conductor industry, publishing industry; there is even the American Truck Stop Owners Association to which I once spoke. What is the purpose of these associations? First, they come together to marshal their forces – in the case of the United States – before Congress and the bureaucracies of Washington. They understand that they have little power divided but considerable power when united. They also come together to share learning and best practices. They even come together to engage in almost ritualistic trust building exercises (golf!) that will allow them to call upon each other if needed. Within each industry competition and cooperation coexist because the members recognize that it is a 'non-zero-sum' game.

All sports are accompanied by rules and referees. These rules and referees do not hinder the competition, rather they facilitate healthy competition. Imagine ten large and athletic basketball players trying to score as often as possible with no rules and no referee.

It would quickly become damaging and not much fun either to play or to watch. The competitors themselves would not want to play in the absence of fair rules and referees. The relationship between business and government must be the same. Business competition without any rules and without fair and consistent enforcement of those rules would exceed the bounds of moderation and would be damaging. In my many years in business I have never heard it argued that there should be no government regulation, only that the regulation should be clear, rational, not excessively burdensome, and fairly administered. Every business person will agree to play by clear and fair rules.

Robert Wright, in his excellent book *Nonzero – The Logic of Human Destiny*,[2] argues that human history and human evolution have a direction. That direction, simply put, is from simple to complex organization, requiring ever wider circles of trust and cooperation. The challenge of unity grows as we move from the simple organization of the family to the complexities of modern organization. He also argues that genetic selection is hard wiring a tendency towards non-zero-sum behavior. It may be hard for us to see the forest for the trees when we are bombarded each night with the miseries and distrust in some corner of the world. Just as we may focus on the competition in sports and fail to see the cooperation, we may fail to see the ever expanding forms of cooperation required for us to survive, and even compete, as a human species.

The nature of competitive–cooperative behavior and the spiritual nature of individuals are inseparable. It is the role of religion to shape the human character towards spiritual attributes. It is those attributes that allow individuals to compete in a manner that leads to human progress and development. If the human character is debased the nature of competition will be debased and destructive. The economic system must allow for healthy competition; government must provide fair rules and just enforcement of rules to facilitate that competition; and the human character must develop in a way that enables healthy competition.

Principles and Practice

The application of Bahá'í principles can be viewed as a matrix, with principles on one axis and management practices on the other. Principles include honesty, unity, a spirit of service, etc. The practices include capital utilization, organization structure, decision-making, etc. Our task is to seek to apply Bahá'í principles to each practice of management. The following chapters are only a start along this journey.

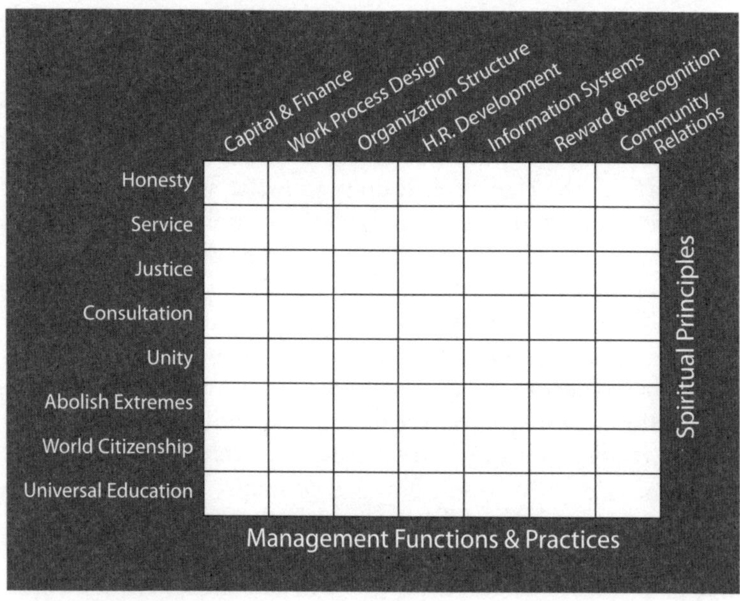

There is another side to the development of a Bahá'í culture of work. There is responsibility on the individual to look within and transform his or her own habits of thought, emotions and behavior. In order to achieve the ideals presented by our writings, we cannot expect a perfect system to be operated perfectly by imperfect individuals. The writings call upon the individual to transform his or her own inner being into a different creature in the work place as well as at home. The following quotation has profound implications for the purpose of commerce and the role of the individual as a consumer, employee or employer.

> All people will have sooner or later to recover, for example, the capacity for contentment, the welcoming of moral discipline, and the devotion to duty that, until relatively recently, were considered essential aspects of being human.[3]

Most economic systems stimulate not contentment but a condition of deprivation and dissatisfaction with one's present condition. Advertising skillfully seeks to stimulate the feelings of deprivation, the creation of need – the need for a new car, a flat belly or a cool drink – a stimulus which, if it were absent, no such need would exist. Only tiny Bhutan has defined a completely different economic goal: 'Bhutan has made an explicit adoption of *Gross National Happiness* (GNH) as its development philosophy. The development of the country is to be guided by this philosophy.'[4] A national philosophy of pursuing and measuring happiness, rather than the increase in production and consumption, would have profound implications for the nature of our economy. Rather than a moral self-discipline, in too many work cultures the individual is doing only what is required to gain material goods and seeking a level of behavior calculated to avoid punishment rather than the higher standard of self-imposed morality. Devotion to duty has been relegated to the status of an out-of-date belief associated with military tradition. The individual, through training, prayer and meditation, must develop these spiritual qualities in order to achieve harmony with an organization operating on Bahá'í principles. There must be a twin-fold process of transformation: a transformation in inner beliefs and spiritual condition and a transformation in the practices of organization and management, each guided by meditation on divinely established principles.

1

Honesty and Trustworthiness

The Foundation of All Virtues

Honesty and trustworthiness are not only the foundation of virtue but of economic activity as well. There is no more self-evident yet intricately complicated principle than that of honesty. The business environment is a great test to this capacity of the individual soul. The merchant is constantly communicating a perception of value – the history of the car, the condition and history of a house, the potential development of a piece of land or the likely appreciation of a stock. The communication is often between one who is expert and one who is not. It is often between one who stands to gain and one who stands to lose. To be dishonest is often very easy and often in one's apparent self-interest. To overcome the temptations of dishonesty one must be detached from one's short-term self-interest and be focused on the value of long-term relationships.

> Beautify your tongues, O people, with truthfulness, and adorn your souls with the ornament of honesty. Beware, O people, that ye deal not treacherously with any one. Be ye the trustees of God amongst His creatures, and the emblems of His generosity amidst His people. They that follow their lusts and corrupt inclinations have erred and dissipated their efforts. They, indeed, are of the lost. Strive, O people, that your eyes may be directed towards the mercy of God, that your hearts may be attuned to His wondrous remembrance, that your souls may rest confidently upon

> His grace and bounty, that your feet may tread the path of His good-pleasure. Such are the counsels which I bequeath unto you. Would that ye might follow My counsels![5]

The business environment is increasingly one in which long-term customer and supplier relationships are essential and are built on trust. The merchant trading in the bazaar of the Middle East was skilled at winning the negotiations by getting the customer to pay as much as possible. The negotiation between customer and supplier was a game played with subtle cultural rules that allowed for a level of dishonesty by both parties. In today's environment, *guaranteed customer satisfaction* is offered by Wal-Mart, L.L. Bean, Home Depot and thousands of other merchants and you can return the item, no questions asked. An Internet search will turn up the medical success rate of hospitals, pharmaceuticals, vitamins, the performance of cars, customer satisfaction of hotels and airlines. Completely unlike the bazaars of the Middle East where the importance of the immediate 'deal' trumped any concern about long-term trust or reputation, the reverse is now true. There are so many mechanisms to share knowledge of merchants, suppliers, restaurants or professionals, there can be no hiding from the good will, the trust, one either generates or destroys. This trust is now the most essential 'capital' of any company.

Companies are all now focused on creating 'brand-equity', the value inherent in a name, a name which can be trusted to represent value. The Toyota Production System, or what has become known as Lean Manufacturing, is built on the creation of long-term and intricately close relationships through the supply chain. In this world class manufacturing model, suppliers invest huge sums to build manufacturing plants next to their customer's plant to provide just-in-time flow of incoming materials. They also share engineering resources, invest time in co-development of component parts and work as one family with their customers to assure continuous uninterrupted flow of materials. No legal agreement, no matter how well constructed, is adequate to assure the close communications and relationships that are required to make this process work. All of these realities of today's business environment require long-term relationships built on trust.

A recent and popular book by Francis Fukuyama[6] presents a well-thought-out argument that 'one of the most important lessons we can learn from an examination of economic life is that a nation's well-being, as well as its ability to compete, is conditioned by a single, pervasive cultural characteristic: the level of trust inherent in the society'.[7] Fukuyama presents a detailed argument for individual virtues which are the bedrock of social relationships, or the tendency towards fluent association, what he calls *spontaneous sociability*.

> Spontaneous sociability is critical to economic life because virtually all economic activity is carried out by groups rather than individuals. Before wealth can be created, human beings have to learn to work together, and if there is to be subsequent progress, new forms of organization have to be developed.[8]

The idea of social capital as a measure of wealth – the intellectual competencies and abilities of the members of society – has been presented before. However, Fukuyama directly relates social capital to the prevalence of trust in a society. High trust societies are more successful at wealth creation; those which are low trust societies demonstrate less ability to generate both social and material wealth. Low trust societies, such as in the Middle East and China, extend trust within, but little beyond, the family association. Economic relationships are often within the family and those relationships beyond are treated with distrust. This is a brake on economic activity. High trust societies such as the US, Japan and Great Britain develop multiple forms of association and ease of relationships beyond the family. These associations include civic clubs, fraternities, political parties, trade and professional associations, as well as religious and other community organizations. This ability to engage in 'spontaneous sociability' is the foundation of economic activity.

This analysis of a high trust society as a foundation of wealth presents a clear warning to cultures such as the United States in which the decline of sociability, the loss of trust, is rapid and visible. The Guardian of the Bahá'í Faith, Shoghi Effendi, said,

> The permanence and stability achieved by any association, group or nation is a result of – and dependent upon – the soundness and worth of the principles upon which it bases the running of its affairs and the direction of its activities. The guiding principles of the Bahá'ís are: honesty, love, charity and trustworthiness; the setting of the common good above private interest; and the practice of godliness, virtue and moderation.[9]

This is how we believe permanence and stability are achieved in business as well as in all other institutions.

> Truthfulness is the foundation of all human virtues. Without truthfulness progress and success, in all the worlds of God, are impossible for any soul. When this holy attribute is established in man, all the divine qualities will also be acquired.[10]

Honesty, the resulting trust and spontaneous sociability equal social capital. If you can imagine a highway or railroad system in a nation as representing an asset to the economy and country, a form of capital, then imagine social capital as a transportation system between human beings in the society. Social capital is the highway of ideas, of trusting conversation, of intellectual discourse and the formation of relationships between individuals and organizations. In the knowledge economy in which we live, social capital – the human idea of discourse – may be far more valuable an asset than any highway or railroad.

The asset of social capital, built on trust, is just as important within a company as within society. Almost all companies today progress to the degree that they are competent at innovation. How does innovation happen? Is it one creative genius sitting in her office with lights going on over her head? Very rarely. Far more often it is the result of brainstorming, the open sharing of ideas without fear of judgment or ridicule. If I fear that you are going to take an idea that I share with you and claim credit for yourself, I am less likely to share that idea. The difficulty is that the idea I share with you is likely incomplete and it is likely that you or someone else will add to that idea or change it slightly, or it may trigger a completely different idea in your mind. This dynamic interchange is the dance of creativity. Distrust shuts down the process just as surely as a train wreck shuts down the railroad line. The cost to the company of shutting down the human dialogue may be greater than the material cost of shutting down material traffic.

I was conducting a workshop on ethics in business at a conference a few years ago. I presented the group with a series of ethical dilemmas and asked them to discuss what they would do in those situations. After discussing these for a while someone raised his hand and said, 'I am not so interested in these cases that are somewhat confusing. What about when someone is stealing from the company?' Somewhat taken aback, I said, 'What is there to discuss? Stealing is stealing, lying is lying. Those aren't ethical dilemmas. Those are clear issues of right and wrong and I am sure everyone here knows what to do in those cases.' I have found that issues of honesty and trustworthiness in the workplace are similar. Simply lying is obviously wrong. That does not require much discussion. But more often the issues are not so clear.

When must one disclose information to be honest? This is a common issue of trust in the workplace. If you must dismiss an employee for poor performance and suddenly all of his associates are imagining why he was fired, do you disclose exactly what this person did to deserve firing? What if you believe the person was doing something dishonest? Do you disclose that? You might at first think: of course you disclose the reasons so other employees can learn from the example. That is certainly a legitimate point of view. But, on the other hand, what will be the effect on the fired individual, his character and reputation? When you disclose what the person did the information will be spread through the larger community and it will no doubt receive editorial interpretation. Now this person will be damaged many times beyond the simple loss of his job. Is this just?

You can decide which concern is most important in the above example. My point is that in the real world of managing organizations, issues of principle, which we would all like to be clear cut-and-dry, are more often issues of balance between competing principles and interests. Managing requires wisdom, not mechanical reliance on obvious principles.

Honesty and trustworthiness are inseparable from the task of leading and following. All organizations, regardless of how democratic they are in their decision-making, no matter how many small groups sit and consult together, all require the example of leadership. Leadership is providing an example for others to follow. Leadership is the human face rather than the cold facts of a decision and that human face creates emotion, enthusiasm, even love. Leadership is creating and articulating common purpose for a group and calling on others to contribute to that purpose. Leadership is creating a positive vision of the group of people whom you seek to lead and calling on others to work towards that shared vision. Leadership is creating energy within a group of people and mobilizing that energy towards a common goal. But leadership is nothing without followers.

The degree to which followers respond to acts of leadership is directly proportional to their degree of trust in the leader. That trust is not only based on telling the truth, it is also built on the record of frank and open sharing of information, of making reliable decisions in the past and of engaging the followers in dialogue. This creates trust. Social capital is not only the fluency of discourse horizontally among peers in the organization; it is the level of trust and the willingness of followers to respond to the calls of leaders. This, too, is an asset of the organization.

The principles I am attempting to define and apply in this book do not stand alone as independent variables. Rather, they form an interdependent web. Honesty and trust are requirements of unity. Unity among people cannot be achieved if they do not trust each other. Many times I have seen within corporations distrust between the manufacturing and engineering organizations, or between the finance and operating organizations, or between workers and managers. The disunity caused by this distrust is a brake on the economic progress of the firm. Just as the decline of the culture of civilizations is typically an act of suicide, the self-created disintegration of the social fabric within the society, in corporations the most common cause of defeat is similarly an act of suicide. Dishonesty, distrust and disunity are the knife used to commit this self destruction. The decline of economic well-being and the disunity brought about by distrust are inseparable.

Questions for Discussion and Reflection[11]

1) You have instituted a profit sharing program within your privately owned company. You are the president and you own the majority of the stock. You have promised your employees that you will share 25 per cent of the profit with them. You previously decided that you personally would take a low salary but would give yourself a bonus when the company was profitable. The company has just made $250,000 in profit. Your compensation is $100,000 annually, which is about half of comparable salaries in other companies. So you decide to take out a bonus of $100,000. Because this is now an expense to the company, it reduces the profit by that amount, which is now $150,000. You are now going to share 25% of this amount. Do you tell the employees about your bonus?

2) You believe that there are too many levels in the structure of your organization. However, these levels represent status and prestige to some of your managers. Although you think these extra levels are counterproductive, you decide to leave them in place out of your compassion and concern for these managers. Do you tell them that this is why you have made this decision?

3) You are a member of a decision-making management team. One member of the team sounds like a broken record. He is constantly bringing up the same points, ones you think are frankly

wrong, and although you have said this in the past, he persists. He believes in persistence. When he brings up these same points, do you honestly tell him and the group how you feel?

4) You have started a training program to prepare managers for higher levels of responsibility. You are now accepting applications. There are 15 openings for the training program. Only 15 managers have applied. One of those managers you strongly believe does not have the potential for a higher level of responsibility owing both to his intelligence and because he is 55 years old and you want to invest energy in training younger managers. Do you accept his application? Do you reject it? And do you tell him why?

5) You manage an advertising agency. You have specialized in print advertising for computer software companies. You are very good at this. This is your core competency. A customer with whom you have worked for several years wants to switch some of his budget to Internet-based advertising. This customer asks you if you can help with this and he wonders whether he should go to another agency experienced in Internet advertising. You would like to expand into this area. What do you advise this client?

Other Quotations and Views on Honesty

Treat those who are good with goodness, and also treat those who are not good with goodness. Thus goodness is attained. Be honest to those who are honest, and be also honest to those who are not honest. Thus honesty is attained. *Lao Tzu*

Confidence in others' honesty is no light testimony of one's own integrity. *Michel de Montaigne*

Honesty is the cornerstone of all success, without which confidence and ability to perform shall cease to exist. *Mary Kay Ash*

Honesty: The best of all the lost arts. *Mark Twain*

We must make the world honest before we can honestly say to our children that honesty is the best policy. *George Bernard Shaw*

As I have said, the first thing is to be honest with yourself. You can never have an impact on society if you have not changed yourself . . . Great peacemakers are all people of integrity, of honesty, but humility. *Nelson Mandela*

Honesty is the first chapter in the book of wisdom. *Thomas Jefferson*

The root of the matter . . . the thing I mean . . . is love, Christian love, or compassion. If you feel this, you have a motive for existence, a guide for action, a reason for courage, an imperative necessity for intellectual honesty. *Bertrand Russell*

People who are brutally honest get more satisfaction out of the brutality than out of the honesty. *Richard J. Needham*

Honesty is as rare as a man without self-pity. *Stephen Vincent Benet*

No legacy is so rich as honesty. *William Shakespeare*

Concentration is my motto – first honesty, then industry, then concentration. *Andrew Carnegie*

The secret of life is honesty and fair dealing. If you can fake that, you've got it made. *Groucho Marx*

2

The Spirit of Service

If we are spiritual beings, rather than simply material or intellectual ones, our relationship to work has a consequence for our spiritual condition. The Bahá'í writings tell us that work performed in the spirit of service is as worship. What does this mean? How can it be true that mere work can be equated to the worship of God? In order to understand this we must have some conception of the human condition, our nature, as it relates to work. If one views human beings from a material perspective, their work life may be little more than the work of a pack animal laboring to haul goods for a master. The animal is rewarded with food and rest at the end of a journey as the human worker may be similarly rewarded. This is the nature of work performed solely for a material reward. The reward is quickly consumed and one then starts the labor anew.

But this is not the conception of the human condition as we understand it. We understand our condition to have more than one nature, material and spiritual:

> As we have before indicated, this human reality stands between the higher and the lower in man, between the world of the animal and the world of Divinity. When the animal proclivity in man becomes predominant, he sinks even lower than the brute. When the heavenly powers are triumphant in his nature, he becomes the noblest and most superior being in the world of creation. All the imperfections found in the animal are found in man. In him there is antagonism, hatred and selfish struggle for existence; in his nature

lurk jealousy, revenge, ferocity, cunning, hypocrisy, greed, injustice and tyranny. So to speak, the reality of man is clad in the outer garment of the animal, the habiliments of the world of nature, the world of darkness, imperfections and unlimited baseness.

On the other hand, we find in him justice, sincerity, faithfulness, knowledge, wisdom, illumination, mercy and pity, coupled with intellect, comprehension, the power to grasp the realities of things and the ability to penetrate the truths of existence. All these great perfections are to be found in man. Therefore, we say that man is a reality which stands between light and darkness. From this standpoint his nature is threefold: animal, human and divine. The animal nature is darkness; the heavenly is light in light.

The holy Manifestations of God come into the world to dispel the darkness of the animal, or physical, nature of man, to purify him from his imperfections in order that his heavenly and spiritual nature may become quickened, his divine qualities awakened, his perfections visible, his potential powers revealed and all the virtues of the world of humanity latent within him may come to life. These holy Manifestations of God are the Educators and Trainers of the world of existence, the Teachers of the world of humanity.[1]

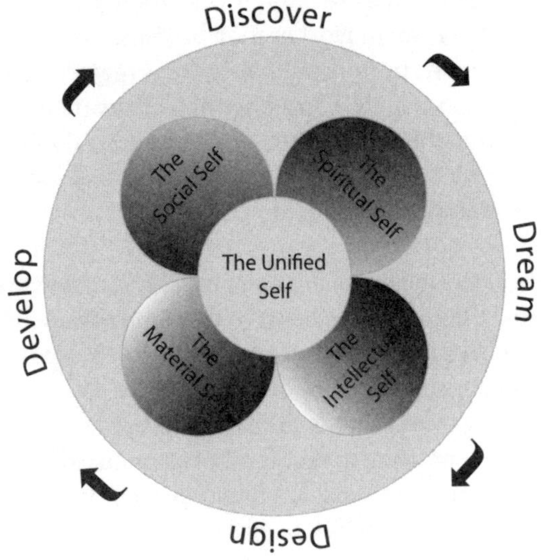

This diagram, as with all diagrams, is an attempt to make the complex simple. Of course, we are more complex than this but it is still helpful to visualize the components of what comprises the human condition. One way to view the different natures of the self is to recognize that we have a material self that requires development and nourishment and is of value to the whole self. How we feel physically affects our emotions and our intellect. Creating some level of material wealth provides for education and emotional and material security and enables us to serve others in material ways. We also have intellectual capacities that are of inherent value and which contribute to our abilities both to perform work that produces material wealth and to apply our mind to the more weighty matters of both science and religion. Similarly, we have a social self, the capacity for strong and healthy human relationships. Our ability to communicate, to create trust with others, strengthens our family, strengthens our team at work and establishes a network of relationships that enable us to both perform our work and enjoy the benefits of associating with others. And, finally, we have our spiritual self, our higher capacity to attain wisdom and to reflect the attributes of God.

One can pursue the development of these four capacities independently. We can spend an hour each day in physical exercise, another hour studying to enhance our intellect and so forth. However, we are not divided into fragments. We are a whole person and all of our capacities are at work at the same time to one degree or another. The Bahá'í Faith is a prescription for a new civilization, an evolution advanced beyond that of any previous or existing civilization. As we have progressed from an existence dominated by the struggle to survive materially, we have progressed to a life more dominated by intellectual activity. We are now a knowledge economy in many parts of the world. One of the effects of advances in efficiency of production has always been to create leisure time, an excess of labor, now to be deployed in new ways.

How will we spend our time in the future? It is reasonable to hypothesize that, rather than devoting most of our life to achieving material, or even intellectual assets, we will increasingly devote our time to acts of service to our fellow man. Life expectancy has been extended approximately 20 years over the past century. It is likely that another 20 years will be added in the coming century. Yet the ability to meet our material needs requires less and less time as our economy becomes more productive. So how will we spend that leisure time? Anyone who has retired (I have retired and un-retired) knows that leisure pursuits – golf, sailing or watching television – quickly become unsatisfying. Energy is lost in activities that lack noble purpose. Energy is created by the pursuit of worthy purpose. Leaders have throughout history energized their followers by instilling a sense of noble purpose.

Something within our nature – perhaps it is a seed planted by God within us – determines that we all seek and will sacrifice for that which is noble. Every leader understands, perhaps intuitively, that followers will sacrifice for a noble purpose and the leader defines the mission of the organization in terms of a worthy purpose. We will sacrifice, even our lives, for a cause we perceive to be noble and worthy. Why? Because we understand the mystery of sacrifice: that when we sacrifice our money, time, energy to that which we hold to be noble, there is no sacrifice but only an investment – one with a guaranteed return – and that return is in that which is most precious to us, our own nobility and worth. The mystery of sacrifice is that we become like that unto which we sacrifice ourselves. When we sacrifice our self to that which is noble, we become more ennobled. A critical component of creating a satisfying quality of life is to do something that you believe to be important, something worthy.

We also know that God has created all humanity in His image. Throughout the Bahá'í writings and those of other religions we are told that service to our fellow man is service to God. A life of leisure is a life of service to self and there is no nobility in serving oneself.

> O thou that hast branched from Mine ancient Stock! My glory and My loving-kindness rest upon thee. How vast is the tabernacle of the Cause of God! It hath overshadowed all the peoples and kin-

> dreds of the earth, and will, erelong, gather together the whole of mankind beneath its shelter. Thy day of service is now come. Countless Tablets bear the testimony of the bounties vouchsafed unto thee. Arise for the triumph of My Cause, and, through the power of thine utterance, subdue the hearts of men. Thou must show forth that which will ensure the peace and the well-being of the miserable and the down-trodden. Gird up the loins of thine endeavor, that perchance thou mayest release the captive from his chains, and enable him to attain unto true liberty.[2]

> It is incumbent upon every man of insight and understanding to strive to translate that which hath been written into reality and action . . . That one indeed is a man who, today, dedicateth himself to the service of the entire human race. The Great Being saith: Blessed and happy is he that ariseth to promote the best interests of the peoples and kindreds of the earth. In another passage He hath proclaimed: It is not for him to pride himself who loveth his own country, but rather for him who loveth the whole world. The earth is but one country, and mankind its citizens.[3]

We also know that God has created all humanity in His image:

> Veiled in My immemorial being and in the ancient eternity of My essence, I knew My love for thee; therefore I created thee, have engraved on thee Mine image and revealed to thee My beauty.[4]

It is therefore logical that service to our fellow human beings is service to God. It therefore falls upon us to conspire to make our work such as to be of service to humanity. This does not necessarily contradict the benefits to the corporation or to oneself. All these can be served together. If one's work is to prepare the meals in a restaurant one can do that with one's heart focused on serving those who will eat the meal, hoping the meal brings them joy as well as nourishment, hoping the environment of the restaurant uplifts their spirit and confirms their relationship with their guests. To the degree to which this preparer of meals is successful, he or she will also be serving the interests of the restaurant itself and will bring credit upon himself.

It is always true that the mystery of sacrifice is that there is no sacrifice because each sacrifice is met with a return. The return is in the satisfaction of knowing one has done the right thing, knowing that one has contributed to a greater cause or has somehow uplifted a fellow human being. Truly, performing work in the spirit of service is vital to one's own spiritual growth and maturity.

> Every individual, no matter how handicapped and limited he may be, is under the obligation of engaging in some work or profession, for work, especially when performed in the spirit of service, is according to Bahá'u'lláh a form of worship. It has not only a utilitarian purpose, but has a value in itself, because it draws us nearer to God, and enables us to better grasp His purpose for us in this world.[5]

If the tactics of the organization are exploitive, seeking to gain the most advantage available from customers and suppliers, without regard for their interests, the organization's managers are in violation of this principle and it will be difficult for a member to behave in a contrary way. In many parts of the world and in many industries it may be hard to conceptualize acting in the spirit of service towards either customers or suppliers. It may be assumed that the game of business is to win-all-you-can and it is the customer's challenge to negotiate the best price or conditions. But if you are serving your customers, you want them to have your product or service at a price and under conditions favorable to them. Business is then an entirely different game.

It is not only beneficial to serve customers with a genuine spirit of service but it is also beneficial to lead others with the attitude and aim of serving the very people you lead. Some authors have promoted the idea of leadership as a form of service in a manner very consistent with Bahá'í ideals of leadership.[6] It has always been an interesting paradox that 'Abdu'l-Bahá is known both as 'the Master' and as 'the Servant'. How can one be master and servant at the same time? Of course, He lived His life in the spirit of service both to God and to humanity. In this He was a 'servant' and from a spiritual perspective this is the highest station of all. Yet He was the Master, Master of the teachings of this Faith, Master as an example of worthy conduct and Master as the leader of the Faith at that time. This is the essence of leadership: to be both the servant of those you lead and to be the perfect example of the qualities you wish to instill into your followers.

The total quality movement has spawned a flood of books with titles such as *The Service Advantage*.[7] Becoming customer focused has been a priority and challenge for most companies. These efforts have resulted in efforts to design products with customer needs in mind, guaranteed money back customer satisfaction and mission statements such as 'Ladies and gentlemen serving ladies and gentlemen' at Ritz-Carlton hotels. Doing work in the spirit of service has become a common goal in those companies striving for total quality. These companies have also experienced the rewards. Customers do business with companies that serve well. One study of the financial performance of those companies that won the National Quality Award of the Commerce Department in the United States demonstrated that their stock price, or shareholder value, increased 30 per cent more than the norm for Standard & Poors Five Hundred.

But there is a dimension to a spiritual approach to work that goes beyond one's own immediate sphere, beyond one's company. So many of the problems and divisions in society are the result of attitudes and decisions made by those in power, the superior class, assuming their wisdom exceeds that of the weak and humble. The imposition of policies and decisions, often by those who are the most learned, may have consequences that are negative, not simply because a decision may be wrong but because it was made from above and imposed below, denigrating the dignity and self-worth of the very people it may have been intended to help. If one believes that one is serving the less powerful or less fortunate, it is wise to enter into that relationship in the spirit of genuine consultation, humility and affection. And this spirit of service opens the door to their receiving whatever knowledge may be possessed by the more fortunate.

> The fundamentals of the whole economic condition are divine in nature and are associated with the world of the heart and spirit. This is fully explained in the Bahá'í teachings, and without knowledge of its principles no improvement in the economic state can be realized. The Bahá'ís will bring about this improvement and betterment but not through sedition and appeal to physical force – not through warfare, but welfare. Hearts must be so cemented together, love must become so dominant that the rich shall most willingly extend assistance to the poor and take steps to establish these economic adjustments permanently. If it is accomplished in this way, it will be most praiseworthy because then it will be for the sake of God and in the pathway of His service.[8]

Questions for Discussion and Reflection

1) In the low income areas of many cities the costs of doing business are high. Insurance rates are high, losses from theft are high and there are increased security costs. For this reason prices in retail stores in these areas are higher than in wealthier areas. You work for a retail chain and your stores are not as profitable as stores in higher income areas. You have been instructed either to bring these stores up to comparable profitability or close the stores. Given your interest in being of service to the less fortunate, what would you do?

2) You are responsible for selecting suppliers of component parts of a product your firm manufactures. You are convinced that it is the supplier's job to be of service to you. Do you have a responsibility to be of service to your suppliers? What form does that service take?

3) You are the president of a small consulting firm. An existing client calls you and asks you if you can help him with a stra-

tegic planning process. Strategic planning is not your primary area of expertise; however it is an area in which you would like to develop and expand your services. What do you do? How is the spirit of service reflected in your decision?

4) Healthcare costs are rising and the insurance premiums that your firm pays are having a very negative effect on your profitability. One of your competitors has just cut their healthcare benefits in half. Your board of directors insists that you maintain your profitability. What do you do?

Other Quotations and Views on Service

To put service above self gives meaning to all three levels and leads us into the Age of Wisdom, the fifth age of civilization. *Stephen Covey*[9]

I know not what your destiny will be, but one thing I know; the only ones among you who will be truly happy are those who have sought and found how to serve. *Albert Schweitzer*

You have not done enough, you have never done enough so long as it is still possible that you have something of value to contribute. *Dag Hammarskjold*

The best way to find yourself is to lose yourself in the service of others. *Mahatma Gandhi*

Teach this triple truth to all: A generous heart, kind speech, and a life of service and compassion are the things which renew humanity. *Buddha*

I know of no great men except those who have rendered great service to the human race. *Voltaire*

Service is the rent we pay for being. It is the very purpose of life, and not something you do in your spare time. *Marian Wright Edelman*

A business absolutely devoted to service will have only one worry about profits. They will be embarrassingly large. *Henry Ford*

Consciously or unconsciously, every one of us does render some service or another. If we cultivate the habit of doing this service deliberately, our desire for service will steadily grow stronger, and it will make not only for our own happiness, but that of the world at large. *Mahatma Gandhi*

If one were to take that goal out of its religious form and look merely at its purely human side, one might state it perhaps thus: free and responsible development of the individual, so that he may place his powers freely and gladly in the service of all mankind. *Albert Einstein*

Joy can be real only if people look upon their life as a service, and have a definite object in life outside themselves and their personal happiness. *Leo Nikolaevich Tolstoy*

There is no higher religion than human service. To work for the common good is the greatest creed. *Woodrow T. Wilson*

Serving God is doing good to man, but praying is thought an easier service and therefore more generally chosen. *Benjamin Franklin*

3

Justice

The Trainer of the World

> The best beloved of all things in My sight is Justice; turn not away therefrom if thou desirest Me, and neglect it not that I may confide in thee. By its aid thou shalt see with thine own eyes and not through the eyes of others, and shalt know of thine own knowledge and not through the knowledge of thy neighbor. Ponder this in thy heart; how it behooveth thee to be. Verily justice is My gift to thee and the sign of My loving-kindness. Set it then before thine eyes.[1]

Justice is an organizing principle upon which successful association and organization must be built. The term 'justice' in popular culture is associated with crime and punishment, the maintenance of order. While this is certainly one of the implications of justice, it is perhaps the most superficial. The Bahá'í International Community in its message on the *Prosperity of Humankind* refers to justice as 'that faculty of the human soul that enables each person to distinguish truth from falsehood'. 'It calls for fair-mindedness in one's judgments, for equity in one's treatment of others, and is thus a constant if demanding companion in the daily occasions of life.' 'At the group level, a concern for justice is the indispensable compass in collective decision-making, because it is the only means by which unity of thought and action can be achieved.'[2]

Justice requires a view of self-interest linked necessarily to the interest and good of others. It requires the consideration of fairness from a detached position in the consideration of every system, function, reward and distribution made by the organization. Ideally, the ability to perceive justice, and the development of this quality of the soul, would be a first requirement of decision-makers. This view is strikingly different from a prevailing perspective among many business people that the only social responsibility of business is to make money. This view holds that if business acts in the interest of shareholders a larger societal good – that of wealth creation through meeting customer needs – will be derived from the natural forces of competition described by Adam Smith.[3]

While there is a certain truth in this perspective, it is an incomplete and unbalanced truth. It fails to deal with the distribution of wealth within the corporation. The rising disparity between those at the bottom and those at the top of the corporation is justified by this Darwinian focus on self-interest as a social good. Self-interest is a social good but not the only social good. Self-interest tends to be a short- rather than long-term good. The demoralization of those below and the corruption of the excess of wealth is, ultimately, not in the stockholders', customers' or society's interest. A faculty of justice provides wisdom in decision-making, not simple calculation. The obsession with short-term gain and the calculation of material things which dominates the culture of most enterprises denies the value of wisdom, the appreciation of the long and collective view of good.

'Abdu'l-Bahá, speaking about industrial justice and the cause of strikes said,

> But the principal cause of these difficulties lies in the laws of the present civilization; for they lead to a small number of individuals accumulating incomparable fortunes, beyond their needs, whilst the greater number remain destitute, stripped and in the greatest misery. This is contrary to justice, to humanity, to equity; it is the height of iniquity, the opposite to what causes divine satisfaction.[4]

The economic system throughout most of human history has been one in which the powerful and wealthy perceived a legitimacy in their accumulation of increasing wealth, wealth they could in no way use, while the poor whom they employed suffered close to starvation and were without any form of healthcare or security in their elder years. In the minds of the wealthy, this was perceived to be just because they believed they were earning this wealth through their greater intelligence. While we have not escaped this perverse logic, we have made progress through the imposition of laws of progressive taxation, social security and government sponsored healthcare.

But these outward remedies do not solve the fundamental problem of how we perceive what is just and unjust. There is some mechanism that allows us to feel that 'if I was able to get it, it must be right and just for me to get it'. The executive of a Fortune 500 company who is earning compensation of one hundred million dollars a year because he was able to climb up the ladder and achieve it, and because his compensation is comparable to that of others in his position, believes it is just and properly earned compensation. That this compensation may be two thousand times that of the average employee in the company does not appear to be an injustice in his mind. To an objective outside observer, there is an obvious injustice in this arrangement.

How then do we develop a sense of justice that helps one escape the relativism that is inevitable when judging one's own worth? It can only be found in the development of spiritual perspectives that allow one to view matters detached from one's own ego.

One of the issues endlessly debated in the world of commerce is the role of government. This is one of those issues by which we falsely divide people into liberal and conservative – liberals favoring a larger government role and conservatives a minimal one. It is very clearly the Bahá'í view that there is a necessary role for government, particularly in matters of justice.

> The court of justice and the government have therefore the right of interference. When a difficulty occurs between two individuals

> with reference to private rights, it is necessary for a third to settle the question. This is the part of the government. Then the problem of strikes – which cause troubles in the country and are often connected with the excessive vexations of the workmen, as well as with the rapacity of manufacturers – how could it remain neglected?[5]

While the Bahá'í Faith is very clear in supporting the rights of capitalists, the protection of private property and the importance of individual initiative, the need for rules and regulations is also recognized. The libertarian view that naively proposes that if we just let the natural forces of competition play out all issues will be solved by the market is clearly rejected. Such a system would return us to the feudal arena of land barons and all-powerful industrialists with masses of poor. The development of the middle class, which has been the backbone of economic progress in western countries, occurred only because laws were established to protect the rights of workers and to establish basic protections of social security.

One of the difficulties of managing a large number of people in any organization is that you will be confronted with all of the ailments of our society manifested in the behavior of your employees. At some time some employee will lie. Some will steal. Some will do damage to other employees in various ways. The manager, or some group of managers in consultation, must now fulfill the role fulfilled by government in the larger society. How do you respond to misbehavior? It is clear that justice does not mean that we are simply to be nice, understanding and merciful at all times. This would lead to chaos and injustice to the majority of well-behaved employees.

> The Kingdom of God is founded upon equity and justice, and also upon mercy, compassion, and kindness to every living soul. Strive ye then with all your heart to treat compassionately all humankind – except for those who have some selfish, private motive, or some disease of the soul. Kindness cannot be shown the tyrant, the deceiver, or the thief, because, far from awakening them to

> the error of their ways, it maketh them to continue in their perversity as before. No matter how much kindliness ye may expend upon the liar, he will but lie the more, for he believeth you to be deceived, while ye understand him but too well, and only remain silent out of your extreme compassion.[6]

It may seem odd that in this passage 'Abdu'l-Bahá is almost admonishing you against extreme kindness. He is actually promoting a sense of justice. And this is also the absolutely practical and realistic understanding of justice present in the Bahá'í writings.

> Justice is the one power that can translate the dawning consciousness of humanity's oneness into a collective will through which the necessary structures of global community life can be confidently erected. An age that sees the people of the world increasingly gaining access to information of every kind and to a diversity of ideas will find justice asserting itself as the ruling principle of successful social organization.[7]

Justice must also be understood in light of the necessity of human development. It is one of the necessary functions of the business enterprise to develop human talents and abilities. All organizations administer justice through their systems of reward and punishment and thereby exert an extreme influence on the shaping of human character, talents and skills. The employee rewarded for rising above his peers in competition will develop a competitive and individualistic nature. The employee rewarded for successfully facilitating a team will develop the talents of listening, empathy and appreciation of diverse views. Seen in this light, this system of the organization must be designed with a view, not merely of exploiting current abilities, but of developing those latent within the human personality.

> O people of God! That which traineth the world is Justice, for it is upheld by two pillars, reward and punishment. These two pillars are the sources of life to the world.[8]

Consider two individuals who have been born with exactly equal natural talent and ability. One, however, has grown up in a family in which there was no access to computers, while the other grew up with her own computer at a very early age and cannot remember a time when she was not connected to the Internet. These two individuals, although born with equal capacity, will soon develop different capacities based on their environment, having little to do with their own choices. In our current culture it is clear that one will do better in school than the other and one will earn a far higher income than the other. Is this just? And what is the role of a corporation in regard to this issue of justice?

'Abdu'l-Bahá said that

> Difference of capacity in human individuals is fundamental. It is impossible for all to be alike, all to be equal, all to be wise. Bahá'u'lláh has revealed principles and laws which will accomplish the adjustment of varying human capacities. He has said that whatsoever is possible of accomplishment in human government will be effected through these principles. When the laws He has instituted are carried out, there will be no millionaires possible in the community and likewise no extremely poor. This will be effected and regulated by adjusting the different degrees of human capacity.[9]

'This will be effected and regulated by adjusting the different degrees of human capacity' is, I believe, an extremely important statement. While we are also told that there will be progressive taxation, that is not the reason there will be no millionaires and no poor. It will be because we will have created laws and processes that will alter human capacity, thereby enabling individuals to earn their fair share of compensation. This, I believe, casts a light on the question in the previous paragraph. Both these children will have access to computers at an early age and both will have the opportunity to develop their capacities.

Issues of justice in the organization often revolve around discipline or dealing with undesirable performance. An effective manager must be willing and able to deal with poor performance in a straightforward and prompt manner. The sooner poor performance is addressed, the less likely it is to develop into a major problem.

We all need feedback. No human being performs well without feedback from those around him. Disciplinary situations often develop because either you have the wrong person (wrong skills and talents) in the job or because of a lack of feedback that may provide the motivation to improve.

I recently received an email from a Bahá'í who asked how she should handle 'unpleasant decisions' that she had to make without it being a bad reflection on her and her Faith. This is how I answered her:[10]

> Regarding your question about 'unpleasant decisions': By 'unpleasant' I assume you mean disciplinary decisions, decisions to fire someone. You also used the term 'unpopular' which might be something entirely different. Here are some random thoughts:
>
> • First, you have an obligation to your employer, as a manager, to do what is in the best interest of the organization. By accepting a management position you are making a contract with the company to do what is right for the company, no matter whether it is unpleasant or unpopular, as long as it is ethical and legal. You simply have to ask whether it is, in fact, the right, the just, thing to do.
>
> • Second, this is an issue of justice. Representing the 'institution' of the company, and unlike in the Bahá'í community where issues of justice are only determined in consultation by the Assembly, you have to act as an institution and make decisions of justice. However, to the degree possible, it is wise and helpful to consult with others regarding these decisions, including the person who may be the problem and may be terminated. Often that person will recognize that his behavior is a problem and will decide either to change his behavior or leave.

• Third, whenever I had to terminate someone, I always asked myself whether I had given this person every opportunity to improve. If you fire someone without having given him feedback so he can improve, it is unjust to hold him accountable. Firing is a last resort, after you have made a number of efforts to redirect his behavior and have given him plenty of warning. As you give him the opportunity to improve, the burden of responsibility shifts from you to him. It is worth asking yourself whether the frequency and quality of feedback you provided has been adequate.

• Fourth, there is an issue of justice for other employees. It is unfair to keep someone employed who is performing in a way that sets a bad example for others or who may be hurting the performance of others or the group. Often you will find that other employees are saying, 'What took you so long?'

• Several times I have fired someone and remained friends. This was because I had given him feedback and the opportunity to improve and he knew he was not performing well and because I did it in a way that was not angry or demeaning, rather saying, 'Look, we both know this isn't working out for us. I think it would be in the interests of both of us if you found another job. I will do what I can to support you in that.' Many people are 'good people' but good people for something else. It reminds me of the Michael Bremer (FEMA) situation – he may be a good person and may be competent at something else. But he is obviously not the right man for that job. It may be that the person you have to fire is a good person for something else and you can help him by helping him discover what type of job he is best suited to. People are generally much happier in a job that is suited to their temperament, skills, etc., even though they don't enjoy the transition.

I don't think there is any conflict between acting justly, including dismissing someone, and being a good Bahá'í. I think if you handle these situations in a just manner and in a manner that

> preserves the dignity of everyone involved, it is a positive reflection on you as a Bahá'í.

For much of humanity the treatment of women is a profound matter of justice.

> Why should man, who is endowed with the sense of justice and sensibilities of conscience, be willing that one of the members of the human family should be rated and considered as subordinate? Such differentiation is neither intelligent nor conscientious; therefore, the principle of religion has been revealed by Bahá'u'lláh that woman must be given the privilege of equal education with man and full right to his prerogatives. That is to say, there must be no difference in the education of male and female in order that womankind may develop equal capacity and importance with man in the social and economic equation. Then the world will attain unity and harmony.[11]

It is perfectly clear from this statement that our organizations, whether business or government, have a spiritual responsibility to treat women as equals and to develop the capacities of women. From the perspective of business and economics, this principle is not only one of religion but is one of simple economic intelligence. In many countries of the world one half of the potential human capacity is suppressed and denied the opportunity to contribute in a full and meaningful way to economic life. This ignorance is crippling the economic development of those societies. For many who do not think deeply about the subject there is a fear of a system that will bring justice to the less fortunate among us. This is based on what Robert Wright has termed 'zero-sum' assumptions, versus 'non-zero-sum' assumptions.[12] A zero-sum assumption assumes that there is a fixed amount of wealth or happiness in the world. If you are going to attain more wealth or happiness, then, clearly, I must lose. Zero-sum assumes that we are all in competition for our share of this fixed amount of money or happiness. This is clearly not the view found in the Bahá'í writings. Rather,

Bahá'ís accept a non-zero-sum assumption: the assumption that the amounts of wealth and happiness are elastic and that, given sound principles, good behavior and a just system, the amount of wealth can increase to meet the needs of all and the wealthy can achieve greater happiness than they currently possess.

> Among the results of the manifestation of spiritual forces will be that the human world will adapt itself to a new social form, the justice of God will become manifest throughout human affairs, and human equality will be universally established. The poor will receive a great bestowal, and the rich attain eternal happiness. For although at the present time the rich enjoy the greatest luxury and comfort, they are nevertheless deprived of eternal happiness; for eternal happiness is contingent upon giving, and the poor are everywhere in the state of abject need.[13]

When a system of true justice is established it will require a new paradigm of thought. Where now it is assumed that the more one accumulates the happier one becomes, the new order will recognize the reality, now proved by science as well, that happiness is contingent not on the accumulation of money or property but rather on the ability to develop and contribute one's talents to a higher and more noble purpose.[14]

> The rich will enjoy the privilege of this new economic condition as well as the poor, for owing to certain provisions and restrictions they will not be able to accumulate so much as to be burdened by its management, while the poor will be relieved from the stress of want and misery. The rich will enjoy his palace, and the poor will have his comfortable cottage.[15]

Questions for Discussion and Reflection

1) You are the purchasing manager for a large manufacturing firm. You are going to put out a contract for cleaning services in your office building. One possible supplier is a large firm

with operations in most cities in your country. They have a long track record and have proved reliable by their service to hundreds of clients. Another possible supplier is a new firm, formed recently by poor members of the local community. They have no track record. They seem to be very anxious to have, and sincerely want, your business. They also appeal to your good nature by explaining that you will be helping local members of your community. The cost of both is the same. You are unsure which contract to accept because, on the one hand, you would like to help the local poor and, on the other, you have a responsibility to the corporation and stockholders to hire vendors who you know to be reliable and trustworthy. How does your sense of justice affect your decision in this case?

2) Your retail store has implemented a guaranteed customer satisfaction policy. Customers may return any item purchased without any explanation or proof that the purchase was in any way defective. You notice that a group of young women are purchasing dresses on Friday afternoon and returning those same items on Sunday or Monday. This is repeated week after week. You also notice that those clothes appear to have been worn, even though the price tags are still on the clothes. What do you do?

3) Your company has contracted with an Indonesian firm to open a manufacturing plant to produce goods for your firm. You visit there to evaluate their progress. You notice that there is a clear distinction in the jobs awarded to women and to men. This is a Muslim country and the managers and workforce are all Muslim. Consistent with their culture, they have separated women and men into different sections, sometimes in different rooms, and the jobs assigned to the women are all the lower paid and lower skill jobs. When you first voice your concern about this inequality the manager of the facility points out that you are not in the West now. This is their culture and he cau-

tions you against what he calls 'cultural imperialism'. What is the just thing to do?

4) You are the manager of a work group comprising ten employees. You are instructed to cut labor costs by 20 per cent. You can achieve this by terminating two workers or by instituting a 20 per cent pay cut for everyone. Which would you do? How would you go about finding the just course of action?

5) The end of year bonus for your division is a lump sum grant by the CEO. You, as division manager, have total discretion regarding its allocation to the employees in your division. Whatever is left, after you have allocated to the employees, is yours to keep. How do you go about determining a just allocation to each member of your team, including yourself?

Other Quotations and Views on Justice

Academic chairs are many, but wise and noble teachers are few; lecture-rooms are numerous and large, but the number of young people who genuinely thirst after truth and justice is small. *Albert Einstein*

Justice that love gives is a surrender, justice that law gives is a punishment. *Mahatma Gandhi*

Justice denied anywhere diminishes justice everywhere. *Martin Luther King, Jr.*

I tremble for my country when I reflect that God is just; that his justice cannot sleep forever. *Thomas Jefferson*

Words like 'freedom', 'justice', 'democracy' are not common concepts; on the contrary, they are rare. People are not born knowing what these are. It takes enormous and, above all, individual effort to arrive at the respect for other people that these words imply. *James Arthur Baldwin*

Recompense injury with justice, and recompense kindness with kindness. *Confucius*

Charity is no substitute for justice withheld. *Saint Augustine*

It is in justice that the ordering of society is centered. *Aristotle*

The slave begins by demanding justice and ends by wanting to wear a crown. *Albert Camus*

Justice is conscience, not a personal conscience but the conscience of the whole of humanity. Those who clearly recognize the voice of their own conscience usually recognize also the voice of justice. *Alexander Solzhenitsyn*

Justice, sir, is the great interest of man on earth. It is the ligament which holds civilized beings and civilized nations together. *Daniel Webster*

As Mankind becomes more liberal, they will be more apt to allow that all those who conduct themselves as worthy members of the community are equally entitled to the protections of civil government. I hope ever to see America among the foremost nations of justice and liberality. *George Washington*

The sentiment of justice is so natural, and so universally acquired by all mankind, that it seems to be independent of all law, all party, all religion. *Voltaire*

4

Consultation

Creating Unity and Collective Wisdom

The Bahá'í Faith makes the most grand of all claims – the power to transform the human condition, human relations and the systems of governance prevalent on this planet. It claims to usher in a new era, even a 'Most Great Peace', a condition of not only political peace but genuine harmony among mankind's diverse religions, ethnic and cultural groups. How is it possible for the educated and rational to accept such an outrageous claim?

The claim to transformative power does not depend on faith alone. In fact, the history of religion would provide little substantiation for a claim that faith in God and one of his Prophets alone would lead to peace in the world. Fortunately, Bahá'u'lláh, who stated clearly that God's greatest gift to humankind is the gift of intelligence, provided far more practical advice, an entire architecture of civilization, and at the heart of that architecture is the process of consultation.

Consultation, from the Bahá'í perspective, is not merely a technique of management or decision-making. Rather it is both a principle and process fundamental to the creation of a new civilization.

> Central to the task of reconceptualizing the system of human relationships is the process that Bahá'u'lláh refers to as consultation. 'In all things it is necessary to consult,' is His advice. 'The

maturity of the gift of understanding is made manifest through consultation.'[1]

It is a fundamental distinguishing feature of the new world order the Bahá'í Faith claims to usher in that the age of rule by kings, priests, mullahs and shahs is done. The future civilization will be one in which governance – the power to make institutional decisions – resides in the collective wisdom of groups. This collective wisdom is realized by the process of consultation. Bahá'ís are just beginning to learn the skills of consultation, a pattern of conversation and thought almost diametrically opposed to the dominant culture of debate in western societies. The collective wisdom of groups, as we all know from our own experience, is not an automatic outcome of most meetings. Rather, it is a rare achievement, an almost magical moment when personalities give way to a unifying process and individual minds come together in a flow of shared creativity, of honest dialogue, and genuine consensus is reached. Unfortunately, we are just beginning to discover how to achieve that state of collective wisdom. Much in our culture stands in our way. A culture of debate and competition hinders our entry into genuine dialogue.

Too often members of the Bahá'í community consider that they are engaging in consultation simply because they are sitting in a group and 'being nice' to each other, attempting to listen and then decide. I suggest that this simplistic understanding of consultation will, in the future, be viewed as a primitive first step. In business and in academia a great deal of work is being done to discover processes to achieve deep understanding, thorough analysis of problems and solutions, and methods for reaching a collective decision. Members of the Bahá'í community must be at the forefront of integrating this knowledge and experience from both academic and applied sources with their principle of consultation and the writings of their Faith.

The purpose of this chapter is to share some guidance on the process of achieving a state of genuine consultation and incorporating some of the lessons being learned in the world of academia and business.

The Quality of Conversation

All conversations are not equal. Have you ever sat down to talk with someone, perhaps someone who you never met before, and felt that he or she was completely understanding, completely aware of what you were saying, how you were feeling and the meaning behind your words? Do you remember how it made you feel to be so well understood? Such receptivity on the part of another is liberating. It frees you to express your thoughts and feelings without fear of rejection or contradiction. If this can be achieved in a group, whose purpose is to reach a decision, it is possible to create a collective wisdom, something far more intelligent, wiser, than may have been possessed by any single member of that group. This is the purpose of consultation.

> He who expresses an opinion should not voice it as correct and right but set it forth as a contribution to the consensus of opinion, for the light of reality becomes apparent when two opinions coincide. A spark is produced when flint and steel come together. Man should weigh his opinions with the utmost serenity, calmness and composure. Before expressing his own views he should carefully consider the views already advanced by others. If he finds that a previously expressed opinion is more true and worthy, he should accept it immediately and not willfully hold to an opinion of his own. By this excellent method he endeavors to arrive at unity and truth. Opposition and division are deplorable. It is better then to have the opinion of a wise, sagacious man; otherwise, contradiction and altercation, in which varied and divergent views are presented, will make it necessary for a judicial body to render decision upon the question. Even a majority opinion or consensus may be incorrect. A thousand people may hold to one view and be mistaken, whereas one sagacious person may be right. Therefore, true consultation is spiritual conference in the attitude and atmosphere of love. Members must love each other in the spirit of fellowship in order that good results may be forthcoming. Love and fellowship are the foundation.[2]

The nature of conversation is largely determined by culture. We learn to talk to each other in ways that become comfortable and acceptable to us. Native Americans will sit and talk with each other in very quiet voices and almost never look each other in the eye, a gesture they regard as a sign of disrespect. A group of old Jewish men in New York will sit on a park bench and to a stranger passing by may appear angry and agitated but in their minds they are simply passing the day in friendly conversation. Native islanders in the South Pacific will sit in complete silence for a long time thinking and then speak only after they have thought about a matter in great depth. These cultural patterns are neither right nor wrong, good nor bad. What is important is, first, that the members of a group develop a pattern that is a common language among them, understood in both language and tone and, second, that this pattern allows the full and frank participation of all so that each voice may be heard with respect, all ideas considered and finally a consensus reached.

> What Bahá'u'lláh is calling for is a consultative process in which the individual participants strive to transcend their respective points of view, in order to function as members of a body with its own interests and goals. In such an atmosphere, characterized by both candor and courtesy, ideas belong not to the individual to whom they occur during the discussion but to the group as a whole, to take up, discard, or revise as seems to best serve the goal pursued. Consultation succeeds to the extent that all participants support the decisions arrived at, regardless of the individual opinions with which they entered the discussion. Under such circumstances an earlier decision can be readily reconsidered if experience exposes any shortcoming.[3]

Different types of organizations require different types of decision-making. The military organization, geared to the crisis and chaos of combat, requires the certain structure of command decision-making in which speed and obedience leads to success and creativity is a subordinate virtue. On the family farm, small groups

– the natural organization of families – provided the mechanism of shared interest and shared decision-making and lacked the necessity of the instant response of battle. The factory organization of the early part of the past century relied on the rigid organization and job definition of Frederick Taylor's industrial engineering model and the work simplification of Henry Ford's factory. This led to the return to hierarchical and individual decision-making which now confronted the human needs of affiliation and intimacy that had been met on the family farm. Today the organizational imperative has again shifted. Conformity and obedience are not the most desired qualities of individual action. Rather, creativity, individual initiative and working in groups are the recognized qualities that lead to economic success. All of these are qualities that require the development of human potential and the ability to engage in work as a collective experience. The process of consultation, or team decision-making, as it is most commonly referred to in business, is rapidly becoming the accepted standard. The process of consultation is not only valued in its ability to bring forth the best decision but in its inevitable secondary effect of developing the mind of the participants. And the human mind is increasingly the most valued asset of the corporation.

Consultation is the process of group decision-making by which unity of thought, unity of knowledge and unity of action are achieved. Consultation requires the deliberate effort of all members of the group to detach themselves from their own ideas and egos and seek collective wisdom. In the past leaders were assumed to have been 'strong' in the sense of asserting personal authority. The requirement today is for a 'strong' leader who is capable of putting aside his or her ego and leading the group in a process that brings forth the contributions of all and allows each contribution to be genuinely understood by other members.

Jim Collins in his book *Good to Great* argues that 'Seemingly ordinary men . . . Level 5 leaders channel their ego needs away from themselves and into the larger goal of building a great company. It's not that Level 5 leaders have no ego or self-interest. Indeed they are incredibly ambitious – but their ambition is first and foremost for the institution, not themselves.' 'The great irony is that the animus and personal ambition that often drive people to positions of power stand at odds with the humility required of Level 5 leadership.'[4] Achieving this type of leadership is consistent with the Bahá'í ideal of consultation.

The Four Containers of Consultation

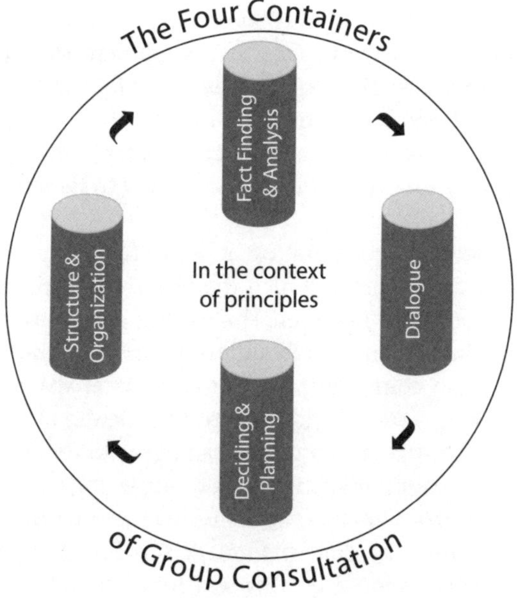

Group decision-making, whether called consultation or by any other name, is not one uniform discussion and it does not – and should not – look and feel the same at all times. There are different stages that a conversation goes through to arrive at a decision. In each of these stages different modes of thought, different patterns of conversation and different techniques are appropriate. One can think of these as different 'containers' that one enters for a period of time. If the members of the group know which container they are in, this can help the group to function in unity.

The term 'container' will be unfamiliar to most readers. It is borrowed from the literature on dialogue. It has proved useful to define a mental space, a mode of conversation that a group agrees to enter together. This space has boundaries that are mutually understood by the group. Knowing the boundaries and nature of the container allows the group to participate together in a constructive manner. We know that different physical spaces evoke different behaviors. When you walk into a library or a place of worship you immediately know that you have entered a 'container', a psychological or spiritual space that is different from the space outside that container. You expect others to conform to standards of behavior that allow you to study in quiet or to pray without distraction. There is an unstated social contract that when you enter this space you agree to behave according to the norms of the 'container'.

In the process of consultation it is useful to have similarly defined space, containers in which the group can agree to engage in productive behavior together. The mental process of gathering and analyzing facts is an entirely different one from the process of dialogue. You can compare them to the physical spaces of a factory or office and those in a library. You think and act differently in these different spaces. If a group can agree to enter that space together it can benefit by the unity of thought appropriate to that container. As a group matures in its understanding of these containers it will enter the dialogue and if someone suddenly says, 'Well I think Mary should do this and John should do that!' the group will have the same feeling you have when someone walks into the library and loudly begins a conversation on a cell phone. Respect for the different types of space will create a spirit of calm and unity that is often destroyed by different members of a group having different assumptions about the type of conversation they are having. It is unfortunately common that members of a group in consultation have very different ideas about what they are trying to accomplish at any given time.

What Bahá'ís refer to as consultation is a process of group decision-making that may often look and feel like other group or team processes. However, the reliance on principles and operating within the context of principles shapes all stages of group process. When Bahá'ís consult they have a common belief in 'divine' principles given to them in the authoritative writings of their Faith. When this process is taken into the work setting the 'faith' aspect may be lacking but the lesson that agreement and adherence to principles is an essential cause of unity and agreement remains true. In the work setting the principles may come from a company's statement of values or the group may define its own principles. This context of principles forms the 'room' in which consultation takes place. Within this room there are different containers that shape the purpose and nature of conversation.

The first container is *structure and organization*. This stage begins before the meeting when you determine the purpose of the group or meeting, the membership and the different roles and responsibilities within the team. This stage also includes understanding the team's relationship to other groups or individuals. Determining the agenda and the time to be allocated to each topic is also included in this container of organization.

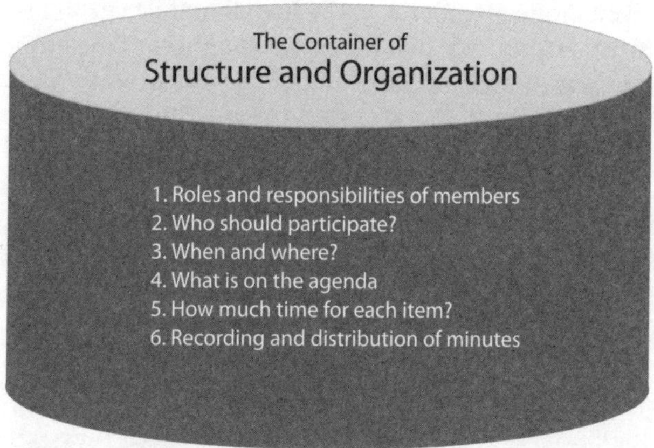

Much of the success of a decision-making meeting is determined by the way the group is structured. I worked for a number of years with the senior executive team of Shell Oil in the United States. The president, who many viewed as authoritarian, worked to implement a team process and create a style of teamwork more consistent with the spirit of consultation. One of the most powerful things he did was to ask that the chairing of the meeting be rotated among the members of his team. The roles of recording secretary and timekeeper were also rotated. In this manner the president had no more formal leadership role in the conduct of the meeting than anyone else. Because each member experienced the role of chairperson they all came to respect the role and to take responsibility for the functioning and success of the team. This change in the culture of the senior management meetings was largely due to a change in the structure and organization of those meetings.

The second container is that of fact-finding and analysis. This container may extend over more than one meeting as the members seek information or data relevant to their decision. It is always amazing to me that a discussion of a problem often starts with members of the group offering their ideas for a solution to the problem. It is part of current culture to jump quickly to conclusions. Even if one member actually has all of the facts in his mind, it is entirely improbable that the other members of the group have the same facts in their mind.

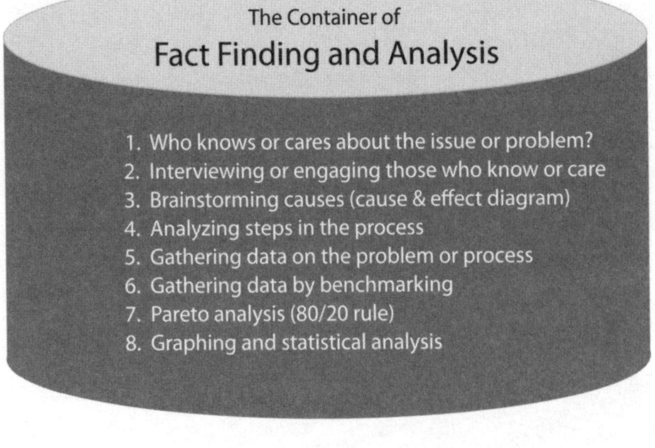

The total quality movement (quality circles, statistical process control or Six Sigma) has promoted and taught fact and statistical analysis of problems. It is not unusual to walk through a factory anywhere in the world today and see hourly workers maintaining statistical control charts, plotting three standard deviations around a mean, identifying 'common' and 'special' causes of variability, analyzing those causes of variability from system performance (a quality variance) and implementing solutions using design-of-experiments techniques. In any world class manufacturing setting today workers and managers are intensely gathering the facts and analyzing those facts using both statistical and non-statistical means.

In other settings it is common for group members to offer opinions based on personal emotions and biases without regard to any facts. If the process that Bahá'ís refer to as consultation is going to be applied to business settings it must be accompanied by rigorous pursuit of facts and analysis. It is beyond the scope of this book to attempt to teach these methods. There are many well-written books on team problem-solving techniques and the development of these skills is a necessary component of effective consultation in the work setting.[5]

The third container is that of dialogue. Dialogue is the process of seeking meaning and understanding. It is the most meditative

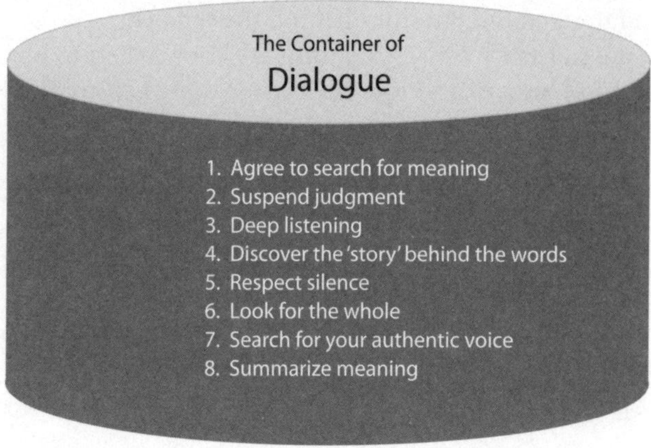

stage of consultation. It is a process that requires patience, silence, finding your own inner voice and the search for what is truly important. This stage is a period of reflection on the subject in order to see things in a different, less obvious way.

Dialogue requires us to escape many of the cultural norms present today. For example, it requires us to suspend judgment rather than quickly jumping to judgment. It requires us to engage in deep inquiry into a matter rather than simply acquiescing to the opinions of others, particularly those who may be held in some respect or authority. And perhaps most difficult of all, it requires us to look deep inside ourselves and find our own voice.

Most conversation occurs at a surface level. We assume that the words out of someone's mouth mean only simple and superficial things and we say, 'Fine, right, what's next?' And this may be fine for 90 per cent of the conversations that occur in our meetings. It is much like in a marriage where 95 per cent of the conversation is 'What's for dinner?' 'What color should we paint the room?' 'What do you want to watch on television?' None of these require deep listening or a search for the meaning or story behind the words. But then suddenly your spouse says, 'I just haven't been feeling very fulfilled lately.' To say, 'Yeah, right, I haven't felt great either. Have you seen that new show on television?' would be to walk right by a person who may be wounded or lost. The first comment has meaning. It requires dialogue. It requires deep questioning to find and understand the story behind the remark.

We are not truly consulting until we know when to engage in dialogue and how to find the story or meaning behind the words. In order to do this, members of a group must strive to think together rather than alone.

One understanding of conversation in a group is to think about the group as a number of different people, individuals with different perspectives or ideas, each member of the group sharing his or her ideas and the group deciding which idea is the best and moving forward with that idea. With this understanding each individual is thinking alone, forming his or her own ideas and opinions and then attempting to convince the others of the value of those ideas. The 'locus' of thought is internal, focused on the self and 'my' ideas, 'my' contribution, the acceptance of 'my' views over those of another.

Another understanding of group conversation is to consider that the group is thinking as one system, one organism or one collective mind. With this understanding the individual members are not so focused on their own ideas or their own opinions. They are less focused on convincing others to accept their ideas. They are not trying to 'win'. They are just as interested in understanding the ideas of others, trying to find the best solution for the group, regardless of who it comes from. When thinking together the members are interested in encouraging and supporting the ideas of others because those ideas become their own. The objective is to create 'collective wisdom', to find the best answer for the group, with no concern for whose idea it is.

It may be helpful to visualize how we communicate with others. The following triangle illustrates the mental 'framework' from which we engage in conversation. In most conversations, particularly those conditioned by current culture in western societies, people are thinking about their own ideas and how to persuade the other person to accept them. Unfortunately, the other person is doing the same. This defeats the opportunity for shared understanding and may result in conflict. When we are in our own corner, thinking alone, we are in a win–lose posture, searching for victory for our position at the cost of defeat for the other person.

A debate among candidates for political office is characterized by an effort to make 'me' look good and make 'you' look bad. Each candidate has his mind, his priority, in his own corner. No one is thinking about what is best for 'us' or how 'we' might mutually benefit. Conversation that is at the bottom of the pyramid is both egocentric and lonely. Unfortunately, this characterizes much of our society. Conversations at the top of the pyramid are inherently unifying because they are not focused on oneself but on shared interest and shared benefit. Conversations at the bottom often have the consequence of increasing disunity and negative assumptions about the other party. Conversations at the top of the pyramid are likely to result in learning and appreciating the view of the other. Those at the bottom are characteristic of a culture of war; those at the top of a culture of peace.

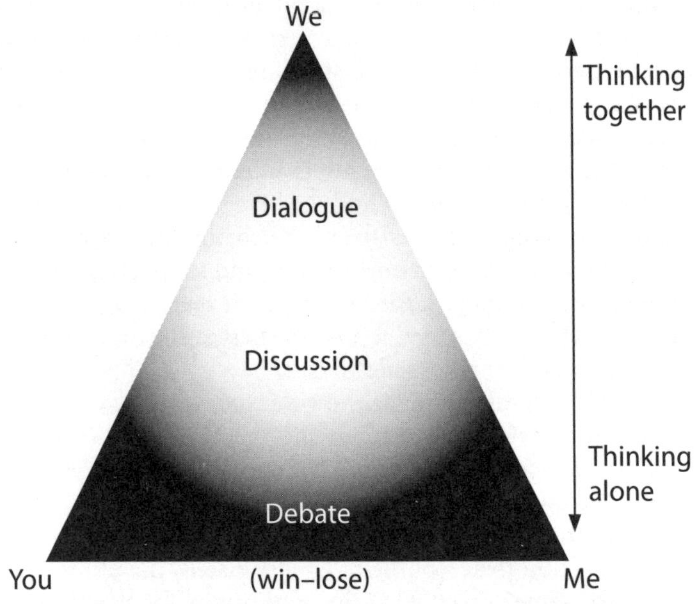

This type of discourse hardens the corners of the triangle and is the exact opposite of dialogue. Debate creates discomfort with opposing views and attempts to lower the stature of anyone who holds those opposing views. Dialogue creates a zone of comfort for others to contribute without fear of being assaulted or insulted. In debate generalizations are used to label a point of view in a manner that discounts its consideration ('That's typical of you liberals!'). In dialogue questions are used to uncover the true meaning of another person's contributions ('If you are in favor of paying teachers more, how do you feel that could be funded?'). In debate you look for the error in the position of another. In dialogue you look for what may be right or helpful in the contribution of another. Debate suffocates intellectual inquiry; dialogue fuels intellectual inquiry. Debate creates or hardens distance or alienation between the parties; dialogue creates connections, appreciation and unity.

Clearly the ideal we strive for in consultation is that of dialogue. However, there is a major difference in the way dialogue is employed today and the requirements of Bahá'í consultation. Dialogue groups are employed today in peace-seeking efforts and other humanitarian efforts to achieve understanding between different ethnic, religious or political groups. There is no purpose other than seeking understanding. There is no requirement to make a decision or take action. For this reason dialogue in its pure form has not become a common practice in business. Consultation, on the other hand, has the purpose of getting to a decision, albeit through unity and understanding. This is why I have placed dialogue in the context of the four containers: so it may be seen as one necessary, though insufficient, step in the process of consultation.

> The standard of truth seeking this process demands is far beyond the patterns of negotiation and compromise that tend to characterize the present-day discussion of human affairs. It cannot be achieved – indeed, its attainment is severely handicapped – by the culture of protest that is another widely prevailing feature of contemporary society. Debate, propaganda, the adversarial method, the entire apparatus of partisanship that have long been such familiar features of collective action are all fundamentally harmful to its purpose: that is, arriving at a consensus about the truth of a given situation and the wisest choice of action among the options open at any given moment.
>
> What Bahá'u'lláh is calling for is a consultative process in which the individual participants strive to transcend their respective points of view, in order to function as members of a body with its own interests and goals. In such an atmosphere, characterized by both candor and courtesy, ideas belong not to the individual to whom they occur during the discussion but to the group as a whole, to take up, discard, or revise as seems to best serve the goal pursued. Consultation succeeds to the extent that all participants support the decisions arrived at, regardless of the individual opinions with which they entered the discussion. Under such

circumstances an earlier decision can be readily reconsidered if experience exposes any shortcomings.[6]

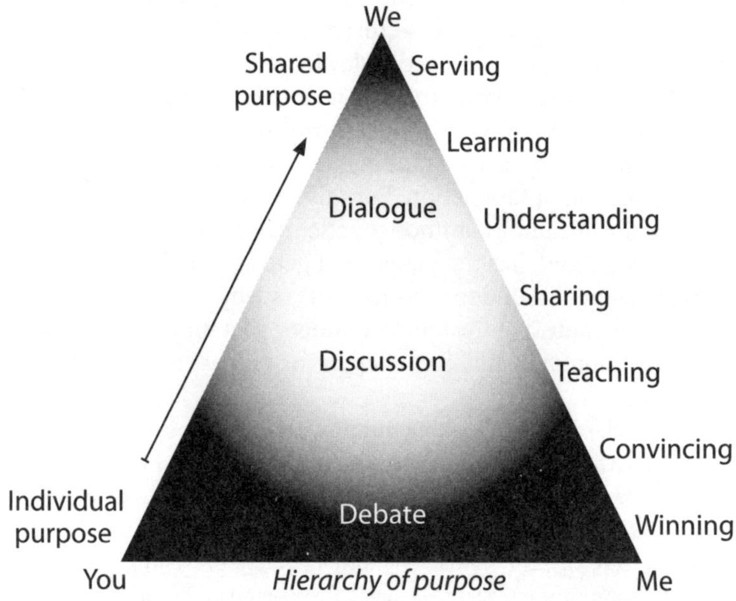

Hierarchy of purpose

The motive or purpose for a conversation among people is critical to understanding its nature. If one is motivated to project one's ego, to win a point, this will largely determine the spirit of the exchange. However, to the degree that the conversation becomes one of serving the other person or learning from the other person, it becomes a process of unity, a process by which the parties come together as one and can achieve that condition of ideal consultation or thinking together.

Finally, there is the container of deciding on alternatives, clarifying the decision and agreeing on an action plan. This is the process of reaching consensus and developing an action plan that specifies what and when things will be done and by whom. This container has an entirely different feel and mode of thought from that of dialogue. Now you become practical. Now you have to judge, whereas in dialogue you intentionally suspended judgment. Now you have to recognize that people are going to take action and actions have consequences that must be considered.

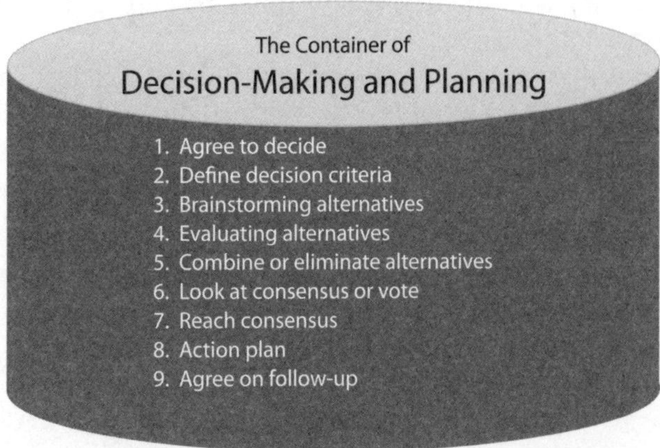

In many meetings a topic is discussed and a consensus point of view appears very easily. The chairperson may simply say, 'Well, it sounds like we are in agreement to . . .' and everyone nods his head. For matters that are not complex and for which the course of action appears to be obvious, this is fine. However, particularly in the business world, matters are often not simple and the possibilities may be many, each requiring careful consideration. For example, the issue may be capital spending for research and development. There may be one million dollars available for research and development but there are proposals for five million dollars in spending. Each proposal presents opportunities for business development and each carries risks. Each proposal requires consideration of the competitive environment, the technology, the marketing channels, a forecast of future technologies and future market demands. If each of these factors is not considered it is likely that the choice will not be the best.

Businesses succeed by making better decisions than their competitors. This decision-making cannot simply be a matter of saying, 'Well, it sounds like we should do this.' It must be more methodical in detailing the risks and opportunities, considering the capabilities of the organization, considering the competitive landscape, etc. This container of decision-making and planning has a completely different feel, a different part of the brain is employed at this stage.

If consultation, as understood by the Bahá'ís, is going to mature in a manner that both employs the spiritual dimensions addressed in the writings and if it is going to be useful in a business environment, it must be able to call upon the tools and competencies required in each of these four stages.

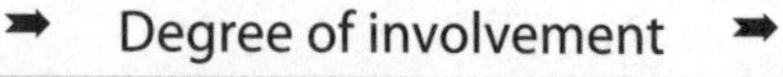

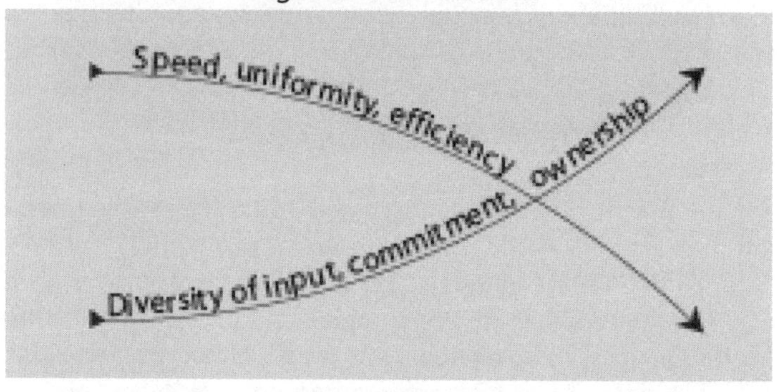

When do we employ consultation or group decision-making? Surely there are times when it is wise for an individual to make a decision without consulting. Imagine a building is burning down. We smell smoke. There are several ways we could get organized to leave the building and we certainly want everyone's understanding and commitment. Shall we gather folks around in small groups and consult on all the different ways we could get out and in what order and reach consensus? Surely this is a time when it would be far wiser for the person who knows where the exits are to stand up and in a loud and commanding voice take charge and march everyone out. This is a good time for obedience in response to command, not endless questioning or conversation.

There is a cost in time and hours consumed in any type of group decision-making. This investment may be worthwhile when more than one member of the group has knowledge and experience that is important to the decision, when there is sufficient time for the group to decide, when several members of the group will need to be committed to the decision and will take action and when the group can benefit from the sharing and learning that will occur in consultation.

It may be wise to delegate decision-making to one person or a few people when speed is of the essence, when an individual or a few individuals possess the critical knowledge (a doctor, for example) required or when the matter is simply not worth the time and cost of group decision-making.

You can divide decision-making along this continuum from command decision-making to consultative decision-making. At one end those who are consulted have knowledge, care or must act; at the other is true consensus or group decisions in which the group gathers together and takes shared ownership for the decision. Effective management requires each of these to be employed as they are most appropriate.

You can summarize consultation in the following way. Consultation is . . .

- the process of creating collective wisdom among a group

- a culture of shared responsibility and ownership for results

- detaching the ego from the idea, contributing, letting go and submitting to the group

- a process of learning, inherent in the process of deciding

- a process of establishing unity of thought and action

- reaching a decision through a focus on principles, honest and frank sharing, completely open listening and detachment from self

- the spiritual quality of humility and unity

How will we achieve this ideal of consultation in our work settings, our spiritual gatherings and in our homes? While there are important skills and habits that can be developed with the help of training, and as important as this will be, it will not be sufficient. What is required in addition is personal transformation and connection with the spiritual qualities we believe to be those of God, as are so well displayed by our Exemplar, 'Abdu'l-Bahá. We are told that the following is a description of 'Abdu'l-Bahá uttered by Bahá'u'lláh and it provides, I believe, a perfect model for the spirit in which we should approach consultation:

> Whatever a person says, hollow and product of vain imaginings and a parrot-like repetition of somebody else's views though it be, one ought to let it pass. One should not engage in disputation leading to and ending with obstinate refusal and hostility, because the other person would consider himself worsted and defeated. Consequently further veils intervene between him and the Cause, and he becomes more negligent of it. One ought to say: right, admitted, but look at the matter in this other way, and judge for yourself whether it is true or false; of course it should be said with courtesy, with kindliness, with consideration. Then the other person will listen, will not seek to answer back and to marshal proofs in repudiation. He will agree, because he comes to realize that the purpose has not been to engage in verbal battle and to gain mastery over him. He sees that the purpose has been to impart the word of truth, to show humanity, to bring forth heavenly qualities. His eyes and his ears are opened, his heart responds, his true nature unfolds, and by the grace of God, he becomes a new creation . . . The Most Great Branch gives a willing ear to any manner of senseless talk, to such an extent that the other person says to himself: He is trying to learn from me. Then, gradually, by such means as the other person cannot perceive, He gives him insight and understanding.[7]

Our challenge, therefore, is to achieve a personal transformation, attain the spiritual qualities that will allow us to enter into a pattern of dialogue with others that will be of similar character. In the world of business and commerce this requires an escape from the habits and norms of our current daily culture.

Questions for Discussion and Reflection

1) You are a member of the management team in a corporation. The culture of the company is adversarial and the normal pattern of conversation is one of debate. It is quite normal for discussion within this management team to be one where only one or two people contribute or the conversation degenerates into a heated argument as one member attempts to win his point over the other. How can you influence this group towards a more consultative pattern of decision-making?

2) You are now the manager of a software development group. The experts who work to develop your software reside and work on three continents and in five different locations. They communicate frequently by email and Instant Messenger. Occasionally there are telephone or video conferences to discuss common issues. Most of their work is done alone, sitting in front of their computers. There are two problems: first, there has been a high level of turnover among this group demonstrating little loyalty to the organization; second, there are frequent disagreements about what was decided in meetings, and even when this seemed to be clear, individuals went in their own direction. What will you do to employ the principle of consultation in this group?

3) You are the owner and manager of a small (about 20 members) professional service firm. All of the members of the firm, with the exception of a couple of young administrative staff, are mature, experienced and very competent. You have a once a month, all day, team meeting to share developments and engage them in decision-making and learning activities. There has been

some dissatisfaction among the group with the compensation system, which they feel does not sufficiently recognize different levels of skill or the contribution to selling new business. In the open meeting one member suggests that a team, composed of the professional staff, be formed to design their own compensation plan. How do you feel about this? Is it a good idea, and if so, would you place any boundaries or provide any guidance to this group? What would cause the exercise to be successful?

Other Quotations and Views on Consultation

If you want to reach a state of bliss, then go beyond your ego and the internal dialogue. Make a decision to relinquish the need to control, the need to be approved, and the need to judge. Those are the three things the ego is doing all the time. It's very important to be aware of them every time they come up. *Deepak Chopra*

War seems to be part of the history of humanity. As we look at the situation of our planet in the past, countries, regions, and even villages were economically independent of one another. Under those circumstances, the destruction of our enemy might have been a victory for us. There was a relevance to violence and war. However, today we are so interdependent that the concept of war has become outdated. When we face problems or disagreements today, we have to arrive at solutions through dialogue. Dialogue is the only appropriate method. One-sided victory is no longer relevant. We must work to resolve conflicts in a spirit of reconciliation and always keep in mind the interests of others. We cannot destroy our neighbors! We cannot ignore their interests! Doing so would ultimately cause us to suffer. I therefore think that the concept of violence is now unsuitable. Nonviolence is the appropriate method. *Dalai Lama*

The most important aspect of freedom of speech is freedom to learn. All education is a continuous dialogue – questions and answers that pursue every problem on the horizon. That is the essence of academic freedom. *William Orville Douglas*

A man's character may be learned from the adjectives which he habitually uses in conversation. *Mark Twain*

The trouble with her is that she lacks the power of conversation but not the power of speech. *George Bernard Shaw*

Silences make the real conversations between friends. Not the saying but the never needing to say is what counts. *Margaret Lee Runbeck*

To listen well is as powerful a means of influence as to talk well, and is as essential to all true conversation. *Chinese proverb*

My God! The English language is a form of communication! Conversation isn't just crossfire where you shoot and get shot at! Where you've got to duck for your life and aim to kill! Words aren't only bombs and bullets – no, they're little gifts, containing meanings! *Philip Roth*

It was impossible to get a conversation going; everybody was talking too much. *Yogi Berra*

When we are debating an issue, loyalty means giving me your honest opinion, whether you think I'll like it or not. Disagreement, at this stage, stimulates me. But once a decision has been made, the debate ends. From that point on, loyalty means executing the decision as if it were your own. *Colin Powell*

The well-run group is not a battlefield of egos. *Lao Tzu*

The greater the loyalty of a group toward the group, the greater is the motivation among the members to achieve the goals of the group, and the greater the probability that the group will achieve its goals. *Rensis Likert*

5

Unity

Uniting Energy and Effort

> Bahá'u'lláh taught, that Religion is the chief foundation of Love and Unity and the cause of Oneness. If a religion become the cause of hatred and disharmony, it would be better that it should not exist. To be without such a religion is better than to be with it.[1]

Systems of organization that have been built upon class distinction are the dinosaurs of our age. Corporations have preserved class structure in the distinctions between management and labor, between salaried and hourly workers, between thinkers and doers. They are all increasingly false and useless baggage, carried forward into a new world from a dying civilization. Class and rank served a useful purpose in the military organization in which obedience to authority was essential. The Church distinguished between those with authority, the clergy, and those who in its early days could neither read nor write and obeyed the authority of the clergy. Early industrial organizations were modeled after military and church organizations with a strong hierarchy and clear class distinctions.

Class distinctions create a barrier to human development, causing those of a perceived lesser class to abdicate their own power of reason, to acquiesce rather than to inquire. This is a block to the potential for both individual and institutional progress. And the privileges of a class-based society are the seeds of corruption and alienation. Only through creating the mechanisms of unity within the enterprise, and recognizing the unity of the entire human race, both in its internal and external relationship, can the enterprise thrive in the modern world.

The concept of unity is profound and requires a great deal of meditation to comprehend its full significance. There are also many different types of unity and different characteristics that promote unity. For the sake of brevity, I will attempt to focus on the unity that affects our work organizations.

Understanding unity requires some systems-thinking, an ability to analyze a part as an interdependent whole-system. This is easy to see through understanding the human body. Medicine has become so specialized that doctors often focus on a part of the body rather than the whole. If you have a pain in your chest you may go to a cardiologist, fearing it is a problem with your heart. But that symptom could also be related to the functioning of your digestive system, respiratory system or even your nervous system. When considering the sub-systems, or parts, of the whole human system it is easy to see their interdependence and interaction. There is an inherent liability in dealing with any one sub-system without considering these interactions, without considering the whole system.

Similarly, in organization life, there are several different sub-systems that comprise the whole system of the organization. There can be unity within sub-systems and there can be unity between them. For example, the human resource system may have internal conflicts or disunity. The training system may not be developing the skills that are called for in the performance appraisal process. Or the compensation system may contradict some of the cultural goals of the human resource system. This is internal disunity. Also, the information system of the organization may not be aligned or unified with the work process. Teams may have been formed to manage steps along the work flow but these teams may not be receiving the information they require to monitor their progress. And the compensation system may contradict the work of the teams by rewarding only individual performance and not group performance. Most of our organizations are misaligned or suffer from internal disunity. This is a major cause of poor performance and a reason why some type of whole-system design process is required.

Another way to consider unity of the organization is to consider the internal and external unity. The beginning of all unity is the unity of self. In an earlier chapter I suggested that we can look at our own unity in terms of the material self, the social self, the intellectual and the spiritual self. Simply put, if an individual is so obsessed with his intellectual development that he does nothing but study, he will suffer in his social relationships. A healthy and happy human being is one who is balanced in his capacities or different characteristics of the self. It is similarly true that if an organization works towards the development of the whole it is more likely to prosper in the long run. If it is entirely focused on material progress (making the most money in the short term), it is likely to damage its relationships with customers and suppliers; it is also likely to damage the motivation and spirit of those who work in the organization and it will fail to develop the human capital which will determine future performance. This is internal unity.

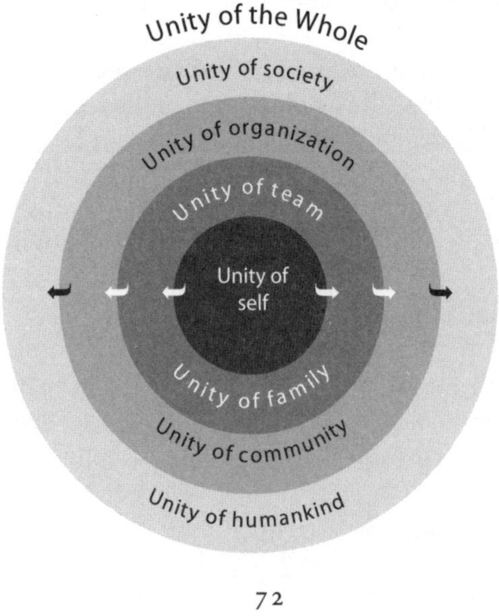

Unity of the Whole
Unity of society
Unity of organization
Unity of team
Unity of self
Unity of family
Unity of community
Unity of humankind

There is also external unity, or the unity of the organization with its larger system. There are many ways to look at the larger system, the environment, in which any organization operates. There is the larger economy that impacts the organization, the social system that determines fashion and other trends. There is an industry environment that also influences performance.

Another way to view this unity is to see unity as a series of concentric circles, beginning with the individual. Individuals who are disunified within are likely to be a source of disunity within their teams and organizations. Individuals who 'have their act together' – who are unified within themselves – are more likely to contribute to the unity of the team and organization. There is then the unity of teams, the immediate work group that, in the organization, serves many of the same functions as the family in society. It is the first social system, the foundation building block of the society of the organization. Then there is the unity of the organization as a whole system. And finally there is the unity of society, the larger socio-economic world within which every organization must function. In the following passage 'Abdu'l-Bahá reflects on a similar understanding of the need for unity within before unity with larger groups can be achieved.

> But the wise souls who are aware of the essential relationships emanating from the realities of things consider that one single matter cannot, by itself, influence the human reality as it ought and should, for until the minds of men become united, no important matter can be accomplished. At present Universal Peace is a matter of great importance, but unity of conscience is essential, so that the foundation of this matter may become secure, its establishment firm and its edifice strong.[2]

Strategic management is a process of continually monitoring the whole system: monitoring the organization's response to the market place, monitoring the internal alignment of the various systems, monitoring the alignment of teams or groups within the organization and monitoring the relationship between the organization and community or society interests. In order to be an executive of any large organization today, one must be a systems-thinker, must be capable of designing and redesigning the whole system as the environment changes. Because the external environment (social, economic, technical) is constantly changing, we must constantly rethink the nature of the system in order to be in unity with the environment.

A major issue of unity within the organization is that of artificial class. We might legitimately refer to class when we refer to those who are distinguished for their accomplishments or knowledge. In addition there is the artificial class associated with rank and position. We have all grown up with hierarchical models firmly implanted in our brains. We are 'moving up' the organization. I am 'feeling up' today. I'm not having a 'downer of a day'. We are conditioned to desire to 'climb the ladder' of the organization. This idea of hierarchy, of a social class system is truly ancient, yet it is one that the teachings of the Bahá'í Faith are clearly designed to alter.

> Most of 'Abdu'l-Bahá's life has been spent in an Eastern prison, which he gladly endured rather than abjure his faith, one of the tenets of which is the absolute equality of souls regardless of physical differences, such as sex and color. He recognizes no class distinctions except those conferred by service and the spirit of brotherly love. For this and other like doctrines he was held prisoner for forty years in the fortress city of 'Akká, in Palestine.[3]

> This is a new cycle of human power. All the horizons of the world are luminous, and the world will become indeed as a garden and a paradise. It is the hour of unity of the sons of men and of the drawing together of all races and all classes. You are loosed from ancient superstitions which have kept men ignorant, destroying the foundation of true humanity.[4]

> This remarkable personage [Bahá'u'lláh] was able by these principles to establish a bond of unity among the differing sects and divergent people of Írán. Those who followed His teachings no

> matter from what denomination or faction they came were conjoined by the ties of love, until now they cooperate and live together in peace and agreement. They are real brothers and sisters. No distinctions of class are observed among them and complete harmony prevails. Daily this bond of affinity is strengthening and their spiritual fellowship continually develops.[5]

Achieving unity of those in an organization is not merely a matter of possessing the right thoughts and saying the right words. It is a matter of designing the organization so the systems and structures minimize unnecessary differences and unite people in a common campaign for the good of the whole.

Some years ago Jack Stack, the plant manager of International Harvester's Springfield Remanufacturing Center, along with other plant managers, sought to purchase this unprofitable, low technology remanufacturer of diesel engines in the heart of the rust belt. For several years the company had tried to find a buyer to divest itself of this drain on profitability. Failing in its efforts to find a buyer with money, International Harvester sold the plant to its managers on favorable terms.

Having invested their meager life savings and now in the possession of a money-losing enterprise, Jack Stack and his compatriots knew they had to do something radically different from the traditional patterns of management. Jack decided that he had to get everyone in the plant playing the same game, what he came to call the 'Great Game of Business'.[6] He broke the plant down into work teams. He taught every hourly employee and manager to read the profit and loss statement and the balance sheet. Every employee was given the company P&L statement every month. Every week they were given a statement for their own department. There were no secrets. Everyone knew the truth about the business. They knew where the money came from and where it went. Everyone was involved in deciding how to improve ratios of income to expense and the variances between budgeted and actual numbers. Every employee was made an owner and given a share of potential profits. People changed. The business changed.

In eight years this business that appeared doomed to failure, without any significant infusion of capital, technology or outside expertise, went from a per share value of ten cents to more than 25 dollars. The employees started 20 new businesses, 18 of which were profitable. Mercedes Benz ships diesel engines to the SRC for remanufacturing and many of the employees have become millionaires. Every employee is in touch with the reality of the financial well-being of the enterprise and every employee takes responsibility.

This story has been repeated dozens of times. It is the story of people who, when placed in a system that acknowledges their potential, that assumes their maturity and eliminates the destructive class distinctions that deny responsibility, sees those people rise to the level of these expectations. First-level employees, even though they work in factories, are today more intellectually able than senior managers of earlier generations. They are fully capable of involvement in the real management of the enterprise.

> . . . Bahá'u'lláh compared the world to the human body . . . Paradoxically, it is precisely the wholeness and complexity of the order constituting the human body – and the perfect integration . . . that permit the full realization of the distinctive capacities in each . . . [7]

Dr Edwards Deming, the late guru of the quality movement, was fond of saying that 95 per cent of the quality problems are caused by management and management is responsible for the system. We blame the person but the problem is in the system. Until we understand how to change the system we will make little progress. Deming was right. The manager of the future is a system engineer, a designer of not only technical but human systems. The system of the organization is the problem. It either creates synergy, integration and unity or it promotes division and distinctions that cripple the inventiveness and energy of the individual. For the rest of our lifetime we will be exploring the challenge of creating institutional structures and processes that unite people in a common cause.

> Clearly, the advancement of the race has not occurred at the expense of human individuality. As social organization has increased, the scope for the expression of the capacities latent in each human being has correspondingly expanded. Because the relationship between the individual and society is a reciprocal one, the transformation now required must occur simultaneously within human consciousness and the structure of social institutions . . . the purpose must be to establish enduring foundations on which planetary civilization can gradually take shape.[8]

In order to achieve unity, either within oneself, within a team or among an organization, what then are the characteristics that must be developed? There are eight pillars of unity that I believe contribute to unity at each level of human organization. I will summarize them here briefly since they are the sole subject of another book.[9]

1) Trust

Just as the unity found in personal relationships is a voluntary act, an act of attraction rather than compliance, the unity that most often results in the success of organizations is discretionary. We choose to share ideas; we choose to think about problems driving in the car or while taking a shower. It is this discretionary effort that is evoked by a culture of trust. The habit of discretionary effort is a form of social capital.

The glue that holds all groups together is trust. Yes, we have a competitive economy and a competitive social system. We compete to be on the baseball team, we compete for grades, we compete for jobs and we finally compete for business. We value those who are highly competitive and who strive to win. Yet even the winner's success depends not only on his ability to compete but on the ability to cooperate as a unified whole.

Robert Wright's thesis in *Nonzero: The Logic of Human Destiny* is that greater degrees of trust are required by complex organizations and, as civilization advances, organizations become more complex or trust dependent. With complexity the challenge of unity becomes more difficult and requires more sophisticated means of trust-building. Wrights says, 'As history progresses, human beings find themselves playing non-zero-sum games with more and more other human beings. Interdependence expands and social complexity grows in scope and depth.'[10] And for this reason, because of the increasing degree of complexity and interdependence, the creation of trust and the resulting unity is an economic necessity.

2) Purpose

The capacity to lead is directly related to the pursuit of worthy purpose. We have a personal responsibility to know and display purpose in our lives. Why? Because it is to the degree that we pursue an ennobling purpose that we tend to attract others. Leaders must attract others if they expect to have followers. Purpose attracts and therefore serves as a unifying force. There is unity to the degree of shared purpose. Our level of satisfaction and our level of energy are directly related not only to our understanding of our own purpose but also to whether the organization, the team, the family to which we contribute share that same purpose.

In this regard let us recall a passage from Chapter 2.

> Something within our nature . . . determines that we all seek and will sacrifice for that which is noble. Every leader understands, perhaps intuitively, that followers will sacrifice for a noble purpose and the leader defines the mission of the organization in terms of a worthy purpose. We will sacrifice, even our lives, for a cause we perceive to be noble and worthy. Why? Because we understand the mystery of sacrifice and that when we sacrifice our money, time, energy to that which we hold to be noble, there is no sacrifice but only an investment – one with a guaranteed return – and that return is in that which is most precious to us: our own nobility and worth. The mystery of sacrifice is that we become like that unto which we sacrifice ourselves. When we sacrifice our self to that which is noble, we become more ennobled. And therefore the leader who promotes a worthy purpose acts to create both energy and unity.[6]

3) Dialogue

Consultation – particularly that type of consultation that is genuine dialogue – builds unity. In every conversation there is a mysterious process by which we are forming attractions and bonds of unity, or we are distancing ourselves, creating separation from the other person. It is not simply a matter of what we say and it certainly is not a matter of being right or wrong. It is in the spirit of the discourse; the spirit of winning a contest by displaying superior wit or the spirit of shared discovery and appreciation. The first creates alienation while the second unites the parties. One is an exercise in thinking and acting alone while the second is an exercise in thinking together. Those who are always thinking and acting alone are likely to be less happy than those who tend to think and discover with others.

4) Teamwork

The principles of unity are mutually reinforcing. Strong trust and purpose, and an understanding of dialogue, enable teamwork. Effective score keeping and an understanding of the flow or processes are also essential to teamwork. In a sense, all of these come together in the work of groups, at every level of the organization. Just as I sincerely believe that a society is no stronger than its families, similarly, no corporation will long be stronger than the effectiveness of work groups.

By 'teamwork' I am not referring simply to good relations among associates. I am referring to people who actually work together in a team, who actually rely on each other to get work done. Work cells, management teams or groups by any other name that share responsibility for a work process, share the responsibility for results and together make decisions about their work, this is genuine teamwork and we must design our organizations so everyone has a home team, a group that is their family at work.

5) Appreciation

The most successful way for a parent to do away with bad behavior on the part of a young child is to consistently reinforce and demonstrate appreciation for the opposite, the positive behavior. In other words, if a child screams and fusses in the grocery store, the parent may punish that behavior. Or the parent may praise the child for how well he behaves when, of course, he does behave well. Strengthening the child's good behavior through appreciation will cause good behavior to replace the bad behavior. Unfortunately, many parents are too consumed with a focus on the negative. In so doing, they not only create miserable children but they make their own lives miserable. Many managers are slaves to the same self-defeating cycle.

At work we reinforce good performance with compensation increases, bonuses and dozens of forms of recognition. We create a climate, a culture, through our own personal behavior by either focusing on desired performance or expressing appreciation; or we create a climate of fear and alienation by looking for the negative case to punish. It is guaranteed chemistry. If you demonstrate appreciation for something I have done, I immediately feel a bond with you. If I demonstrate appreciation for something you have done, you are more likely to share with me, discuss problems openly and generally engage in consultation. Appreciation creates bonds of unity.

6) Score keeping

Score keeping is not only essential to the motivation of a team but it is a system that creates unity in groups. Imagine the scoreboard at a basketball or football game – everyone watches it, everyone cheers when it changes and without it there would be no fans in the stands. What is the magic of the scoreboard? If you understand this then you understand how to create great score keeping systems at work. Something about the way we are internally wired causes us to derive great pleasure in seeing the numbers change. Watching the ball go through the hoop, everyone cheers. Then their eyes turn to the scoreboard and they are pleased with the change in score. The entire process helps to bond the team and fans together.

7) Flow

Mihaly Csikszentmihalyi described flow as the psychology of optimal experience:

> It is what the sailor holding a tight course feels when the wind whips through her hair, when the boat lunges through the waves like a colt – sail, hull, wind, and sea humming in a harmony that vibrates in the sailor's veins. It is what the painter feels when the colors on the canvas begin to set up a magnetic tension with each other, and a new *thing*, a living form, takes shape in front of the astonished creator.[11]

This experience of flow is not a serendipitous accident or surprise. The sailor has studied her course and angle to the wind, has set the right sail for the conditions and has practiced her hand on the tiller and knows how her boat responds to this wind and these waves. The appearance of natural or effortless performance is the result of trained competence.

This flow is the flow of a process, a series of steps leading to a result, and these steps are so well known that their performance appears effortless. Processes at work rarely provide a similar sense of exhilaration. Notice that processes that are exhilarating, that flow, are without interruption, have an efficiency of no unnecessary steps and are controlled by those who are engaged in the performance. Processes are a horizontal flow through the source of interruptions we call organization. In a unified organization the process controls the organization, not the other way around.

8) Discipline

All cultures, all organizations, dance to the beat of their own drums. The beat of the drum creates unity of motion, unity in the spirit of the group. It must be in the human genetic code, a natural and universal need to bring order and energy to people. Every culture has a calendar that proclaims a regular drumbeat – days, weeks, months and years. It is fixed rhythm of 2/2 or 2/4 time. The religion found in every culture, has its drumbeat of daily and weekly worship, annual periods of sacrifice and self-reflection.

All work, going back to ancient times, progresses with the rhythm of the drum. All work songs – sea shanties to which sailors hauled in the lines, the drums of the galley slaves, the field songs and hollers of African-American slaves and prison camps that are the most fundamental roots of blues and later rock 'n' roll – reflect the primal need in our souls to dance to the rhythm of the drum. Without drumbeats we would all be 'doing our own thing', on our own time and at our own pace.

Each of these eight pillars of unity in the organization are behavioral characteristics and processes. They are not a mystical or illusive phenomena. They are things that managers create through the design of organizational processes, system, structure and skills. Creating these mechanisms of unity is the job of the manager.

Questions for Discussion and Reflection

1) Let us assume that you have a friend whose life may not be well balanced. His parents placed great value on academic achievement; he did well in school and excelled in college. His favorite activity is, to this day, reading almost any book that challenges his mind. Almost every night he is occupied reading. He never enjoyed going to dances or going out to parties or other group activities. He does not have many friends. What would you advise this person to do for his development? What are the challenges he must overcome and why? How is this case similar or dissimilar to your own life?

2) In your workplace you are a member of a team responsible for serving a group of customers. While your customers are not complaining, you feel that the work your group does is far less

than it could do. You feel that with some creativity and extra effort you could build into your services features that would be of great benefit to the clients, and when they understood those benefits, would be extremely pleased. However, the majority of your group is satisfied with the current work they do and they don't want to 'rock the boat'. You have grown increasingly frustrated with this attitude and other members of the team sense that you are becoming alienated from the group. You are beginning to feel that you are a source of disunity. What should you do? What is the greatest priority in this case? Why?

3) The information systems manager has just purchased a major software package that will impact the way almost everyone does their work in your organization. A team of consultants working for the software company have come into the organization and are now designing the implementation of the software. These consultants know very little about the actual work your group does and they do not know that there are major problems in the flow of the work that need to be fixed. Fixing these problems in the flow of the work may result in a redesign of the organization around a new process, changes in responsibilities and changes in the need for information. You mentioned this to one of the consultants and he responded as if this was not his problem. You are faced with the potential for major disunity in the organization if things continue down this path. How do you handle this situation when you are not the one with actual power or authority to affect either of these changes? How is this similar to issues within your own workplace and how are you dealing with those?

Other Quotations and Views on Unity

He who experiences the unity of life sees his own Self in all beings, and all beings in his own Self, and looks on everything with an impartial eye. *Buddha*

When you make the sacrifice in marriage, you're sacrificing not to each other but to unity in a relationship. *Joseph Campbell*

Where there is unity there is always victory. *Publilius Syrus (1st century BC Roman author)*

For the unity of freedom has never relied on uniformity of opinion. *John Fitzgerald Kennedy*

It is a magnificent feeling to recognize the unity of complex phenomena which appear to be things quite apart from the direct visible truth. *Albert Einstein*

Do not follow the ideas of others, but learn to listen to the voice within yourself. Your body and mind will become clear and you will realize the unity of all things. *Dogen (Japanese Buddhist monk and philosopher 1200–53)*

By faithfulness we are collected and wound up into unity within ourselves, whereas we had been scattered abroad in multiplicity. *Saint Augustine*

The reason why the world lacks unity, and lies broken and in heaps, is, because man is disunited with himself. *Ralph Waldo Emerson*

The essence of the beautiful is unity in variety. *William Somerset Maugham*

Only peril can bring the French together. One can't impose unity out of the blue on a country that has 265 different kinds of cheese. *Charles de Gaulle*

Unity to be real must stand the severest strain without breaking. *Mahatma Gandhi*

Buddhism has the characteristics of what would be expected in a cosmic religion for the future: It transcends a personal God, avoids dogmas and theology; it covers both the natural and the spiritual, and it is based on a religious sense aspiring from the experience of all things, natural and spiritual, as a meaningful unity. *Albert Einstein*

In the East the wilderness has no evil connotation; it is thought of as an expression of the unity and harmony of the universe. *William Orville Douglas*

Civilization is a process in the service of Eros, whose purpose is to combine single human individuals, and after that families, then races, peoples and nations, into one great unity, the unity of mankind. Why this has to happen, we do not know; the work of Eros is precisely this. *Sigmund Freud*

I know that my unity with all people cannot be destroyed by national boundaries and government orders. *Leo Nikolaevich Tolstoy*

As the unity of the modern world becomes increasingly a technological rather than a social affair, the techniques of the arts provide the most valuable means of insight into the real direction of our own collective purposes. *Marshall McLuhan*

From of old the things that have acquired unity are these: Heaven by unity has become clear; Earth by unity has become steady; The Spirit by unity has become spiritual; The Valley by unity has become full; All things by unity have come into existence. *Lao Tzu*

6

Moderation

The principle of moderation is one of those most conducive to a spiritual life. Moderation enhances the environment to enable dialogue and appreciation of diverse points of view. It uplifts the spirit of a group or community. It creates a framework for justice.

When we think about moderation in business we are likely to think first about money. We are told, 'Fear ye God, and take heed not to outstrip the bounds of moderation, and be numbered among the extravagant.'[1]

When considering moderation, material excess is certainly an important aspect that needs our attention, particularly in western developed countries. However, there are other aspects of life that require moderation – moderation in how one uses one's time, moderation of speech and behavior – while moderation in our views and priorities can prevent us from committing important errors.

True dialogue among people is impossible without moderation. The ambition for excess material goods or an excess of speech causes separation and alienation. They hinder unity. Much of the difficulty within groups, between individuals and in public affairs is caused by a lack of moderation. In many countries the culture has promoted and rewarded those with the most immoderate speech and denigrated those who speak with a balanced or moderate view. This is very often a source of conflict. Imagine the family situation in which one party, pressured and dedicated to her work, announces that she has to work all weekend. The husband, frustrated that he will once again be taking the children to events alone, says, 'All you care about is your work. If you really loved your family you would sacrifice work and spend more time with your children!' It is not hard to write the words that would follow: it is likely to be in the same tone. It may well be that the woman's work pattern is immoderate but the language used by the husband – 'if you really loved your family', implying that she does not – is also immoderate. For both, moderation is a source of unity and immoderation is a source of conflict and disunity. Speaking of the conditions required for consultation, 'Abdu'l-Bahá said,

> They must then proceed with the utmost devotion, courtesy, dignity, care and moderation to express their views. They must in every matter search out the truth and not insist upon their own opinion, for stubbornness and persistence in one's views will lead ultimately to discord and wrangling and the truth will remain hidden. The honoured members must with all freedom express their own thoughts, and it is in no wise permissible for one to belittle the thought of another, nay, he must with moderation set forth the truth, and should differences of opinion arise a majority of voices must prevail, and all must obey and submit to the majority.[2]

The culture in the year 2006 in the United States is particularly one that promotes a lack of moderation. Television and radio talk show hosts publish books with titles like *Slander, Libel* and *Liberalism is a Mental Disorder* to emphasis the author's disagreement and disdain for those with differing opinions. This exaggerated language is the product of a media that creates or exaggerates enemies for audience appeal. Television talk shows have, for the most part, become a form of entertainment, much like a staged wrestling match, with the entertainment value in the heat and passion of the debate rather than in any depth of meaning or intellectual inquiry. Immoderation sells TV time. Moderate talk is much less exciting. In this we have a problem. The freedom to compete for audience share, the freedom to appeal to an audience in any way, no matter how debasing that may be, leads to immoderate behavior. This can only be resolved by the promotion of spiritual values that cause viewers to turn the channel and ignore immoderate language and behavior.

The issue of executive compensation is probably the most obvious, but not the only, example of a lack of moderation. There is also no set of facts that does more to harm the credibility and legitimacy of corporations and their officers. It is hardly a global problem, however. In Japan, executive compensation is 11 times that of first level factory workers. In Germany it is 12 times, France 15 times, Canada 20 times, Britain 22 times, Mexico 47 times and, finally, in the United States the top executive receives approximately 500 times the compensation of the first level employee. This is the result of an entirely deficient system of corporate governance at the board level.

Many studies have been made to determine whether or not executive compensation is related to the performance of the executive. Unfortunately, it has been demonstrated that there is little or no correlation between compensation to senior executives and the financial performance of their companies. This is the immoderate excess of the free economy.

Many aspects of the free economy have promoted increased standards of living for all and the general wealth of the western world is largely attributable to a system of entrepreneurship. This however, should not distract one from the fundamental purpose of business enterprises in society. The purpose of business is to create aggregate wealth, to efficiently transform resources into goods and services that meet the needs of consumers and to develop human capacity towards productive ends. Making people and resources productive is the heart of the management task. To the degree that aggregate wealth, the wealth of society, is increased, poverty is diminished. If poverty is diminished then society as a whole becomes more moderate. You can approach immoderation from either end: the excess of wealth at the top or the wealth deficit at the bottom. Understanding the concept of productivity is essential to understanding the creation of aggregate wealth. The ability to make resources productive is the key to alleviating poverty.

Poverty is bad for business. Henry Ford understood it. He was not the first to produce cars. He was, however, the genius behind mass production with both its good and bad qualities. He was bigoted against the wealthy, particularly bankers. Unfortunately, he had to rely on bankers to start up his company. All of the other car manufacturers were making cars for the wealthy, those who had the money to afford a car. One might say they were operating on the simple principle of the great bank robber Willy Sutton who, when asked why he robbed banks, frankly explained, 'That's where the money is.' The bankers understood it too and wanted Ford to make cars for the wealthy. Ford had a different idea. He wanted to make cars for what he called 'the common man'. When the bankers protested that the 'common man' didn't have the money to buy a car, Ford replied that that was OK because he would hire a lot of them and pay them enough so they could afford to go out and buy one. Ford paid his workers five dollars a day, more than the going rate of three and half dollars paid by the Dodge brothers. Paying workers more than he had to didn't make a lot of sense to the bankers but he did it.

This was the *miracle of mass production*. With the improved efficiency of the system wealth was increased and individuals could afford to buy cars. Common men and women in industrialized countries were many times wealthier than before Ford's system. While there were negative effects of his system Ford had discovered a basic truth that is recognized by all economists: poverty is bad for business. Productivity is the ratio of input to output of any system. If 40 hours of work (input) produces x number of bushels of corn, widgets or cars (output), that is a measure of productivity. If the same input can produce 2x the output, then wealth is increased. The productivity of capital, energy and other inputs can be measured and improved, as well as work hours. Technology has continually had the effect of increasing productivity and wealth. This was true of the automated looms in textile mills, the combine and tractor on the farm, the assembly line and the computer. As a result of these improvements in productivity children do not need to work on the farm or in factories.

Unless one has this macroeconomic understanding of how wealth is created, one cannot begin to think intelligently about the elimination of poverty or abolishing the low end of the extremes of wealth. The most powerful force for the elimination of poverty today is education, increasing human capacity to be productive.

> But if conditions are such that some are happy and comfortable and some in misery; some are accumulating exorbitant wealth and others are in dire want – under such a system it is impossible for man to be happy and impossible for him to win the good pleasure of God. God is kind to all. The good pleasure of God consists in the welfare of all the individual members of mankind.[3]

Bahá'ís have been called to contribute to the process of social and economic development. In communities all over the world Bahá'ís are initiating projects dealing with education, justice, the training of children and other ways to address the needs for social and economic development. These initiatives address the fundamental issues of poverty.

If Bahá'ís are to be of genuine assistance in the field of economic development and help eliminate the extremes of wealth and poverty there are two essentials which must be understood. The first is the imperative to create rather than redistribute wealth. Many Bahá'ís have been conditioned by the academic anti-capitalist sentiment of the 1960s that was grounded in the adversarial assumptions of Marxist thought. Although progressive taxation is certainly just and justified, redistributing wealth has no potential to lift up the poor from poverty. Only the process of enabling the creation of new wealth among all segments of global society can eliminate the evils of poverty. Second, Bahá'ís must understand the currency of development in today's world. Until the last ten or 20 years, and for the previous 100 years, the critical currency of economic development was the control and productivity of capital and material resources. It was an age of *materialism* in the most literal sense of the word. However, we no longer live in an age in which the primary mechanism of development is the productivity of natural resources, capital or labor. We are now engaged in the second miracle of production.

Peter Drucker explained it well:

> The basic economic resource – 'means of production', to use the economist's term – is no longer capital, nor natural resources (the economist's *land*), nor labor. It is and will be knowledge. The central wealth creating activities will be neither the allocation of capital to productive uses, nor labor – the two poles of nineteenth and twentieth century economic theory, whether classical, Marxist, Keynesian, or neo-classical. Value is now created by 'productivity' and 'innovation', both applications of knowledge to work. The leading social groups of the knowledge society will be 'knowledge-workers' – knowledge executives who know how to allocate knowledge to productive use; knowledge professionals; knowledge employees. Practically all these knowledge people will be employed in organizations. Yet unlike the employees under capitalism, they will own both the 'means of production' and the 'tools of production' – the former through their pension funds, which are rapidly emerging in all developed countries as the only real owners; the latter because knowledge workers own their knowledge and can take it with them wherever they go. The economic challenge of the post capitalist society will therefore be the productivity of knowledge work and the knowledge worker.[4]

While it is obvious that not all societies have entered this post-capitalist era, it will not be necessary for economies in the earliest stages of development to go through the same stages of industrialization and mass production with all of their social consequences. With education and technology there is no reason why people in Samoa cannot participate in the knowledge work society and with less disruption to their culture and ecology than the traditional route of development.

Malaysia is a good case in point. Malaysia defies many stereotypes held in the West about socio-economic development. Malaysia is very aware of the information economy and the government is officially pursuing a strategy of becoming a leader in the information age. A multi-billion dollar 'MultiMedia Corridor' is being constructed outside of Kuala Lumpur with a billion dollars of investment from Microsoft. There are eight fiber optic cable plants in Malaysia and this high capacity cable is being laid throughout the country. Recently in the paper there were pronouncements of official policies to reach the indigenous and underprivileged people with Internet access, computers and education to bring them into the development process and to allow them to voice their views to the country and the world. On 21 September 1996 a headline in the *New Straits Times* proclaimed: *Making known our concept of civil society through IT.* The article states 'Malaysia must make known its concept of civil society to the world through information technology to make sure it is not overwhelmed by the Western dominated global concept of civil society.' Virtually every day in the newspaper there are stories about government and industry efforts to promote information technology and one recent article declared that companies must not move manufacturing to Malaysia to seek low skilled, low pay labor: there is no more. Only high value-adding jobs will be allowed. One could make a case that Malaysia, recently considered a less developed country, may surpass many so-called developed nations in their entry into the information age.

If we are to assist in abolishing the extremes of wealth and poverty we must understand the vehicle, the currency of wealth and poverty. Central to increasing that currency is the ability to access and utilize knowledge or information. This enables human capacity and development, the key to human productivity.

The principles of moderation and the elimination of the extremes of wealth and poverty quickly lead to the issue of the role of government and taxation. It is clear that the writings of the Bahá'í Faith endorse some form of progressive taxation, a system by which those in great need will not pay taxes and those with increasing amounts of income will pay an increasing percentage of that income in taxes. In the following passage 'Abdu'l-Bahá describes the creation of a storehouse in an agricultural village. In it He describes how taxes will vary by income.

First and foremost is the principle that to all the members of the body politic shall be given the greatest achievements of the world of humanity. Each one shall have the utmost welfare and well-being. To solve this problem we must begin with the farmer; there will we lay a foundation for system and order because the peasant class and the agricultural class exceed other classes in the importance of their service. In every village there must be established a general storehouse which will have a number of revenues.

The first revenue will be that of the tenth or tithes.

The second revenue (will be derived) from the animals.

The third revenue, from the minerals, that is to say, every mine prospected or discovered, a third thereof will go to this vast storehouse.

The fourth is this: whosoever dies without leaving any heirs all his heritage will go to the general storehouse.

Fifth, if any treasures shall be found on the land they should be devoted to this storehouse.

All these revenues will be assembled in this storehouse.

As to the first, the tenths or tithes: we will consider a farmer, one of the peasants. We will look into his income. We will find out, for instance, what is his annual revenue and also what are his expenditures. Now, if his income be equal to his expenditures, from such a farmer nothing whatever will be taken. That is, he will not be subjected to taxation of any sort, needing as he does all his income. Another farmer may have expenses running up to one thousand dollars we will say, and his income is two thousand dollars. From such an one a tenth will be required, because he has a surplus. But if his income be ten thousand dollars and his expenses one thousand dollars or his income twenty thousand dollars, he will have to pay as taxes, one-fourth. If his income be one hundred thousand dollars and his expenses five thousand, one-third will he have to pay because he has still a surplus since his expenses are five thousand and his income one hundred thousand. If he pays, say, thirty-five thousand dollars, in addition to the expenditure of five thousand he still has sixty thousand left. But if his expenses be ten thousand and his income two hundred thousand then he must give an even half because ninety thousand will be in that case the sum remaining. Such a scale as this will determine allotment of taxes. All the income from such revenues will go to this general storehouse.

Then there must be considered such emergencies as follows: a certain farmer whose expenses run up to ten thousand dollars and whose income is only five thousand, he will receive necessary expenses from the storehouse. Five thousand dollars will be allotted to him so he will not be in need.

Then the orphans will be looked after, all of whose expenses will be taken care of. The cripples in the village – all their expenses will be looked after. The poor in the village – their necessary expenses will be defrayed. And other members who for valid reasons are incapacitated – the blind, the old, the deaf – their comfort must be looked after. In the village no one will remain in need or in want. All will live in the utmost comfort and welfare. Yet no schism will assail the general order of the body politic.

Hence the expenses or expenditures of the general storehouse are now made clear and its activities made manifest. The income of this general storehouse has been shown. Certain trustees will be elected by the people in a given village to look after these transactions. The farmers will be taken care of and if after all these expenses are defrayed any surplus is found in the storehouse it must be transferred to the national treasury.

This system is all thus ordered so that in the village the very poor will be comfortable, the orphans will live happily and well; in a word, no one will be left destitute. All the individual members of the body politic will thus live comfortably and well.

For larger cities, naturally, there will be a system on a larger scale. Were I to go into that solution the details thereof would be very lengthy.[5]

From this it is clear that 'Abdu'l-Bahá thought carefully about the welfare of the poor and the distribution of profits. While this prescription does not provide a detailed set of guidelines for most societies today, it certainly makes clear the principles of taxation and moderation.

Also in the writings of the Bahá'í Faith are provisions for progressive taxation: the assumption that those who are better off should contribute relatively more than those who are less fortunate. While there are those in the West who argue for a flat tax, contending that it would be more fair, it would clearly not be more fair to tax the person earning 30,000 a year the same as the person earning 30 million. Most millionaires agree with this proposition. Ross Perot, the billionaire, when asked how he felt about paying millions each year in taxes, replied that it gave him great pleasure to look at his tax statement and realize how fortunate he was to have been able to earn so much income that he would have to pay so much in tax. While the debate about how much progressivity is fair and reasonable will most likely continue forever, there can be no doubt that Bahá'ís agree with Ross Perot, at least on this issue – it is a blessing to be able to pay a higher tax rate.

> Then rules and laws should be established to regulate the excessive fortunes of certain private individuals and meet the needs of millions of the poor masses; thus a certain moderation would be obtained. However, absolute equality is just as impossible, for absolute equality in fortunes, honors, commerce, agriculture, industry would end in disorderliness, in chaos, in disorganization of the means of existence, and in universal disappointment: the order of the community would be quite destroyed. Thus difficulties will also arise when unjustified equality is imposed. It is, therefore, preferable for moderation to be established by means of laws and regulations to hinder the constitution of the excessive fortunes of certain individuals, and to protect the essential needs of the masses.[6]

Moderation can never be a set of rules with clear guidelines. Moderation is a matter of personal judgment. We must develop a sense of moderation – moderation in our temperament, our speech, our ambitions and our treatment of others. The principle of moderation is necessarily linked to our understanding of the unity of humankind. It is forms of excess that have divided humankind throughout the ages. Excessive displays of wealth, excess in consumption, behavior and speech, even within a society that may appear homogeneous, are the mechanisms of class separation.

> In his summary of significant Bahá'í teachings, Shoghi Effendi wrote that Bahá'u'lláh 'inculcates the principle of "moderation in all things"; declares that whatsoever, be it "liberty, civilization and the like", "passeth beyond the limits of moderation" must "exercise a pernicious influence upon men"; observes that western civilization has gravely perturbed and alarmed the peoples of the world; and predicts that the day is approaching when the "flame" of a civilization "carried to excess" "will devour the cities".'[7]

Our society has conditioned us to perceive immoderate behavior as pleasing or associated with happiness. Constant messages from the television associate gold chains, fast cars, immoderate dress and huge houses with the fruits of success. In reality these things do not lead to happiness but rather to misery. It will require a huge culture shift to understand the falsehood of these messages. It is clear that the teachings of the Bahá'í Faith are in fact a prescription for happiness, not a call to asceticism or suffering. But it is our very extreme obsession with liberty that challenges us to rise above the commercialization of happiness to find what truly leads to a happy and worthy life.

> Thus, we hold to this ultimate perspective: Bahá'u'lláh came to set humanity free. His Revelation is, indeed, an invitation to freedom – freedom from want, freedom from war, freedom to unite, freedom to progress, freedom in peace and joy.
>
> You who live in a land where freedom is so highly prized have not, then, to dispense with its fruits, but you are challenged and do have the obligation to uphold and vindicate the distinction between the licence that limits your possibilities for genuine progress and the moderation that ensures the enjoyment of true liberty.[8]

Questions for Discussion and Reflection

1) Your great ambition was to start your own company and achieve financial security. You have succeeded. You are the founder and owner of a professional services firm. Your revenue is between five and six million dollars each year. After paying all of your expenses, including salaries that are at or above comparable market levels, you have a profit of approximately one million dollars. If you pay this out in bonuses, either to staff or to yourself, it will become compensation and therefore you will not owe corporate tax on that amount. If you retain the earnings or pay it to yourself as a dividend it will be taxed at the corporate tax rate of approximately 35%. What do you decide to do with these one million dollars? How does the principle of moderation apply in this case?

2) Warren Buffet is widely recognized as one of the world's great investors. He drives an old car, lives in a modest house and wears clothes that might be described as those of an absent-minded professor. In a recent year the shares of his company, Berkshire-Hathaway, underperformed the S&P 500. He announced in his annual letter to shareholders that he was personally responsible for this failure and advised his shareholders that if he could do no better there was no reason for them to invest their money in his company. In an interview with a group of students Buffet put his own talents into perspective. He said 'I was born wired to allocate capital well. If I was born in Bangladesh and I walked down the street explaining that "I allocate capital well", the townspeople would say "get a job". Bill Gates told me that if I were born 1000 years ago, I wouldn't survive because I am not fast or strong. I would find myself running from a lion screaming, "But, I allocate capital well!"' You should know that Warren Buffet's net worth is approximately 41 billion dollars. What does this information about him tell you about the principle of moderation? If you were successful enough to acquire a net worth of more than

one billion dollars, small by comparison, what would be your life style?

3) You work for a large corporation in their sales and marketing department. Your company is a close second to the market leader in your industry and the third place player is way behind. Your company is gaining in market share and revenue on the market leader. The vice president of sales and marketing can be described as a 'warrior' engaged in a passionate fight for first place. Becoming number one is his driving purpose, his passion, and everything the organization does is to serve this motive. In meetings to discuss marketing tactics it is common to employ the military metaphor such as 'this will kill them' or 'this will outflank them and be a surprise attack that can crush them in this market'. Everyone in the organization is caught up in this competitive spirit and this is expected as a sign of loyalty and commitment to the organization. How does this affect you? Is this relevant to the issue of moderation, and if so, how?

Other Quotations and Views on Moderation

The man who makes everything that leads to happiness depends upon himself, and not upon other men, has adopted the very best plan for living happily. This is the man of moderation, the man of manly character and of wisdom. *Plato*

Complete abstinence is easier than perfect moderation. *Saint Augustine*

The heart is great which shows moderation in the midst of prosperity. *Seneca*

A wise man is superior to any insults which can be put upon him, and the best reply to unseemly behavior is patience and moderation. *Molière*

Moderation is an ostentatious proof of our strength of character. *François de la Rochefoucauld*

The choicest pleasures of life lie within the ring of moderation. *Benjamin Disraeli*

Out of moderation a pure happiness springs. *Johann Wolfgang von Goethe*

To go beyond the bounds of moderation is to outrage humanity. *Blaise Pascal*

When the sword is once drawn, the passions of men observe no bounds of moderation. *Alexander Hamilton*

Throw moderation to the winds, and the greatest pleasures bring the greatest pains. *Democritus*

Moderation, which consists in an indifference about little things, and in a prudent and well-proportioned zeal about things of importance, can proceed from nothing but true knowledge, which has its foundation in self-acquaintance. *Plato*

The virtue of justice consists in moderation, as regulated by wisdom. *Aristotle*

Trade is the natural enemy of all violent passions. Trade loves moderation, delights in compromise, and is most careful to avoid anger. It is patient, supple, and insinuating, only resorting to extreme measures in cases of absolute necessity. Trade makes men independent of one another and gives them a high idea of their personal importance: it leads them to want to manage their own affairs and teaches them to succeed therein. Hence it makes them inclined to liberty but disinclined to revolution. *Alexis de Tocqueville*

My experience through life has convinced me that, while moderation and temperance in all things are commendable and beneficial, abstinence from spirituous liquors is the best safeguard of morals and health. *Robert E. Lee*

7

World Citizenship

The World of Commerce

Kenichi Ohmae, one of the most observant of management writers, has declared the death of the nation state in the borderless world:

> What we are witnessing is the cumulative effect of fundamental changes in the currents of economic activity around the globe. So powerful have these currents become that they have carved out entirely new channels for themselves – channels that owe nothing to the lines of demarcation on traditional political maps. Put simply, in terms of real flows of economic activity, nation states have already lost their role as meaningful units of participation in the global economy of today's borderless world.[1]

The nation state still exerts influence and control on commerce but with a decreasing effect each day. The national origin of goods and services is no longer clear, meaningful or recognized by consumers. Do you know where your car was produced or how much of it was produced in which country and do you care? Most nations are composed of diverse economic regions, not a homogeneous economy, and these regions are just as economically linked and interdependent with regions in other nations as within their own. The nation state is increasingly an anachronism.

In the last century to be engaged in multinational business

meant to be a large and powerful corporation. General Motors and ITT were multinational conglomerates with all of the connotations of excessive power and dominance. Today it is not at all unusual for a small professional service firm to serve multinational clients. My own firm had approximately 25 employees yet did business in Canada, the US, Mexico and South America, Malaysia, Oman and Egypt. We were certainly not large or powerful but we were multinational. Place – the predominant reality of the previous age and the material world – is becoming less and less relevant. Even large corporations like GE and ABB are preaching the gospel of thinking globally and small at the same time. The CEO of ABB, the world's largest power-engineering group, recently remarked that 'We are not a global business. We are a collection of local businesses with intense global coordination.' Consistent with the trend towards dispersed power, this company's headquarters shrank from 4,000 down to 200.[2] So much for the fear of the large centrally controlled company.

Tom Friedman, a *New York Times* columnist and keen observer of the international scene, recently published a book titled *The World is Flat*. Well, of course he is not suggesting that the world is actually flat but what he is suggesting is that the global economy has created a form of parity, as it is called in sports, in which players are traded and move from one team to the other, creating a level playing field. The global economy is rapidly creating a more level playing field, hence the world is flat. A good example of this is IBM's recent sale of its entire personal computer business to Lenova, a Chinese company that previously was just a contract manufacturer. There was a time when we were surprised that Japan was making quality cars. Now that is taken for granted. We then thought that Chinese labor was only capable of producing textiles or low technology manufactured goods. This is no longer true. China and India, two countries that have long been known for their masses of poor, are both becoming technology leaders and highly competitive economies. India has established a solid reputation in software development and services and China is now graduating more engineers and MBAs than the United States.

From its inception the Bahá'í Faith has recognized the emergence of global civilization and the economic and political systems that will be essential to its achievement. While much of the world is debating the issue of 'globalization', the business community is waiting for no one. The great leveling of the global economy is not controlled by the World Bank or International Monetary Fund; rather it is the organic process of free trade. The fastest growing economy and the one in which wealth is rising at the most rapid pace is China. And that growth is largely attributable to capital investment from wealthier countries that established manufacturing facilities to take advantage of (one could say 'exploit' but that implies a judgment I am not willing to make) cheap labor. However, with the rapid growth in the Chinese economy labor shortages are beginning to appear and that inevitably produces a rise in wage rates. This is as it should be and is the natural process of economic development. This is exactly the same process that led to both Japan and Korea becoming relatively wealthy and developed nations.

To understand the transformation of the global economy a simple set of numbers will help. A recent issue of *Road and Track* magazine published a report on the development of the automotive market in China. In 1986 there were a reported 986,000 automobiles on China's roads. In 2004 alone an estimated 2.36 million cars were sold in China. There were 168 miles of highways in China in 1989. By the end of 2003, during which year China spent $42 billion and used 40 per cent of the world's cement building roads, there were 18,500 miles. And if all goes according to plan, by 2008 there will be 51,000 miles, more than America's 46,000 miles of Interstates. In 2003 China became the second largest consumer of oil. The effects of that have already been felt at gas pumps around the world. If the Chinese were to continue following the model of the US, that is, ultimately to have the same number of cars per person, some project that China would burn 24.8 million barrels of oil every day – approximately what OPEC now produces. This growing demand for oil and the absence of major new oil finds is going to produce an increasing competition for petroleum resources and push prices higher. This will have dramatic implications for all of the world's economies. It will also, and is now, fueling investment in alternative energy sources and technologies.

We are so linked together by the network of supply chains and economic interdependence that we will be required to cooperate in the development of alternative energy sources and the management of global debt and currencies. The United States is rapidly becoming one of the larger debtor nations. Who is lending money to offset this debt? Japan and China are the two largest lenders to the United States. Put another way, China and Japan are gaining ownership of America. It is an odd irony. The US is dependent on China to produce cheap goods to sell in Wal-Mart, China is dependent on the US for jobs, the US is dependent on China to finance its excessive spending and/or under taxation and China is again dependent on the ability of the US to repay the money it has loaned. This interdependence may be viewed with horror by some but it may also be viewed as part of God's plan to create a global society that includes the entirety of the human race in one unified system.

Shoghi Effendi, the Guardian of the Bahá'í Faith wrote that

> A world community in which all economic barriers will have been permanently demolished and the interdependence of Capital and Labor definitely recognized; in which the clamor of religious fanaticism and strife will have been for ever stilled; in which the flame of racial animosity will have been finally extinguished; in which a single code of international law – the product of the considered judgment of the world's federated representatives – shall have as its sanction the instant and coercive intervention of the combined forces of the federated units; and finally a world community in which the fury of a capricious and militant nationalism will have been transmuted into an abiding consciousness of world citizenship – such indeed, appears, in its broadest outline, the Order anticipated by Bahá'u'lláh, an Order that shall come to be regarded as the fairest fruit of a slowly maturing age.[3]

The step-by-step process by which global integration would occur could not have been foreseen by the central figures of the Bahá'í Faith but the direction and mechanisms of integration they predicted are now emerging and no one has the power to stop those forces.

When I first encountered the Bahá'í Faith I was somewhat astonished by the claim that it included a pattern, a prescription, for a new world order. My thoughts immediately went to the totalitarian and messianic ambitions of communism, the wild ambitions of Napoleon and the conquest and inevitable collapse of the Roman Empire. Here was yet another fanatic religion set on imposing its order over all others. I think mine was a common initial reaction. However, with more careful study of the proposed 'new world order' and with the constant march of global communications, culture and commerce, its inevitability becomes more apparent each day. Another way to view the emergence of global order is to compare the state of affairs today with those at the founding of the United States. During the revolution of 1776 a soldier in George Washington's army wrote a letter home explaining that he didn't understand why he was fighting alongside these people who had a completely different language, a different religion, a different culture and values. He was from Connecticut and he was talking about fellow soldiers from Pennsylvania. Each state had its own militia and its own currency, as well as a different religious history. It was not certain at all that they belonged together in one nation. However, those with a more farsighted vision were able to see the benefits of union, the benefits of one common currency, a common language, a common set of laws and principles. We are in much the same place today as every country struggles with the issue of globalization, understanding how we either benefit or are damaged by our integration in the global economy. In every country there are voices advocating tariffs and protection against global forces of commerce while at the same time there are entrepreneurs seeing opportunities and taking advantage of the mechanisms of integration.

As we go down the path towards the globalization of the economy it would be worth considering the nature of the new world order described by Shoghi Effendi:

> Let there be no misgivings as to the animating purpose of the world-wide Law of Bahá'u'lláh. Far from aiming at the subversion of the existing foundations of society, it seeks to broaden its basis, to remold its institutions in a manner consonant with the needs of an ever-changing world. It can conflict with no legitimate allegiances, nor can it undermine essential loyalties. Its purpose is neither to stifle the flame of a sane and intelligent patriotism in men's hearts, nor to abolish the system of national autonomy so essential if the evils of excessive centralization are to be avoided. It does not ignore, nor does it attempt to suppress, the diversity of ethnical origins, of climate, of history, of language and tradition, of thought and habit, that differentiate the peoples and nations of the world. It calls for a wider loyalty, for a larger aspiration than any that has animated the human race. It insists upon the subordination of national impulses and interests to the imperative claims of a unified world. It repudiates excessive centralization on one hand, and disclaims all attempts at uniformity on the other. Its watchword is unity in diversity such as 'Abdu'l-Bahá Himself has explained.[4]

Today the most important resources are intellectual capital and the access to information. With these two elements you are in business and access to knowledge is the great equalizer. The potential transformation in commerce and the implications for social and economic development are so significant that our minds, conditioned by the assumptions of the pre-information age, can barely begin to comprehend. Within a few years, there is no reason why a student sitting on an island in the Pacific Ocean or in a village in South America will not be able to access all knowledge and presentations by the world's best teachers, to interact daily with other students, to access experts and resources from all over the globe, to gain every degree and engage in intellectual commerce without physically leaving the village. Without appreciating this potential we demonstrate our own enslavement to the industrial age. This access to common communication – total freedom to access information and communicate with others on the planet – is the most irresistible force creating a sense of world citizenship. One hundred and fifty years ago Bahá'u'lláh instructed that 'It is not for him to pride himself who loveth his own country, but rather for him who loveth the whole world. The earth is but one country, and mankind its citizens.'[5] For those around Him in prison cells in 'Akká and in exile in Constantinople and Palestine it must have seemed a strange vision. Today it is simple common sense.

World citizenship is a state of mind. It is not a passport or a place you call home. The leaders in business during the coming years will be those who possess the mind set of world citizenship. Every parent would do well to consider how to raise his children to have a global perspective, to have empathy and understanding of different cultures and people of diverse religions and ethnicity. My wife and I encouraged each of our three children to participate in some international experience every summer during their high school years. Those experiences shaped their perspectives in college and in their careers. Over the past several years I have consulted with AIESEC International, the global youth leadership organization that is entirely youth run and operates in 87 countries and with approximately 30,000 members. The very purpose of the organization is to help students gain international understanding and experience. Participating in organizations such as this helps young people understand global economic development and the issues that are on the minds of young people in other countries. And, perhaps as important, it is a forum for developing a personal global network of friends who may become helpful business contacts in the future.

The importance of a global perspective is well stated in this message prepared by the Bahá'í International Community:

> History has thus far recorded principally the experience of tribes, cultures, classes, and nations. With the physical unification of the planet in this century and acknowledgment of the interdependence of all who live on it, the history of humanity as one people is now beginning. The long, slow civilizing of human character has been a sporadic development, uneven and admittedly inequitable in the

> material advantages it has conferred. Nevertheless, endowed with the wealth of all the genetic and cultural diversity that has evolved through past ages, the earth's inhabitants are now challenged to draw on their collective inheritance to take up, consciously and systematically, the responsibility for the design of their future.[6]

In a few short years everyone will be connected to everyone, all knowledge will be available to all and place will be irrelevant. This is the context of business in the 21st century. The ability to compete and conduct business in the globally interconnected context is the challenge of the future. The village is the globe and it is now.

> World citizenship begins with an acceptance of the oneness of the human family and the interconnectedness of the nations of 'the earth, our home'. While it encourages a sane and legitimate patriotism, it also insists upon a wider loyalty, a love of humanity as a whole. It does not, however, imply abandonment of legitimate loyalties, the suppression of cultural diversity, the abolition of national autonomy, nor the imposition of uniformity. Its hallmark is 'unity in diversity'. World citizenship encompasses the principles of social and economic justice, both within and between nations; non-adversarial decision making at all levels of society; equality of the sexes; racial, ethnic, national and religious harmony; and the willingness to sacrifice for the common good.[7]

Questions for Discussion and Reflection

1) Your firm publishes training manuals for management development. It is a normal practice in the United States to provide a free copy to a company that may be a prospect for a large quantity purchase. Companies are also likely to purchase one copy to help them decide whether they will buy a quantity. You have reached an agreement with a Latin American training and development firm to represent you in Latin America. They advise you that you should not send out single copies of your materials because it is common to take that material and make

copies without respect to the copyright or fee. You feel that this is prejudicial and would be discriminating against Latin American companies. On the other hand, you respect the local knowledge of your affiliate. What do you do?

2) You work as a research scientist for a multinational pharmaceutical firm. You have been sent to the Amazon jungle to research natural health and healing practices among native tribal people. You have found that there is a tea that the tribal people make that they claim reduces pain. You gather samples of the plant used to make this tea which you take back to the research lab. From your research you discover that there is a chemical ingredient in the leaves of this plant that does have the reported effect. Your company then works for several years developing and testing a way to formulate those chemical elements and test the results. The results are positive. The new product will be made without using any of the native plants. It was only the knowledge of those plants that led to the discovery. Does your company have any financial or other responsibility to the native people? Why? In the course of making this decision you contact an expert in the tribal culture of these people. The expert advises you that paying any significant amount of money to the tribal people would destroy their culture that is not now dependent on any form of money. He tells you that if you pay them money you are imposing your values on them and this is a form of cultural imperialism. What do you do?

3) You are a young manager working for a major oil company. You have been asked to transfer to an Arab country where your company is a partner in the exploration and production of oil. You are newly married and your wife is also a young professional. If you accept this transfer you may bring your wife with you. However, she will not be allowed to work in this country and she will be required to conform to certain Islamic laws. She finds conforming to these laws a violation of her rights and culture. This move is very advantageous for your career and if

you turn this down it is likely to limit your success in this company. What do you do?

Other Quotations and Views on World Citizenship

We cannot wait for governments to do it all. Globalization operates on Internet time. Governments tend to be slow moving by nature, because they have to build political support for every step. *Kofi Annan*

It has been said that arguing against globalization is like arguing against the laws of gravity. *Kofi Annan*

We must ensure that the global market is embedded in broadly shared values and practices that reflect global social needs, and that all the world's people share the benefits of globalization. *Kofi Annan*

Globalization is not something we can hold off or turn off . . . it is the economic equivalent of a force of nature – like wind or water. *Bill Clinton*

Globalization could be the answer to many of the world's seemingly intractable problems. But this requires strong democratic foundations based on a political will to ensure equity and justice. *Sharan Burrow*

This is a very exciting time in the world of information. It's not just that the personal computer has come along as a great tool. The whole pace of business is moving faster. Globalization is forcing companies to do things in new ways. *Bill Gates*

From the suites of Davos to the streets of Seattle, there is a growing consensus that globalization must now be reshaped to reflect values broader than simply the freedom of capital. *John J. Sweeney*

A human being is part of a whole, called by us the Universe, a part limited in time and space. He experiences himself, his thoughts and feelings, as something separated from the rest, a kind of optical delusion of his consciousness. This delusion is a kind of prison for us, restricting us to our personal desires and to affection for a few persons nearest us. Our task must be to free ourselves from this prison by widening our circles of compassion to embrace all living creatures and the whole of nature in its beauty. *Albert Einstein*

All the ills of mankind, all the tragic misfortunes that fill the history books, all the political blunders, all the failures of the great leaders have arisen merely from a lack of skill at dancing. *Molière*

Most of the luxuries and many of the so-called comforts of life are not only not indispensable, but positive hindrances to the elevation of mankind. *Henry David Thoreau*

8

Universal Education

Creating Human Capital, the Engine of Growth

Every organization is in the business of developing people. The wealth of a country is now determined more by its human capital than by its material capital or natural resources. The success of every company is in the knowledge, competence and creativity of its people. All businesses are 'knowledge' businesses. The success of every individual today is based on his own management of his own competence. We are all in the business of human development.

Ignorance is poverty and knowledge is wealth, individually and collectively. Education is not the problem of educational institutions alone. In the United States corporations spend close to 50 billion dollars a year in training and development and the better corporations devote more than a week a year to training for each employee. Constant improvement in competence is an essential requirement of competition in today's business. Economies cannot develop without the increased capacity of its individual members.

But what is *human capital* and what does it mean to develop human capital? We know what *financial capital* is: money in the bank, the value of our real estate, inventory and other material assets. *Market capital* is the value placed on your company's products or services by the market place. It is your reputation or respect in the market place. This is also called brand equity. *Social capital* is the level of trust among members of the organization and with external stakeholders. *Human capital is the sum of all the skills or competencies of the people within your organization.* These competencies are the foundation of competitive performance in the marketplace.

Then one must ask, what is human development? What are the competencies or skills and knowledge that are important? In order to answer that question it is useful to have a model that describes the whole person. This illustration is one way to describe four major sets of characteristics of any human being. Often human development is out of balance. For example, one may focus entirely on one's material self, the physical body and appearance, or on money, to the exclusion of the intellect. When someone is developed in a balanced manner we can describe their qualities as a unified whole. Why do we say someone 'has her act together'? Or we might say, 'he is falling apart'. What does this mean and why has it become common language in our culture? In fact, many people are not 'together' because only one aspect of their character is sufficiently developed.

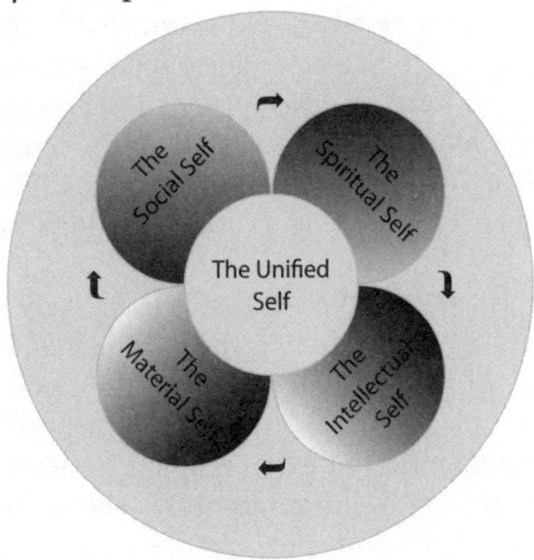

We can describe four components of a 'unified self'. The most apparent is the *material self*. This includes our physical body, our health, as well as our financial worth. A materialistic culture quite naturally causes people to focus largely on the development of the material self. Developing our material self is good. A healthy, energetic or attractive body is certainly a good thing, as is money, and they can contribute to the development of our other characteristics if we understand our purpose.

The *social self* is our relationships, our ability to develop and maintain friendships, trust and communication. Perhaps no one more than young people in high school understand the importance of social relationships but the ability to develop and maintain relationships is a foundation of business success in today's world. Very few people succeed on technical skills alone. Most companies are organized into teams that engage in problem-solving and take shared responsibility for their work. Social skills such as effective communication are critical to the success of all work groups.

The *intellectual self* is our reservoir of knowledge and our competence in problem-solving and decision-making. At work, intellectual development is likely to be thought of as development of functional knowledge, technical expertise. In every field technical knowledge is essential. However, those who are likely to become managers, particularly senior managers in an organization, are going to need to develop their intellect with a broad perspective. Knowledge of international affairs, economics, psychology and history will all be drawn upon as the executive travels from country to country seeking to understand markets and cultures.

And, then, the aspect of the self that is least likely to be recognized in the world of organizations is the *spiritual self*. I believe that the development of the spiritual self is not the same as religion. Religion may be a means towards the development of spirituality. It is certainly the intention of every religion to develop spiritual capacities. I also do not feel that businesses should promote any religion. On the other hand, they should be conducive to the development of spiritual qualities.

It is the clear intention of the Bahá'í teachings to promote spirituality, not at the expense of the material, but rather to achieve a golden mean, the best results that can come from the development of both material and spiritual qualities together. In the following passage 'Abdu'l-Bahá presents this principle in terms of merging the best qualities of East and West.

> In the western world material civilization has attained the highest point of development, but divine civilization was founded in the land of the East. The East must acquire material civilization from the West, and the West must receive spiritual civilization from the East. This will establish a mutual bond. When these two come together, the world of humanity will present a glorious aspect, and extraordinary progress will be achieved. This is clear and evident; no proof is needed. The degree of material civilization in the Occident cannot be denied; nor can anyone fail to confirm the spiritual civilization of the Orient, for all the divine foundations of human uplift have appeared in the East. This, likewise, is clear and evident. Therefore, you must assist the East in order that it may attain material progress. The East must, likewise, promulgate the principles of spiritual civilization in the western world. By this commingling and union the human race will attain the highest degree of prosperity and development.[1]

But what are spiritual qualities and why should business be concerned about these? Some people feel spiritual when they sit on a mountaintop and watch the sunset or experience a spiritual high when the endorphins kick in while they are running ten miles. You may experience a spiritual connection to the universe when staring up at a star-filled sky. But is this spirituality or just a good feeling? I think it is a component of spirituality but it is not sufficient. I believe that true spirituality requires some connection to a source, something unchanging, something that we believe is a source of eternal and infallible values and guidance for our personal life. Of course, for most, this is religious faith in a Supreme Being. Those with religious faith tend to suffer less anxiety and are generally happier people.[2] This contributes to the development of the other three aspects of the self. Spiritual development does not mean, in my opinion, the absence of material things. Nor does it require a divorce from the intellectual self. And I believe our spiritual development is necessarily related to our social relationships, trust in our family and friends, appreciation for others and the ability to engage others in unifying dialogue.

The concepts of stability and trustworthiness are related to spirituality and this is where it becomes a significant issue for business. There are two types of stability: dynamic and inherent. If you think of a bicycle you can see these clearly. A bicycle has low inherent stability. A tricycle has more inherent stability. The design itself produces stability; it is inherent in the structure. Dynamic stability is generated by motion. A bicycle moving at two miles per hour is very unstable. Speed up to ten or 20 miles an hour and it become far more stable. Human beings are much the same. Spiritual values provide both inherent stability and energy directed towards a worthy purpose that becomes dynamic stability.

Spiritual values, like the third wheel on the tricycle, create a structure, a framework that provides stability. In our business careers we are faced with thousands of decisions, thousands of different circumstances, about which we must make decisions. Of course businesses provide some guidelines for decision-making. However, the complexity of our world presents so many decisions and difficult issues that the ability to call upon a source of certitude, a source of reliable values, a source of examples of right conduct, causes the spiritual person to be more confident and more likely to make sound judgments.

My understanding of a spiritual life, as incomplete as it may be, includes a belief that your life is purposeful. If you believe that your life only has meaning in terms of the here and now, what you achieve or possess in the current life, your judgments, will be short sighted. If, on the other hand, you believe that your life is to serve a more noble and worthy purpose, to contribute in a meaningful way to the advancement of civilization, that purpose produces an energy, a forward movement, that may be similar to dynamic stability, the forward movement of the bicycle. For these reasons the development of the spiritual self is good for business. It is an asset to the organization as well as to the individual.

While much training is required by the rapid evolution of technology, corporations are increasingly concerned about the development of social competencies, the skill of group decision-making, the ability to share work and knowledge within the organization and the ability to communicate, inform and persuade customers and suppliers. The work of my firm and dozens like mine are devoted largely to the development of social skills essential to the flat organization in which employees are empowered to make decisions and control their work processes.

Even senior executives are dedicating serious efforts to learning new forms of behavior. I worked with the senior team of a major oil company and watched the president literally perspire when asked to verbally reinforce the good work of another. He later told me that his wife had often told him that he needed to do more to recognize the good qualities in his children but he found this enormously difficult. This simple competence of expressing appreciation for a job well done had never been developed, and perhaps more shocking, had never been required as he made his way to the highest level of the company. But to his credit, he now recognized the importance of this simple skill and was willing to exert the effort to develop the habit.

This same team of executives reported that one of the most powerful development experiences they participated in was *action learning* in which they took on a community project, working together as a team. They rebuilt a home in a poverty-stricken section of town. As a work team these executives evaluated the house, bought paint and other materials and showed up on weekends to do manual labor. It may seem somewhat odd that a very highly paid senior executive team of a large oil company would engage in such an effort. However, they reported that they gained new insights and appreciation of each other's qualities and found that they worked together better as an executive team as a result of this experience. They considered this one of their most memorable experiences in their entire working careers. I think this says something about the relationship between the spiritual, social and intellectual selves. Serving others is a spiritual act. It enhances one's spiritual capacities. At the same time, when it is a shared activity it enhances the social relationships within the group. It also provides a forum for looking at group process in a different setting, providing lessons that may be less evident in the routine of the workplace.

While corporations are devoting much effort to technical skill-building, it is in the area of the social, interpersonal skills of problem-solving and decision-making that the most effort is being applied. The skills of group decision-making are a strong advantage in the modern workplace. Worldwide businesses are seeking managers who possess the qualities that allow for groups to reach unity and consensus and which draw out the unique contributions of diverse members.

International corporations are among the most significant forces of human development in the world today. They are training the future leaders of society everywhere they operate. They are establishing patterns of institutional process that will inevitably be modeled by non-profit and government agencies. For this reason the development of human capacities within the organization has an effect on the direction and capacities of the larger society.

One of the distinct differences between the Bahá'í Faith and earlier religions is the importance and legitimacy placed on science and intellectual development.

> God has conferred upon and added to man a distinctive power, the faculty of intellectual investigation into the secrets of creation, the acquisition of higher knowledge, the greatest virtue of which is scientific enlightenment.
>
> This endowment is the most praiseworthy power of man, for through its employment and exercise, the betterment of the human race is accomplished, the development of the virtues of mankind is made possible and the spirit and mysteries of God become manifest.[3]

This acknowledgment of the value of scientific and intellectual development is so important because it is these capacities that are the basis of so much commerce in today's world. If one examines those cultures that are poor there are two distinct cultural characteristics that are related to that poverty. One is the failure to utilize the talents and abilities of women. You cannot have an economically healthy society if you fail to call on the contribution of one half of the population. Second is the suppression of scientific and objective intellectual thought in the name of religious dogma. It is perfectly clear that in the new world order the spiritual and intellectual capacities must both be developed, side by side.

The following statement by the Bahá'í International Community makes clear the necessity of developing objective thought.

> People need, for example, to learn how to separate fact from conjecture – indeed to distinguish between subjective views and objective reality; the extent to which individuals and institutions so equipped can contribute to human progress, however, will be determined by their devotion to truth and their detachment from the promptings of their own interests and passions. Another capacity that science must cultivate in all people is that of thinking in terms of process, including historical process; however, if this intellectual advancement is to contribute ultimately to promoting development, its perspective must be unclouded by prejudices of race, culture, sex, or sectarian belief. Similarly, the training that can make it possible for the earth's inhabitants to participate in the production of wealth will advance the aims of development only to the extent that such an impulse is illumined by the spiritual insight that service to humankind is the purpose of both individual life and social organization.[4]

Here, clearly, is the call to combine both the discipline of objective analysis along with spiritual insight and guidance.

There is no question that the primary requirement for the elimination of poverty and the creation of wealth is education. Knowledge equals the capacity for business and economic development. Therefore anything that business organizations can do to promote the education of their members, and the quality of education in the society in which they live, is a contribution to the development of that society.

> In the same way he must establish human education – that is to say, he must educate intelligence and thought in such a way that they may attain complete development, so that knowledge and science may increase, and the reality of things, the mysteries of beings and the properties of existence may be discovered; that, day by day, instructions, inventions and institutions may be improved; and from things perceptible to the senses conclusions as to intellectual things may be deduced.[5]

The central concept of the Bahá'í Faith is that of unity. Unity has many meanings. It includes the unity of religion, the unity of the races, the unity of nations and it also implies unity of cultural characteristics and fields of knowledge. In our universities we divide up knowledge. Sociology, psychology and history are all separate departments and fields of study. But can you truly separate sociology from psychology or history? Certainly not. Knowledge is a unified whole, a series of interconnected complex relationships. In the past spiritual knowledge or the development of spiritual capacities was seen as something entirely separate from secular study, the study of science or history, for example. But I believe that in this era we will see the unity of knowledge, the unity of science and religion; spiritual, intellectual, material and social capacities will be recognized as interdependent parts of a whole.

Questions for Discussion and Reflection

1) You are working at your first job after college. Most of the other new employees in the company are trying to make the best possible impression they can and establish a reputation for hard work and initiative in the company. You also want to make a great impression during your first year. It is very normal for these colleagues to spend 12 hours a day at work

and to work on the weekends. It is their life. Because you find yourself in this competitive environment and with these time demands you have not had time to attend religious activities and you have little social life. How do you reconcile the demands for attention to the development of material capacity and the needs for social and spiritual development?

2) You are the training and development manager for a medium-sized company. Half of the company works in field service, out delivering and installing computer hardware, and the other half works in sales and marketing. You have presented the idea to your manager, the vice president of human resources, that it is important to develop the whole person, including material, intellectual, social and spiritual capacities. She understands and appreciates this. She suggests that you proceed to develop a program that will do that. What will this program include? How might it be structured and who would participate? Discuss any ideas you have for the development of such a program.

3) You work for a manager who considers himself a born-again Christian. He is very sincere in his beliefs and wants others to appreciate and value his Christian point of view. He has established a voluntary prayer session each day at noon that lasts approximately 30 minutes. It is apparent that those attending tend to be his 'favorites', those who are personally close to him. Do you attend these meetings? Is your motive sincere? Do you discuss this with the manager? How else might you react to this situation?

Other Quotations and Views on Education and Development

Education's purpose is to replace an empty mind with an open one. *Malcolm S. Forbes*

The principal goal of education is to create men who are capable of doing new things, not simply of repeating what other generations have done – men who are creative, inventive and discoverers. *Jean Piaget*

Formal education will make you a living; self-education will make you a fortune. *Jim Rohn*

The function of education is to teach one to think intensively and to think critically . . . Intelligence plus character – that is the goal of true education. *Martin Luther King, Jr*

Education is simply the soul of a society as it passes from one generation to another. *G. K. Chesterton*

An education which does not cultivate the will is an education that depraves the mind. *Anatole France*

One's work may be finished some day, but one's education never. *Alexandre Dumas Père*

Dancing in all its forms cannot be excluded from the curriculum of all noble education; dancing with the feet, with ideas, with words, and, need I add that one must also be able to dance with the pen? *Friedrich Nietzsche*

The only thing more expensive than education is ignorance. *Benjamin Franklin*

Education without values, as useful as it is, seems rather to make man a more clever devil. *C. S. Lewis*

Excellence is an art won by training and habituation. We do not act rightly because we have virtue or excellence, but we rather have those because we have acted rightly. We are what we repeatedly do. Excellence, then, is not an act but a habit. *Aristotle*

The only real training for leadership is leadership. *Anthony Jay*

Perhaps the most valuable result of all education is the ability to make yourself do the thing you have to do, when it ought to be done, whether you like it or not. It is the first lesson that ought to be learned and however early a man's training begins, it is probably the last lesson that he learns thoroughly. *Thomas Henry Huxley*

The biggest job we have is to teach a newly hired employee how to fail intelligently. We have to train him to experiment over and over and to keep on trying and failing until he learns what will work. *Charles F. Kettering*

Part Two

Practical Spirituality: Putting Principles to Work

Applying principles to practice is the challenge of daily life. The unity of science and religion, the unity of form and spirit, the unity of prayer and action all illustrate the imperative to walk the spiritual path with practical feet. This challenge permeates life in any organization today. The purpose of the second part of this book is to apply the principles to the most critical functions of management.

I think the more experienced one is in the field of management, the more humble one becomes in his or her assertions of how best to do things. I was never more certain of how to raise children than before I had them. Applying principles to the practice of management is much like parenting. You meditate on the meaning of principles, you seek to apply those principles to each practice as best you can, you then observe and learn and then modify your application to incorporate your experience.

I am not necessarily an expert in the following practices of management. I am not expert in information systems, financial management or others. I have done a good bit of observing, however, and I have meditated on the principles and how they may be applied. I offer my own thoughts and some references from the Bahá'í writings on each, simply to assist you as a starting point for your own journey of discovery as you seek to apply spiritual principles within your organization.

9

Capital and Finance

There has always been a strained relationship between religion and money. In previous religious dispensations the lending of money for interest was viewed with either condemnation or at least suspicion. Jesus entered the temple and turned over the tables of the moneylenders. Jews have been reviled for the image of Shylock, the moneylender, and Islam directly forbids the charging of interest. In the past century Marxism vilified the owners of financial capital, the capitalists, as the source of most of the evils in the world. And it is a common theme of movies and literature that someone of wealth and power is abusing or taking advantage of a poor victim. It is little wonder that we have come to associate wealth with ungodliness and poverty with piety. Lacking a sound theory for the true sources of wealth and poverty, good and evil, happiness and misery, it is convenient to have a scapegoat and those who control capital have served as easy targets. There is no doubt that this was often justified. However, attacking the moneylenders and capitalists has led only to more misery and more poverty and not once to wealth for the poor.

> No, Bahá'u'lláh did not bring a complete system of economics to the world.
>
> Profit-sharing is recommended as a solution to one form of economic problems.
>
> There is nothing in the teachings against some kind of capitalism; its present form, though, would require adjustments to be made.[1]

Money may be the source either of misery or of happiness, good or evil, and is not inherently either. Whether money leads to good or evil is entirely determined by the values and decisions of those who control that money. You can invest in guns or hospital beds, gambling establishments or agriculture, and you can personally spend to educate your children or buy fancy cars. It is not the money but the human character that is the source of good or evil.

There are two central issues regarding capital and money in business. The first is who controls the capital and who decides how that capital is used. Essentially there are only two choices: the private ownership of capital and investment decision-making or the ownership and investment by some government or government agency. The second issue is how are the returns on capital distributed? Bahá'ís have clear, although general, teachings on both of these matters.

In the teachings of the Bahá'í Faith there is no question that there is a recognition of the legitimate need for the creation, investment, lending and profit on private capital. The Báb, Bahá'u'lláh and 'Abdu'l-Bahá were all either merchants or owners of property and encouraged others to invest in the creation of wealth-producing businesses. The teachings of the Faith reflect their understanding of the essential nature of capital formation and exchange in the economy.

It is important to make a distinction between a formal definition of capitalism and the current culture of capitalism. Formally, capitalism is an economic system in which land and capital are privately owned and operated for profit and where investments, production, distribution, income and prices are determined largely through the operation of a free market rather than by centralized state control. Nothing in the writings of the Bahá'í Faith is contrary to this formal understanding of capitalism. Nowhere is there a suggestion that private ownership or control of land and capital is wrong or that profits and free markets should be replaced by state control. In fact, several passages in the writings clearly support a private capital market. On the other hand, the current culture of capitalism is something entirely different. Clearly, there is no support for a culture that values the pursuit of profit as a supreme objective, one that can be used to justify any degradation or exploitation of the less fortunate. It is clear that the free market must be balanced with sensible regulation and concern for the less fortunate.

This simple example of 'Abdu'l-Bahá is a perfect example of the proper use of capital:

> His means of livelihood was his business partnership with me. That is, I provided him with a capital of three krans; with it he bought needles, and this was his stock-in-trade. The women of Nazareth gave him eggs in exchange for his needles and in this way he would obtain thirty or forty eggs a day: three needles per egg. Then he would sell the eggs and live on the proceeds. Since there was a daily caravan between 'Akká and Nazareth, he would refer to Áqá Riḍá each day, for more needles. Glory be to God! He survived two years on that initial outlay of capital; and he returned thanks at all times.[2]

The ownership, distribution and benefits of capital have been the subject of the greatest economic schism and experiment in the past century, if not in all human history. Communism sought to eliminate the private control of capital and place it in the hands of an allegedly beneficent state which would eventually disappear. Communism was a misguided response to the evils of an era of capitalism in which the mechanisms of capital formation and distribution were essentially unjust and led to the enrichment of the few and impoverishment of many. However, one injustice often leads to a response that is equally unjust. Speaking of economic problems 'Abdu'l-Bahá said,

> The solution of this problem is one of the fundamental principles of His Holiness Baha'u'llah [*sic*]. But it must be solved with justice and not with force. If this problem is not solved lovingly it will result in war. Perfect communism and equality are an impossibility because they would upset the affairs and the order of the

> world. But there is a fair method which will not leave the poor in such need, nor the rich in such wealth.[3]

Speaking of the Báb and accusations of communism leveled at his followers, Shoghi Effendi said:

> The only communism known to and recommended by Him (the Báb) was that of the New Testament and the early Christian Church, viz., the sharing of goods in common by members of the Faith, and the exercise of alms-giving, and an ample charity.[4]

And again, Shoghi Effendi made very clear his disdain for communism:

> God Himself has indeed been dethroned from the hearts of men, and an idolatrous world passionately and clamorously hails and worships the false gods which its own idle fancies have fatuously created, and its misguided hands so impiously exalted. The chief idols in the desecrated temple of mankind are none other than the triple gods of Nationalism, Racialism and Communism, at whose altars governments and peoples, whether democratic or totalitarian, at peace or at war, of the East or of the West, Christian or Islamic, are, in various forms and in different degrees, now worshiping. Their high priests are the politicians and the worldly-wise, the so-called sages of the age; their sacrifice, the flesh and blood of the slaughtered multitudes; their incantations outworn shibboleths and insidious and irreverent formulas; their incense, the smoke of anguish that ascends from the lacerated hearts of the bereaved, the maimed, and the homeless.[5]

Communism emerged from the economic period of the 'great' capitalists, when the Carnegies, Rockefellers, J. P. Morgan and Mellons gained their enormous wealth. It might be argued that the evolution of economic development required a period of centralized capital control, the period of the building of railroads, steel mills and other industrial infrastructure that required large amounts of concentrated capital. It is equally arguable that this period was a carryover from a feudal period of extremes of wealth and poverty and economic progress required the dispersion and democratization of capital control.

The essential idea of communism failed to recognize that human beings are simply not equal in their capacity, their motivations or their choices. It defies the essential concept of free will that determines the course an individual pursues and the outcomes that result. Equality of opportunity is essential but equality of rewards is not. The balance is found in the desire to eliminate the extremes of wealth and poverty while still providing for differences in achievement.

> Then rules and laws should be established to regulate the excessive fortunes of certain private individuals, and limit the misery of millions of the poor masses; thus a certain moderation would be obtained. However, absolute equality is just as impossible, for absolute equality in fortunes, honors, commerce, agriculture, industry, would end in a want of comfort, in discouragement, in disorganization of the means of existence, and in universal disappointment: the order of the community would be quite destroyed. Thus, there is a great wisdom in the fact that equality is not imposed by law: it is, therefore, preferable for moderation to do its work.[6]

The system of capitalism has changed. Peter Drucker[7] has called the current age in western countries the age of *democratic socialism* when the majority owners of most major corporations are the employees themselves and the majority owners of most large companies are employee pension and retirement funds. Capital control has become highly dispersed when it was once concentrated. If there is excessive control of capital today it can be found in the managers of large mutual funds or other investment organizations. There is no doubt that damaging manipulation of the markets, whether those of stocks or commodities, is still a perversion that needs to be controlled.

The ability to move capital, to take risks with capital, is the engine that drives entrepreneurship and wealth creation. When two college students started Yahoo, the Internet search service, in their college dormitory, they were besieged by offers of capital before they had an office or a business suit. Those who control capital are constantly seeking out those with ideas; those who have the intellectual seed of enterprise require the material nourishment of capital resources. In the past, and in many societies today, capital is excessively centralized and controlled for the benefit of too few people. The following clearly points to the need to more broadly distribute capital and its benefits:

> No more trusts will remain in the future. The question of the trusts will be wiped away entirely. Also, every factory that has ten thousand shares will give two thousand shares of these ten thousand to its employees and will write the shares in their names, so that they may have them, and the rest will belong to the capitalists. Then at the end of the month or year whatever they may earn after the expenses and wages are paid, according to the number of shares, should be divided among both.[8]

Virtually every nation has now reached some point of moderation in the assumptions about private versus public capital deployment. Both Russia and China are no longer communist countries in that they have both encouraged the flow of private capital and the profit motive. But every country has sought to find a point of moderation to prevent the excesses of power that can derive from the accumulation of capital. In the United States, the Security Exchange Commission, the Congress and the courts seek to regulate the free market to create transparency. As the Enron and WorldCom cases have demonstrated, the free market is not free of corruption. Markets will always be subject to the ills of dishonesty and bad character. Dishonesty occurs in academia, government and every other endeavor in which human beings have the opportunity to exercise free will.

Public capital funding, even in free market economies such

as the United States, has been found necessary to provide broad based public service, such as the postal service, highways and small loans to entrepreneurs. Public capitalization might be desirable, for example, in funding minority ownership business or businesses in less developed areas of a nation or the world. This funding would be justified to develop the human resources of that area though the risks might outweigh those acceptable to private capital sources. I suspect that future institutions will, on the other hand, be careful not to subvert the natural process of risk calculation that the private markets engage.

Capital markets have already become entirely international. The investor in Kansas wakes up and goes to his computer to check the oil tanker rates recorded that day in Greece and the Arab Gulf and enters a trade that morning from his bedroom before the stock markets open in New York. Late in the evening the investor is watching CNBC Asia to see how the markets in Singapore and Hong Kong are reacting to the latest news. A well-known Arab sheik meets with tribesmen seeking favors in a tent while three flat screen televisions have been set up in the tent so he can monitor the markets in New York and London and simultaneously make trade decisions on his cell phone. The capital markets are at once electronic, instantaneous and global. The price and the effect of a stock purchase will be exactly the same whether it is being made by a farmer in Kansas or an Arab sheik in a tent. Perhaps the most important thing that is happening is the growing consciousness of a unified global economy.

The flow of capital to less developed nations and areas of the world is obviously desirable in the promotion of equality and the elimination of the extremes of poverty. There are now literally thousands of analysts scouting the less developed nations for investment opportunities. And the World Bank has the express purpose of funneling capital for the purpose of social and economic development. Undoubtedly this flow of capital does not sufficiently reach down to 'micro-enterprise', the development of individual and family businesses that require little capital and primarily benefit those doing the work, rather than the provider of capital. However, the Grameen Bank has proved that lending to the poor is not only effective in developing small business but is also a sound investment.

The following passage from a recent publication of the Bahá'í International Community lends credence to the view that future institutions will take into account not only economic return but the social diversity and common value to be derived from the earth's resources, when making capital utilization decisions.

> In His later writings Bahá'u'lláh made explicit the implications of this principle for the age of humanity's maturity. 'Women and men have been and will always be equal in the sight of God,' He asserts, and the advancement of civilization requires that society so organize its affairs as to give full expression to this fact. The earth's resources are the property of all humanity, not of any one people. Different contributions to the common economic welfare deserve and should receive different measures of reward and recognition, but the extremes of wealth and poverty which afflict most nations on earth, regardless of the socio-economic philosophies they profess, must be abolished.[9]

The issue of the employment of capital is necessarily linked to the individual sense of justice, that quality of the soul, referred to by the House of Justice. The individual must develop an understanding of the need and desirability of making capital and resources available to others, particularly the poor, in order to achieve their advancement, advancement which must represent progress desirable to all members of the society. But material capital is only one small component of economic success. The human capital, the skills and intellect, are even more important and if the institutions fail to develop these they will be disappointed by the poor return on their investment in monetary capital.

There is perhaps more guidance in the Bahá'í writings on the subject of the distribution of profit, the return on capital, than on any other business practice. The guidance is clear. It should be shared by both the owner and the worker. These writings confirm the essential process of capitalism, individual investment judgments and corresponding return (or loss) to the individual investor. There is no debate as to whether capitalism is a legitimate system in the Bahá'í Faith, only the nature of the system, the process by which it is carried out.

> For instance, the owners of properties, mines and factories should share their incomes with their employees and give a fairly certain percentage of their products to their workingmen in order that the employees may receive, beside their wages, some of the general income of the factory so that the employee may strive with his soul in the work.[10]

What is clear in a careful reading of the Bahá'í writings on this subject is a complete balance and recognition of legitimate interests of all parties and the interdependence, the common benefit for all of humanity that is derived from a just and equitable system. Members of western society must overcome their adversarial assumptions that have so long dominated any discussion of capital, capitalism and profit. The focus must shift from who is a winner and loser in the game of business to how the benefits are best shared in service to humanity.

> Since the body of humankind is one and indivisible, each member of the race is born into the world as a trust of the whole. This trusteeship constitutes the moral foundation of most of the other rights – principally economic and social . . . The security of the family and the home, the ownership of property, and the right to privacy are all implied in such a trusteeship. The obligations on the part of the community extend to the provision of employment, mental and physical health care, social security, fair wages, rest and recreation, and a host of other reasonable expectations on the part of the individual members of society.[11]

The sharing of profit is not a simple matter. Profit is very elastic. How much profit is to be made is determined by price, competition, scarcity, government regulations and decisions of management.

Do pharmaceutical companies make excessive profit when they charge a dollar for a tablet that costs two cents to produce? Or is this justified by the billions they invest each year in pharmaceutical research that must be offset by those profits? Does the entrepreneur reinvest her gross profit in the business or distribute it as gross profit? It is possible never to share any profit by continually reinvesting or paying high executive bonuses. How does one decide? These only become simple judgments when one looks at one side of the issue in isolation from the other.

In several places the Bahá'i writings call for sharing 20 or 25 per cent of the profit of the enterprise with the workforce. This may mistakenly be viewed as a legalistic definition that can be applied without further discussion. Nothing could be further from the truth.

> Therefore, laws and regulations should be established which would permit the workmen to receive from the factory owner their wages and a share in the fourth or the fifth part of the profits, according to the capacity of the factory; or in some other way the body of workmen and the manufacturers should share equitably the profits and advantages. Indeed, the capital and management come from the owner of the factory, and the work and labor, from the body of the workmen. Either the workmen should receive wages which assure them an adequate support and, when they cease work, becoming feeble or helpless, they should have sufficient benefits from the income of the industry; or the wages should be high enough to satisfy the workmen with the amount they receive so that they may themselves be able to put a little aside for days of want and helplessness.[12]

Profit is generally regarded as 'the bottom line', that which is left over after all expenses are subtracted from revenue. That is simple enough. But the devil is in the detail. What are legitimate expenses? It is very easy for an owner, particularly of a small or private firm, to minimize profit and thereby that which is to be shared or taxed. For example, the owner of a business with ten million dollars of revenue may produce one million dollars of profit. However, this owner may decide to pay himself a very large bonus, purchase cars or airplanes in the name of the company or create other expenses that may eliminate or minimize the profit. This may be entirely legal and result in great benefit to the owner but no profit to be taxed or shared by the workers.

It is common practice in privately held firms to minimize profit in order to minimize the amount taxed by government. Should profit sharing be a percentage of the actual amount of declared profit, thereby taxed, or should the amount to be shared come out as an expense before profit is declared? The latter approach would provide for a greater amount to be shared with the workers but less would be paid to the government. Is this a proper judgment? Whatever initial profit is paid out in bonuses then becomes an expense and is, therefore, technically not profit sharing. And is the amount paid into retirement plans, which can vary based on the performance of the firm, to be considered as profit sharing, or simply a form of compensation? What these question illustrate is that profit sharing is not so simple a matter and if viewed as a legalistic formula, rather than understanding the true spirit and intention, it can be manipulated for one advantage or another.

Another perversion of profit can occur if the owners attempt to maximize profitability and the amount to be shared. For example, profit can easily be increased, and thereby shared, by failing to make expenditures for research and development or other investments in future growth. Imagine that the pharmaceutical company starved its research labs to pay out the maximum amount to shareholders and workers. Would this be just or would the company be failing in its essential social responsibility to discover new drugs to alleviate the suffering of the sick?

Another complication arises with an understanding of ownership. In the past there was a clear distinction between owners and workers. This is no longer true. Today, most workers are owners through pension funds or profit sharing plans of the company. If a worker is both an owner and a worker, which amount does he share? Do managers share the same amount as workers?

The writings of the Bahá'í Faith provide no legalistic definitions or specific guidelines regarding the definition of profit and what is allowable above the bottom line. When attempting to apply this principle it is also important to recognize that every country has its own laws governing accounting practices that will impact these computations. Therefore, this writer, at least, assumes these guidelines to represent 'guidance', not legalistic definition. It is the spirit of sharing 20 or 25 per cent and arriving at this in a manner that is perceived to be fair and just that is most important.

There are many plans to share profit that have become widespread in business. There are plans such as the SCANLON[13] and Gainsharing plans that provide for sharing bonuses with workers for improvement in the performance of the organization. In both the United States and Europe laws have been established to encourage direct employee ownership of stock in their companies. One of the most popular in the US is the ESOP (Employee Stock Ownership Plan), whereby an owner can sell her shares to an ESOP, whose shares are distributed among employees, and the owner can receive the proceeds of this sale without paying capital gains taxes. This accomplishes employee sharing in the benefits of ownership. The federal government has established this incentive to encourage owners of privately held firms to sell their firms to their employees.[14] The US government, as well as others, has decided as a matter of policy and law that employee ownership and sharing in profit is a societal good.

Profit sharing is not only a moral good. Several studies have demonstrated that profit sharing and employee ownership result in improved business performance over companies that do not share or provide for employee ownership.[15] But the benefit is not only in the fact of sharing. It is in the process. How it is done makes all the difference. It is entirely possible to share 20 per cent of the profit, yet deal with employees in a manner that causes them to feel disenfranchised. Several attempts at employee ownership failed because the new managers under employee ownership, the former union presidents, were just as autocratic and insensitive when they became the managers as the former owners had been.

In one case the union members voted to sell their shares of the company back to the original owner. This clearly illustrates that ownership is more than a piece of paper or a check received in the mail.

Ownership is as much in the process of inclusion and empowerment in decision-making as in the sharing of the profit or ownership of shares. I know several companies in which the employees feel very committed, empowered and feel like owners despite the absence of formal legal ownership. They feel this sense of ownership because they are treated with the dignity of owners. They are involved in important decisions. They own the relationship with the customers, the process by which work gets accomplished and the process by which resources are managed within the firm. In addition they may share in the economic well-being through some form of variable compensation. These factors may have much more benefit to the spirit than legal ownership or profit sharing.

> When matters will be thus fixed, the owner of the factory will no longer put aside daily a treasure which he has absolutely no need of (for, if the fortune is disproportionate, the capitalist succumbs under a formidable burden and gets into the greatest difficulties and troubles; the administration of an excessive fortune is very difficult and exhausts man's natural strength). And the workmen and artisans will no longer be in the greatest misery and want; they will no longer be submitted to the worst privations at the end of their life.[16]

It is interesting that 'Abdu'l-Bahá says that 'the administration of an excessive fortune is very difficult and exhausts man's natural strength'. I don't know how many of the extremely wealthy would acknowledge that their wealth is exhausting. I suspect not many. However, what seems to me to be very apparent is that as one's wealth grows, earned through the exercise of one's natural talents, one increasingly devotes time and energy to studying investment options, watching the stock market or fantasizing about doubling one's money in ways other than through one's core strengths or business. This diversion of talents and energy does frequently reduce the effectiveness of the entrepreneur whose talents did create something of genuine value to society.

Pension and retirement plans, while not strictly profit sharing, are clearly consistent with the Bahá'í writings encouraging society to provide for the care and well-being of the worker after retirement. Laws have been established in many countries that encourage such plans and provide for their regulation, although in most of the world there are no such plans or regulations.

> It would be well, with regard to the common rights of manufacturers, workmen and artisans, that laws be established, giving moderate profits to manufacturers, and to workmen the necessary means of existence and security for the future. Thus when they become feeble and cease working, get old and helpless, or leave behind children under age, they and their children will not be annihilated by excess of poverty. And it is from the income of the factory itself, to which they have a right, that they will derive a share, however small, toward their livelihood.[17]

Business men and women will be required to make judgments regarding these issues, balancing the many interests of employees, customers, government, the local community and their own. The day will come when in every town there will be a local consultative body, a Spiritual Assembly or House of Justice, to which the owner or manager may go to receive assistance in these considerations. The decision about how to allocate funds to various types of compensation or profit sharing is a good example of the type of decision that should not be made by one individual, who will inevitably be conflicted by self interest and other emotions. The process of consultation, involving others who are detached from self-interest, will certainly result in a wiser decision.

As one acquires wealth one may become consumed by the game of business and come to see each additional million as some great prize without thinking deeply about its meaning. However, many who have succeeded in business have thought deeply about the purpose of business and the meaning of money. I particularly enjoyed Jacob Needleman's *Money and the Meaning of Life* in which he takes the reader on a spiritual quest to understand the meaning of both money and life and the relationship between the two. He said,

> It may seem a long step from Donald Trump to an inept 'spiritual' shopkeeper in the Haight-Ashbury, but they are not so far apart as it may appear. The first represents the attempt to find life's meaning in money; the other tries to make money out of the search for meaning. I know them both too well – they live inside of me, and perhaps inside of most of us. They represent the confusion of two directions of life within us. This confusion prevents us from seeing the real difference between the search for God and the need to live normally in the material world.[18]

It seems to me that every human being in this age must similarly struggle with these two sides of life. What the writings of the Bahá'í Faith make clear is that one of these impulses is not exclusive of the other and that we all must seek a point of moderation, a balance in our pursuit of the material gain and the pursuit of spiritual health.

There is increasing research on the effect of money and happiness. Understanding this research can be very helpful when considering one's own aspirations and attitudes. Many people naively assume that money equals happiness. If I had a million dollars I would be really happy; and if I had ten million I would be ten times as happy. One does not have to rely on spiritual teachings to know that this is simply false. There is now sound research that points to both the value and the false hopes of money. In *Authentic Happiness* Martin Seligman summarizes much of this research. A cross-national survey of life satisfaction and purchasing power, involving tens of thousands of adults, illustrates several interesting points.

> Overall national purchasing power and average life satisfaction go strongly in the same direction. Once the gross national product exceeds $8,000 per person, however, the correlation disappears, and added wealth brings no further life satisfaction. So the wealthy Swiss are happier than poor Bulgarians, but it hardly matters if one is Irish, Italian, Norwegian or American . . . there are also plenty of exceptions to the wealth-satisfaction association: Brazil, mainland China, and Argentina are much higher in life satisfaction than would be predicted by wealth.
>
> Real purchasing power has more than doubled in the United States, France and Japan, but life satisfaction has changed not a whit . . . In the United States, the very poor are lower in happiness, but once a person is just barely comfortable, added money adds little or no happiness. Even the fabulously rich – the Forbes 100, with an average net worth of over 125 million dollars – are only slightly happier than the average American.[19]

I would suggest that their slight increase in happiness is not so much from the money itself but rather from their more substantive accomplishments, the success of their companies, for example.

I believe these data are profoundly important. Materialistic society is founded on the pursuit of material things with the assumption that attaining material things will lead to happiness. That is virtually a definition of *materialism*. We have all experienced the desire for a new car and imagined how great we would feel driving around in it. Once we have the car, very quickly we find that driving around in it is little different from driving around in the old car. This failed pursuit of happiness is then depressing. What we must all do now is to educate ourselves on the true sources of happiness.

'Abdu'l-Bahá spoke often about happiness. There are many dozens of references to the pursuit and conditions of happiness. It seems to be something that He thought about often. In the following passage He fully appreciates the need for material progress, while explaining its limitations. If we keep these things in mind, we will be guided in our pursuit and handling of money.

God is not partial and is no respecter of persons. He has made provision for all. The harvest comes forth for everyone. The rain showers upon everybody and the heat of the sun is destined to warm everyone. The verdure of the earth is for everyone. Therefore there should be for all humanity the utmost happiness, the utmost comfort, the utmost well-being.

But if conditions are such that some are happy and comfortable and some in misery; some are accumulating exorbitant wealth and others are in dire want – under such a system it is impossible for man to be happy and impossible for him to win the good pleasure of God. God is kind to all. The good pleasure of God consists in the welfare of all the individual members of mankind.

A Persian king was one night in his palace, living in the greatest luxury and comfort. Through excessive joy and gladness he addressed a certain man, saying: 'Of all my life this is the happiest moment. Praise be to God, from every point prosperity appears and fortune smiles! My treasury is full and the army is well taken care of. My palaces are many; my land unlimited; my family is well off; my honor and sovereignty are great. What more could I want!'

The poor man at the gate of his palace spoke out, saying: 'O kind king! Assuming that you are from every point of view so happy, free from every worry and sadness – do you not worry for us? You say that on your own account you have no worries – but do you never worry about the poor in your land? Is it becoming or meet that you should be so well off and we in such dire want and need? In view of our needs and troubles how can you rest in your palace, how can you even say that you are free from worries and sorrows? As a ruler you must not be so egoistic as to think of yourself alone but you must think of those who are your subjects. When we are comfortable then you will be comfortable; when we are in misery how can you, as a king, be in happiness?'

The purport is this that we are all inhabiting one globe of earth. In reality we are one family and each one of us is a member of this family. We must all be in the greatest happiness and comfort, under a just rule and regulation which is according to the

> good pleasure of God, thus causing us to be happy, for this life is fleeting.[20]

Here 'Abdu'l-Bahá reminds us of one of the major reasons to pursue material wealth: so that one may achieve happiness through generosity. We all know that sharing wealth leads to greater happiness than simply building up a greater horde of wealth:

> But in the divine teachings equality is brought about through a ready willingness to share. It is commanded as regards wealth that the rich among the people, and the aristocrats should, by their own free will and for the sake of their own happiness, concern themselves with and care for the poor. This equality is the result of the lofty characteristics and noble attributes of mankind.[21]

Questions for Discussion and Reflection

Bill Samuels started a management consulting and training firm. He soon recruited his key partner, Jennifer Smith. Samuels owns 80 per cent of the stock in the firm and Smith owns 20 per cent. There are 13 other consultants and four administrative staff who work in the office.

Samuels started the firm and fulfills three major roles in the firm: he develops a lot of the intellectual capital in the form of books and manuals, he gives public talks and his books and talks serve as the primary marketing activity of the firm.

Jennifer Smith does the majority of the 'people management' activities and directly manages the work for several key clients. The 13 consultants deliver the work and do some marketing, mostly in terms of creating follow-on business, continuing the work with existing clients.

The revenue of the firm comes from daily billing of consulting work, seminars and the sale of manuals and other related materials. Competitive compensation for consultants is in the range of between $75,000 and $150,000. Typical administrative compensation is in the range of $22,000–$30,000. When the firm is billing

70 per cent or more of available billing days it is profitable. They have a total of 76 per cent committed for this year, which equals $4.1 million. Adding materials and seminars the firm is assured of doing a total of $4.8 million for the year. If projected, but not yet committed, business comes through, they will do $5.6 million. The figures produce a projected 'gross' profit of either $1.45 or $1.74 million.

Gross profit is above the bottom line, in other words, it is not yet the taxable, reported profit. It includes all operating expenses such as office costs, base salaries, travel, healthcare, etc. It can also include bonuses.

It is important to understand that this figure includes a minimum base salary for all consultants and the owners and a per billed day bonus. Consultant base salaries are $50,000 and with the per day bonus, they will earn between $100,000 and $150,000 each depending on the amount they billed to clients. It also includes a $100,000 for each of the two owners.

Assuming these figures and data, answer the following questions:

1) What principles apply to deciding how to determine the distribution of the approximately $1.6 million in gross profit?

2) Approximately what percentage of this total should be distributed to
    a) the consultants
    b) the administrative staff
    c) the two owners

3) How should the funds be distributed among the consultants? On what basis?

4) How will the compensation reward individual effort and skill?

5) How will the compensation reward teamwork, sharing intellectual developments and cross-training among consultants?

6) On what basis will the administrative staff earn bonuses?

7) How much will the owners each earn and how will it be divided among them? Will it be distributed as a 'bonus' or as 'dividends'; in other words, above or below the bottom line?

8) How much will drop to the 'bottom line' for declared net profit?

Other Quotations and Views on Money and Wealth

Wealth is the ability to fully experience life. *Henry David Thoreau*

I know of nothing more despicable and pathetic than a man who devotes all the hours of the waking day to the making of money for money's sake. *John D. Rockefeller, Jr*

The Roots of Violence: Wealth without work, Pleasure without conscience, Knowledge without character, Commerce without morality, Science without humanity, Worship without sacrifice, Politics without principles. *Mahatma Gandhi*

You aren't wealthy until you have something money can't buy. *Garth Brooks*

A man is usually more careful of his money than he is of his principles. *Ralph Waldo Emerson*

It's a kind of spiritual snobbery that makes people think they can be happy without money. *Albert Camus*

Some people think they are worth a lot of money just because they have it. *Fannie Hurst*

Money never starts an idea. It is always the idea that starts the money. *Owen Laughlin*

If a person gets his attitude toward money straight, it will help straighten out almost every other area in his life. *Billy Graham*

Let us not be satisfied with just giving money. Money is not enough, money can be got, but they need your hearts to love them. So, spread your love everywhere you go. *Mother Teresa of Calcutta*

Most people never feel secure because they are always worried that they will lose their job, lose the money they already have, lose their spouse, lose their health, and so on. The only true security in life comes from knowing that every single day you are improving yourself in some way, that you are increasing the caliber of who you are and that you are valuable to your company, your friends, and your family. *Anthony Robbins*

All the breaks you need in life wait within your imagination. Imagination is the workshop of your mind, capable of turning mind energy into accomplishment and wealth. *Napoleon Hill*

A man's true wealth is the good he does in the world. Beauty is eternity gazing at itself in a mirror. But you are eternity and you are the mirror. *Kahlil Gibran*

Prosperity in the form of wealth works exactly the same as everything else. You will see it coming into your life when you are unattached to needing it. *Wayne Dyer*

10

Design of Work

The design and organization of work, how we get things done, may seem to be a merely technical matter that could be left to engineers or others with a purely practical mind. Isn't it simply a matter of breaking the job down into its component tasks and then assigning them to those who are best able to accomplish them? Or isn't it a matter of buying the right equipment and arranging it efficiently in the manufacturing plant and then training and assigning people to use that equipment? What could it have to do with spirituality in the work place?

When speaking before business groups a simple example has proved helpful in making the connection between work process and the spirit of work. I ask the group if anyone enjoys doing carpentry, making things with wood, as a hobby. Inevitably someone does. I then ask if he has made a chair. He has. I then ask what he did with the chair and he may say something like 'I gave it to a loved one', his spouse or child. I then ask the rest of the audience if anyone thinks he is crazy to spend his free time doing something like this, which looks like 'work'. No one thinks he is crazy. I then ask, 'What if instead of making a chair, he said "I just make legs."' Just legs! Why would anyone just make legs? If someone went home on the weekend and spent his spare time just making legs, you might call him 'crazy'. No one just makes legs – at least, not as a hobby. Our intuitive reaction to making a chair and making legs is entirely different. One gives us a warm and pleasant feeling. The other seems almost insane. And now ask yourself, how have we organized work? Do we make chairs or do we make legs? In all too many cases we have broken the job down into the making of legs.

The difference between making a chair and making legs is the difference between making something that is 'whole' – something that clearly meets the need of a customer, something that brings him pleasure – and something that is a part, something without meaning unto itself. On the family farm and craft shop, they made chairs. In Henry Ford's factory, the factories of mass production, they made legs. The difference is profound. It is the difference between meaningful and meaningless. It is the difference between boredom and monotony, and self-satisfaction and pride. It is the difference between a task that puts the mind to sleep and one that calls on creativity and one's aesthetic talents. The nature of work design has a profound effect on the spiritual well-being of those who labor within the work system. We know how to give meaning and satisfaction to work and we know how to create work systems that denigrate the human spirit. And the difference is not one that engineers are trained to recognize. The work process must be designed so that it is experienced, not as fragmented and isolated parts, but as an integrated holistic process resulting in a discernible output, thereby giving the individual a sense of fulfillment. The individual alone does not need to accomplish the entire work process. But that individual can be a member of a team that accomplishes the whole and the individual will gain the satisfaction of the output of the group. This is the family system that must be restored to our workplace.

The work process is the definition and arrangement of activities that result in the output, the product or service, of a work system. Every work system, including education, government and businesses, contain work processes and those can be studied and improved. A work process may isolate an individual from his or her customer or it may require the individual to understand the flow of work to the customer. Walls between departments of an organization block the sight of the customer to those doing the work. To the degree that those working in a process understand the entire flow they will empathize with the customer and experience the spirit of service. It is illogical to design a work process that does not allow knowledge of the customer yet expects the individual to work in the spirit of service to that customer. Responsibility rests with the manager of the system to design the system consistent with principles.

The effective organization of work accomplishes two critical things: first, it enables the individual to experience the spirit of service, the satisfaction of knowing that your work meets the needs of another human being; second, it provides an opportunity to exercise one's mental faculties in the improvement of the work or the product of work. 'Abdu'l-Bahá said that 'In this great dispensation, art (or a profession) is identical with an act of worship and this is a clear text of the Blessed Perfection.'[1] He also said that

> This is highly suitable. Strive as much as possible to become proficient in the science of agriculture for in accordance with the Divine Teachings, the acquisition of sciences and the perfection of arts is considered as acts of worship. If a man engages with all his power in the acquisition of a science or in the perfection of an art, it is as if he has been worshiping God in the churches and temples. Thus as thou enterest a school of agriculture and strivest in the acquisition of that science thou art day and night engaged in acts of worship – acts that are accepted at the threshold of the Almighty. What bounty greater than this that science should be considered as an act of worship and art as service to the Kingdom of God.[2]

In the above passage 'Abdu'l-Bahá speaks of work, agriculture, the pursuit of arts and science, all as acts of worship. He is not, therefore, speaking of any one kind of work. But, importantly, there is a qualification. 'If a man engages with all his power in the acquisition of a science and in the perfection of an art, it is as if he has been worshiping God . . .' I believe that this 'if' is extremely important. It doesn't say that if a person simply shows up at work and puts in his time, it is as if he were worshiping God. It is only if he is 'engaged with all his power' and is seeking perfection in that work. I believe this is a natural law, much like the exercise of the human muscle: in order to be strong, to grow and develop, the muscle must be exercised. Similarly, the mind and spirit must be exercised at work and only then, *when engaged with all his power*, is it an act of worship.

The ability to exercise one's mental powers in the pursuit of perfection and to serve one's customers in the spirit of service are very dependent on the design of the work system. Many work systems make these conditions impossible and thereby deny the ability to achieve this state of worship. What then are the conditions that enable this achievement? The following are conditions that are both the responsibility of the managers in their design of the system and also of the individual who may choose how he or she approaches the work.

1) Organize for customer focus

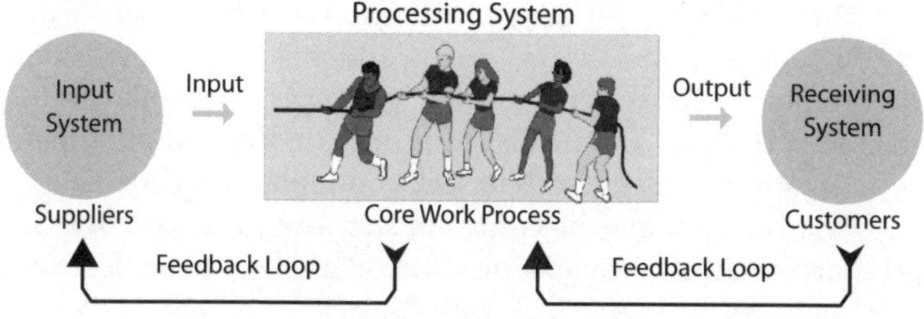

In order to feel concern for a customer and to feel the motivation to improve one's work the work must be organized so that clear segments are completed by a group of associates who can see the flow of the work from a supplier through to a customer. This flow in the quality improvement field is known as SIPOC: Supplier, Input, Process, Output and Customer. Quality results from the attention not to one but to this entire flow of work. The work of the team and its members is defined to include inspecting the work received from suppliers and providing the suppliers with immediate feedback so they can improve. It is also their job to continually improve their work process, inspect their own work and receive feedback from their customers. Defining work around this work flow and with the specifically stated responsibility to improve their work is the most basic work design factor that will enable work to be performed in the spirit of service.

2) Continually seek improvement and appreciate past performance

When a child takes his or her first steps we applaud and squeal with delight. While we appreciate this humble beginning, wobbly and uncertain as it may be, we also expect natural and continuous improvement. In the larger scheme of things we are all children taking wobbly steps and hoping to do better next time. It is most important that we both encourage improvement in the efforts of others and appreciate the value of the efforts they have made. While we appreciate what has been done, we remember that 'If a man engages with all his power in the acquisition of a science or in the perfection of an art, it is as if he has been worshiping God . . .' This seeking of perfection means never being satisfied with the current state and always seeking a higher level of perfection. No product or the work process that produces that product is in a state of perfection. To be satisfied is to cease forward movement; to be creatively dissatisfied is to seek continuous improvement.

Dissatisfaction may be either constructive or destructive. The great artist, athlete, scientist or writer is unlikely to be described as someone who is 'satisfied' with himself or herself. In fact, he is most often his own worst critic, most aware of the deficiency of his work and energetically seeking the next level of improvement. This dissatisfaction is 'creative' because it creates direction and energy, energy motivated by the awareness of the gap between where he is and where he could be.

When is dissatisfaction destructive? It is usually destructive when it is directed at others or when it fails to recognize prior success. When it is not accompanied by the confidence in one's ability to improve it is unlikely to lead to helpful change. To be helpful to others we must give them this confidence, recognize their success, as well as give them a vision of how things could be improved.

3) Problems are normal – each an opportunity

If you follow baseball, for example, you know that even the world's best hitters go into slumps during which they appear no better than the worst players. You know that this is a normal cycle. The world's best pitchers will have bad games in which they have poor control and leave the game early. This is normal. The most creative geniuses, Thomas Edison, for example, had hundreds of ideas that failed. Edison tried thousands of ideas to create the lightbulb, each resulting in failure, until he finally found the one that worked. But from each he learned. Successful entrepreneurs in business have more often than not had previous business failures. But they pressed on, each time honing their skills.

Trial and error, failures, slumps and losing streaks are all experienced by those who, in the long run, prove to be successful. The Bahá'í writings tell us that tests and trials are for our benefit. They both strengthen our spiritual will and provide an opportunity to learn important lessons. The question is whether or not we view tests from a perspective of continuous improvement, asking ourselves the question, 'What can I learn from this experience so I may do better the next time?'

> Thou hast written concerning the tests that have come upon thee. To the sincere ones, tests are as a gift from God, the Exalted, for a heroic person hasteneth, with the utmost joy and gladness, to the tests of a violent battlefield, but the coward is afraid and trembles and utters moaning and lamentation. Likewise, an expert student prepareth and memorizeth his lessons and exercises with the utmost effort, and in the day of examination he appeareth with infinite joy before the master. Likewise, the pure gold shineth radiantly in the fire of test. Consequently, it is made clear that for holy souls, trials are as the gift of God, the Exalted; but for weak souls they are an unexpected calamity. This test is just as thou hast written: it removeth the rust of egotism from the mirror of the heart until the Sun of Truth may shine therein. For, no veil is greater than egotism and no matter how thin that covering may be, yet

> it will finally veil man entirely and prevent him from receiving a portion from the eternal bounty.[3]

4) Time matters

Improvement occurs in time. Imagine the student in school. The student studies and turns in a required paper. Time goes by – weeks, months. Six months after turning in the report, the teacher hands it back with feedback, both corrections and commendations. Now imagine the same student turns in another paper in a different class with a different teacher. Two days after turning in the report to this second teacher the student receives feedback, with similar corrections and commendations.

In which of these cases will learning be most enhanced? Why?

There is a great deal of research on the effect of feedback. It is conclusive – the more immediate the feedback, the greater the positive effect on learning and motivation. The more delayed the feedback, the more diminished its effect.

The rate at which problems are addressed defines the rate of learning in an organization. If problems that occurred yesterday are addressed and solved today, the cost of that problem will be diminished, while the learning will be increased. If problems are allowed to go without correction and learning for a month, for example, that problem is likely to be compounded and learning is far less likely.

5) Consider knowledge, skill and motivation

All learning is not the same. There are different types of learning that impact different competencies. Knowledge is information – data in the data bank of your mind. Education increases knowledge. Reading a book or listening to a lecture may increase your knowledge of a subject.

Skill is entirely different. Imagine that you want to learn to touch type at 80 words per minute. Will knowledge of the keyboard, the location of the keys, achieve this? No. Typing is a skill and is acquired in an entirely different way from knowledge. Skills such as speaking a language, playing a musical instrument or a sport, are only acquired through some knowledge but then much practice and feedback. Practice, practice, practice – this is the essential element in developing skills.

Motivation is different again. Motivation is the 'want to' rather than the 'can do'. Knowledge and skill enable, the 'can do'. What creates the motivation? Motivation is largely the result of consequences – particularly reward, recognition or appreciation.

Each of these types of learning will address different problems in a process. Sometimes a work process may be slow to deliver a product to a customer because employees are not motivated to deliver the product in a speedy manner. However, the late delivery may result from good motivation but a lack of skill in completing the task. It is important that each problem be analyzed to determine whether it is one of motivation, skill or knowledge.

6) Most problems are in the process, not the person

Most problems are in the process, how we do things, yet most often we blame the person and fail to fix the process. We change the person and then are surprised to find that the new person performs in a manner similar to the previous person. Dr W. Edwards Deming said that '95% of the quality problems are in the process, and 95% of the time we blame the person and fail to fix the process.'

It is very common to do damage by blaming individuals for the cause of problems, create fear and guilt and drive away those who could make contributions to our community. A process is a set of activities, a sequence of steps, coordinated to achieve a result. Planning children's classes is a process. Planning worship services, a teaching campaign or a conference is a process.

Imagine that you asked someone to plan a conference. You told him you want to have five hundred people attend, you want nationally recognized speakers, you want it to be held in a very dignified setting, to be held in four weeks and the costs should be minimal. Great! Imagine the frenzy of activity the good-hearted soul would engage in who attempted to meet these criteria. Of course, he would fail. The conference would probably be a mass of confusion, failing to meet most of the stated criteria. The organizer might be blamed for his poor conference planning skills. He would be disheartened and discouraged from future service. Is he to blame? Of course not. The process that led up to this conference is to blame. How it was planned, the steps leading up to it, made it impossible. This is a process problem, not a problem that can be solved by blaming someone.

7) Keeping score leads to improvement

The experience of results increases both learning and motivation. Every sport includes a mechanism for score keeping. This is not only because one athlete or team competes against another. The runner seeking to improve his or her own fitness measures the miles run each day, week or month; the minutes per mile; the pulse rate at the end of a number of miles. Why do they keep score on their own performance? We measure, or keep score, because we are motivated to see improvement. Crowds cheer, athletes practice and runners perspire to experience results.

Businesses have learned that sharing results, visualizing results, for all employees to see has a positive impact on motivation. Virtually every quality improvement process includes the graphing and charting of quality performance as well as visualizing processes and opportunities for improvement. This visualization is one of involvement, giving employees a feeling of ownership and participation in improvement.

Some may fear that charting and visually posting scores may produce undesirable competition. It will only produce undesirable competition if the managers have created an assumption of a zero-sum game rather than a non-zero-sum game. In other words, if everyone improves, everyone can be applauded. One team's success or improvement does not have to come at the expense of others.

8) Map the process

We have all heard the saying that a picture is worth a thousand words. There is some magic in being able to see a diagram, a graph of data or the map of a process. There is also power in a group, mapping a process together, asking 'which step comes first?', 'which step comes after that?' and 'who does this step?' The simple act of mapping a process on a wall or a flip chart and discussing the order of each step is an exercise that helps the group to become more systematic in its thinking.

The following is an example of a simple 'relationship map' that illustrates not only the steps in the process but also who is responsible for each step.

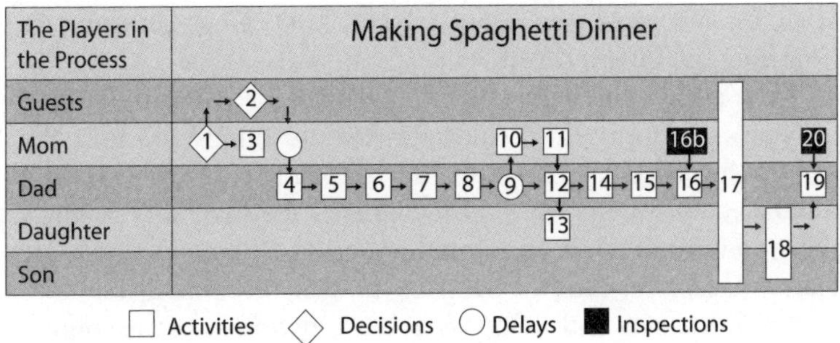

This example, of a family preparing a meal for guests, is a very simple process. But looking at it, you immediately learn something. What does this map tell you about Dad? What does it tell you about the role of the children? Of course, each number step is defined. For example in step #1 Mom makes a decision to invite the guests to dinner. Obviously she does this by herself. In step #2 the guests decide to come. In step #3 she comes home and informs the family that the guests are coming. In step #4 Dad goes shopping to buy the ingredients. In the following steps Dad prepares the meal. Finally, in step #17 the guests arrive and they all eat together. In #18 the son and daughter clear the table. In step #19 Dad washes the dishes and, #20, Mom inspects and provides feedback.

The process map not only tells you how the work got done – and therein may lay the causes of problems and opportunities for improvement – but it also tells you about relationships, roles and responsibilities. This provides the 'facts' around which an intelligent discussion of how we can improve may be centered. It is a common practice to first map out the 'current state' process, then discuss problems, what works, etc., and then create an 'ideal state' map of how we will do things in the future. It is best to do this in a group, the group responsible for the process, and to put the process on the wall for all to see and discuss.

This is a detailed work process. In a business setting you will also have high level process maps that define the basic flow of work between research and development, engineering, manufacturing, sales, etc. These process maps explain how things get done and how they can be improved.

Even within the Bahá'í or other religious communities, process maps can be used to study how we do things and how they can be improved. For example, the following is a map created by a Bahá'í community that had recognized the need for 'caring' in their community and appointed a Caring Response Team. This team was responsible for caring for the sick, recognizing birthdays and anniversaries and welcoming new individuals to the community. They mapped out the processes they would use to accomplish this. It served as a guide to their work and making this visible to the entire community (along with a map of a teaching process, children's class process, etc.) enabled everyone to understand the process and contribute to its improvement.

The Players in the Process	Community Caring Response Process
LSA	1 → 4 → 6 →
LSA Secretary	7
Caring Response Team	2 → 3 → 5 → 8 → 10 →
Feast	9 →
CRT Member	11 → 12 →
CRT Member	→ 13 →
Community Member	14

□ Activities ◇ Decisions

All of these steps are ways to insure that individuals are engaged in their work in a manner that will lead them to achieve the guidance: 'If a man engages with all his power in the acquisition of a science or in the perfection of an art, it is as if he has been worshiping God . . .'

Questions for Discussion and Reflection

1) Imagine that you have been named the manager of an accounting department of a large organization. The department is currently organized into functions: tax, accounts payable, accounts receivable and payroll and benefits. Your department does the accounting for 12 different business units that are in various locations. Given the principles regarding process discussed above, how might you organize the work of this department to maximize the degree to which employees feel ownership of their work and are motivated to serve their customers?

2) You work in a manufacturing plant with five hundred employees. There is a plant manager, five department managers and three staff heads that comprise the plant manager's team; 25 supervisors; and 30 working team leaders who are members of work teams and who take leadership responsibilities for their teams. The department managers each have functional departments such as warehouse and shipping and maintenance and three manufacturing departments. Your company has decided to reduce the number of levels throughout the organization. You now have four levels and must redesign the organization to reduce one level. What would you do? In addition to the simple structure of the organization, what other implications for other systems (human resource, information, etc.) would this change have?

3) You have been asked to establish work teams in a manufacturing organization. Other than simply grouping people into

teams, what other implications will this have? Imagine that you have been given the mandate to 'optimize the capability of these teams'.

Other Quotations and Views on Work Process

Your work is to discover your work and then with all your heart to give yourself to it. *Buddha*

Man was made at the end of the week's work, when God was tired. *Mark Twain*

How do I work? I grope. *Albert Einstein*

By the work one knows the workman. *Jean de La Fontaine*

As for me, prizes are nothing. My prize is my work. *Katharine Hepburn*

Don't waste life in doubts and fears; spend yourself on the work before you, well assured that the right performance of this hour's duties will be the best preparation for the hours and ages that will follow it. *Ralph Waldo Emerson*

11

Structure and Organization

Does structure affect the spirit? Does it matter how many levels, departments, divisions are in a firm? Can't one possess the same spirit, motivation or focus on performance in an organization of a dozen levels as in one with three? Isn't organization structure a simple distraction, a materialistic view of the world we should be able to rise above?

Many years ago while stationed in Europe with the US Army, a friend and I traveled from town to town around Europe, casually seeing the countryside and trying to understand the culture of each country. In the center of most French or German towns of any size is the church or cathedral. When entering these cathedrals for the first time I would walk in and my head would almost automatically go back, staring up into the great arches and the stained glass windows. As my eyes went up towards heaven I felt something within, some change in spirit, some emotion and some inner reply to the architect's magic. Cathedrals are amazing for their arches, for the incredible engineering feat that results in a spiritual response. If one had no idea of the intended purpose of the building one might consider it entirely impractical, a huge waste of space and effort, unnecessarily difficult to build. But the architect was not only an engineer, not merely concerned with structural strength or cost of construction. The architect knew his purpose and the relationship between structure and spirit. This is the essence of the 'art' of architecture, distinct from the engineering of buildings.

Those who design organization structures are, at their best, architects, not merely engineers. An organization is not merely a practical thing. It is a structure, like a building, that will affect how its inhabitants think, feel and act. Form and spirit interact.

To the reader who may not be entirely familiar with the Bahá'í Faith it is important that we review a few of the most significant features of its teachings related to its own structure. The Bahá'í Faith is the first major religion whose founders provided an administrative process and a structure. We are taught that this is a model for future governments. If we accept that this structure, and the decision-making processes it implies, is the future structure of not only religious institutions but of government as well, may it not also be applied to the institutions of commerce? What better model could there be but the model provided by God's own hand? I have found nowhere in the Bahá'í writings where it says that this model must be followed in business organizations. However, it is only logical to find what is superior, what works best, in this new structure and seek to apply those lessons to our business organizations. This discovery process is likely to extend over the period of several generations. While it is certainly beyond my capability to forecast exactly how this model will eventually apply to businesses, it is worth beginning a dialogue and imagining how we may learn from this example.

The claim of this Faith, whether believed or not, is somewhat astounding, yet it is perfectly clear and must be confronted.

> He has ordained and established the House of Justice which is endowed with a political as well as a religious function, the consummate union and blending of church and state. This institution is under the protecting power of Bahá'u'lláh Himself. A universal or international House of Justice shall also be organized. Its rulings shall be in accordance with the commands and teachings of Bahá'u'lláh, and that which the universal House of Justice ordains shall be obeyed by all mankind. This international House of Justice shall be appointed and organized from the Houses of Justice of the whole world, and all the world shall come under its administration.[1]

Nowhere in the Bible or the Qur'án is there a similar claim that a clearly defined institution, and the processes of election and decision-making, will come to serve as world embracing administration. It is a claim so bold that it cannot be ignored. It must either be rejected as spurious or investigated for its possibilities. A discussion of all of its rationales and implications is beyond the scope of this book or chapter. However, there are several characteristics and implications of this claim that are relevant to our discussion of business management.

The first concerns the animating purpose of the institutions defined in the Bahá'í texts. No institution or structure exists in form alone. Like the cathedral, the structure is derived from purpose and serves that purpose. Any analysis of its elements must be judged according to the degree to which it helps to fulfill that purpose.

> This New World Order, whose promise is enshrined in the Revelation of Bahá'u'lláh, whose fundamental principles have been enunciated in the writings of the Center of His Covenant, involves no less than the complete unification of the entire human race.[2]

Who among us could design such an organizational system? Who among us is capable of being the 'Founding Father' of a constitution that would have not only the structural integrity but the spiritual power to accomplish the unification of the entire human race? Bahá'ís believe that no mortal man or woman could found such a system but rather that this is the very purpose animating and central to God's revelation in this age.

The Guardian of the Bahá'í Faith, Shoghi Effendi, makes clear just how stupendous is this claim and how profound its implications for the human race:

> The Revelation of Bahá'u'lláh, whose supreme mission is none other but the achievement of this organic and spiritual unity of the whole body of nations, should, if we be faithful to its implications, be regarded as signalizing through its advent the *coming*

> *of age of the entire human race.* It should be viewed not merely as yet another spiritual revival in the ever-changing fortunes of mankind, not only as a further stage in a chain of progressive Revelations, nor even as the culmination of one of a series of recurrent prophetic cycles, but rather as marking the last and highest stage in the stupendous evolution of man's collective life on this planet. The emergence of a world community, the consciousness of world citizenship, the founding of a world civilization and culture – all of which must synchronize with the initial stages in the unfoldment of the Golden Age of the Bahá'í Era – should, by their very nature, be regarded, as far as this planetary life is concerned, as the furthermost limits in the organization of human society, though man, as an individual, will, nay must indeed as a result of such a consummation, continue indefinitely to progress and develop.[3]

One could (and should) meditate on this paragraph for a long time. Its implications encompass everything presented in this book and a hundred times more. But the phrase 'the furthermost limits in the organization of human society' strikes me as particularly significant for our task. The order prescribed by this Faith is not merely an order for the administration of another religion. It is a prescription for all of human society and for the unification of all societies on this planet. While none of us in the world of business or other organizations can dream of such profound intentions, nevertheless this organizational form is predicted to permeate all forms of organization in human society.

It is clearly justified to say that 'if this system is to bring about the unity of the entire human race, then my humble business, my organization with far more modest ambitions, with a far more narrow focus, surely does not need to adopt this system in its entirety'. And that is most likely correct, particularly at this time in our culture when many aspects of this order may seem too foreign, too extreme, to be comfortably accepted by those managers and employees for whom we are responsible. But consider the matter another way. In my experience the adherents of the Bahá'í

Faith have often been too modest or conservative in their willingness to assert the principles of Bahá'í administration as they may apply to work organizations. Too often it has been from other sources that principles of spirituality, the process of reliance on group decision-making and other qualities of administration have been promoted and taken root because of their practical application while such principles were made clear a hundred years earlier in the Bahá'í writings. It seems to me that it is long past the time when Bahá'ís should be bold in proposing the adoption of the fundamental principles of their administrative order.

What then are the key characteristics of this new organizational structure that may be considered for adoption by secular organizations?

The Twin Branches of Governance: The Rulers and the Learned

In the government of the United States and many others there are three separate branches of government: executive, legislature and judiciary. Each branch is designed to accomplish entirely different missions and functions with some independence. In many parts of the world there is the separation of royalty, inherited rank and status, from that of elected parliaments and executives. This 'separation of powers' has proved useful, not only as a check on the misuse of power but in order to provide different perspectives, temperaments and skills. A judge with a lifetime appointment is able to view matters with a detachment and perspective not available to a congressman who is elected every two years, for example. The two views are complementary and valuable for a different purpose.

Within most business organizations there is essentially one structure of authority and decision-making, although one could argue that in some corporations the staff organizations of accounting, human resources, etc. serve as an independent source of authority from line operating groups. In most organizations there is a tension between members of operating units who would almost always like to have complete control over their internal staff and the corporate staff structure that views these staff as independent extensions of their expertise and as a control function. However, in many cases it is clear that the function of accounting has been used by operating managers to achieve their operating goals or to hide the failure of operational attainment, when those very functions should have been clearly reporting the facts with an independent discipline. The lack of clear independence of accounting and operations is one of the explanations for the Enron, WorldCom and other recent fiascos.

In the Bahá'í system of administration there are two branches that function in different ways and each with a different purpose. On the one hand there are the elected institutions that are elected from the bottom up and make all decisions in a process of group consultation; on the other are the appointed institutions, appointed from the top down. The elected are clearly and unequivocally designated as the 'rulers'. The structure of the Bahá'í Faith seeks to gain the benefits of individuals who are 'learned' and who are capable of providing guidance, inspiration and a detached view to those who bear the responsibility for making decisions and exercising authority, while at the same time eliminating the failings of previous institutions in which individuals exercised personal authority because of their rank. The entire history of previous institutional forms is a litany of the ills of personal ego – the corruption of power. It is hard for us to imagine institutions in which the element of personal power, ego, and the resulting corruption is eliminated but this is exactly what the structure of the Bahá'í Faith is designed to accomplish. To document the ills of personal power would consume an entire volume of work and its reading would be rather depressing. But we all know of individuals who entered government, for example, with the best and most noble of intentions and succeeded in gaining a position of power and prestige. And very soon the forces of influence bore down on this individual, every interest group or party seeking to gain influence, those around him seeking to gain favor by reinforcing and restating his views until they seem to be assuredly correct, only because of the absence of alternative views. The mind and the spirit are gradually corrupted even though the individual's intentions remain good. The weight of personal power grows exponentially with growing rank and authority until it is more than almost any human being can bear to remain clear-headed and objective in his views. The structures of the Bahá'í Faith have removed this burden and replaced it with the authority of the group and the gentle guidance of the individual.

The Structure of Spiritual Authority

In any society there must be authority. There must be the ability to say, after the sharing of ideas and gathering information, 'we will go this way and not that way'. The absence of a clear source of authority leads to anarchy and anarchy leads to the tyranny of might over right. The Bahá'í system places authority in groups called Assemblies. Group decision-making in the corporate world has become well accepted, although there is an ongoing discussion about when individuals versus groups should make decisions. The model of group decision-making presented in the Bahá'í Faith cannot properly be understood without understanding the spiritual nature of Assemblies and the connection to the primary source of authority – God's revelation. The spiritual nature of man, the human character, cannot be divorced or in any way separated from the outward structure of organization or decision-making.

Bahá'u'lláh, in His Book of Laws, the Kitáb-i-Aqdas, states:

> The Lord hath ordained that in every city a House of Justice be established wherein shall gather counselors to the number of Bahá, and should it exceed this number it does not matter . . . It behooveth them to be the trusted ones of the Merciful among men and to regard themselves as the guardians appointed of God for all that dwell on earth. It is incumbent upon them to take counsel together and to have regard for the interests of the servants of God, for His sake, even as they regard their own interests, and to choose that which is meet and seemly. Thus hath the Lord

> your God commanded you. Beware lest ye put away that which is clearly revealed in His Tablet. Fear God, O ye that perceive.[4]

The number 'Bahá' is the number nine. What is most significant about this quotation is its clear instruction regarding the motivation, the spirit that should guide those who take counsel together. To 'have regard for the interests of the servants of God, for His sake' makes clear that their interests are not to be their own but rather those they serve. This spirit of service to others, as an act of service to God, entirely changes the nature of the group process from that most common in organizations today. Imagine if the board of directors of major corporations actually met and consulted with this spirit. It would entirely transform the very purpose of the corporation and the very nature of our economic system.

'Abdu'l-Bahá, speaking of the nature of the Assemblies and the requirements for their successful functioning said:

> The prime requisites for them that take counsel together are purity of motive, radiance of spirit, detachment from all else save God, attraction to His Divine Fragrances, humility and lowliness amongst His loved ones, patience and long-suffering in difficulties and servitude to His exalted Threshold. Should they be graciously aided to acquire these attributes, victory from the unseen Kingdom of Bahá shall be vouchsafed to them. In this day, assemblies of consultation are of the greatest importance and a vital necessity. Obedience unto them is essential and obligatory. The members thereof must take counsel together in such wise that no occasion for ill-feeling or discord may arise. This can be attained when every member expresseth with absolute freedom his own opinion and setteth forth his argument. Should any one oppose, he must on no account feel hurt for not until matters are fully discussed can the right way be revealed. The shining spark of truth cometh forth only after the clash of differing opinions. If after discussion, a decision be carried unanimously, well and good; but if, the Lord forbid, differences of opinion should arise, a majority of voices must prevail.[5]

One could meditate for a long time on the spiritual nature, the high standard of human character, called for in this passage. How many of us can honestly say that we meet this standard of 'purity of motive, radiance of spirit, detachment from all else save God, attraction to His Divine Fragrances, humility and lowliness amongst His loved ones, patience and long-suffering in difficulties and servitude to His exalted Threshold'? I for one would have to excuse myself from any service on any Assembly if I felt I had to confess to 'detachment from all else save God' for example. But these standards give us the direction, the goal, the lofty station to strive for.

Again, attempt to imagine if groups at work, from the board room to the team at the first level, were able to even strive towards such standards of spiritual conduct. Imagine that they had this passage posted on the wall of their work area as they now have quotations about quality and customer service. The mere acceptance of the standard as one to strive for is, in itself, transformative.

Applying Bahá'í Principles to Structure and Organization

How might these twin pillars be applied to the world of business or secular institutions? This is a matter that no one can answer with certainty but we can speculate, experiment and innovate. Over the years we will learn how to extract the wisdom of this model and find its application to business organization.

Before suggesting some specific applications there is a principle that must be considered. This concerns the relationship between voluntary behavior and that which requires external control. Religions largely function owing to high voluntary behavior. This volunteerism, or discretionary effort, is based on commitment to values or a 'cause'. Business organizations may also elicit discretionary effort. To the degree that members are committed to the principles of the organization and are motivated by those principles, external control is required only to provide gentle steering or direction to the effort. The Bahá'í institutions rely to a very great extent on voluntary effort and one may thereby question the applicability of its loose structure to the world of business.

Business also requires greater conformity. While in local religious communities it is permissible, even necessary, to have very diverse activities depending on the local resources and conditions; a business is not likely to find such diversity of activity acceptable. McDonald's or Starbucks succeed largely because of the conformity of local stores to making hamburgers and coffee in the same way.

Every organization must assess the degree to which its members may be guided by principles and process versus direct supervisory control. To the degree that the leaders have defined motivating principles that build unity of effort and trust there is less need for supervisory control. To the degree that processes are well defined (as in fast food preparation) and employees are trained in the process, less supervision and control is required. Maximizing self-control and minimizing the requirement of supervision is a critical factor in cost competitiveness. Structure can be loose, costs of management can be reduced, if the leaders have succeeded in instilling a culture of strong values and clearly defining processes.

Let us attempt to imagine the workings of an 'Institution of the Learned' in business. It is first worth noting that the most important function in most businesses these days is the development and application of knowledge. Perhaps the second most important function is the motivation and encouragement of the members of the organization. Neither of these functions are ones of formal decision-making or the exercise of authority. Yet the sharing of knowledge and personal motivation are both essential to the success of any organization. In order to compete successfully a business must be a 'learning organization' and it is motivated individuals who learn.

Universities often have *scholars in residence*, who may teach a course or two, but whose primary purpose is simply to continue with their own research and to make themselves available to emerging scholars in their field – in other words, to provide inspiration, encouragement and guidance. At Honeywell some years ago they created a somewhat similar position in critical technology fields. For example, they had done some of the most important work in the development of lasers and the application of laser technology. This resulted in the 'three ring laser gyro' that now guides most commercial aircraft. One of the senior scientists who had been responsible for much of this work held a position very similar to that of a scholar in residence with no formal duties other than to continue the pursuit of the work he loved, advanced research in lasers, and to be available to consult with others seeking to apply laser technology.

Corporations should identify their core competencies, those competencies essential to their core work processes that serve their customers. In the case of Honeywell Aerospace and Defense, laser technology was a core competence. To a technology company there is no more important function than the development and utilization of its core competencies. Managing projects and people is a very different set of skills than developing laser technology, for example. In fact, it is likely that the world's greatest laser scientist may very well be a poor manager of people and projects. Yet in most companies there is only one path to promotion and that is the path of decision-making and the exercise of authority in line management. Most companies have assumed that line managers will be both the technological experts and the experts in managing people and projects. It is an entirely erroneous assumption.

You can see in this example of a separate organization of scholars, scientists or 'the learned' the opportunity to give people responsibility for those areas that they most enjoy and at which they are most adept. Separate compensation and evaluation processes must support the promotion of personal expertise without any regard to managing people or ongoing operations. It is not hard to imagine the identification of experts in core sciences, marketing, human resources, financial management, law and other areas of knowledge essential to the well functioning of an organization and giving those who are most expert individual responsibility for the development and promotion of those areas of expertise. These 'counselors' would then be available to consult and advise, encourage and inspire, those working on projects or in the line operations of the organization. They would not be responsible for meeting financial goals, the short term needs of customers or the organization of work. Their evaluation and compensation would not be dependent on those with operating management responsibility.

The number of individuals serving in such a capacity would be small relative to the number serving in line management or operating positions. Similarly, in the Bahá'í community the number of individuals who serve within the Institution of the Learned is relatively small compared to the number serving in the community and on Assemblies.

The Organization of Authority in Groups

Currently in government and business organizations the primary organizing structure is that of individual managers, who report to other individual managers and who exercise their individual authority of decision-making. There will always be a role for individual decision-making when speed is a requirement or when only one person has the expertise to make a decision (a surgeon in an operating room, for example). However, the Bahá'í system of organization is entirely different. It recognizes that in most decision-making groups there is collective wisdom, collective experience and diverse perspectives that are best brought to bear on a problem or decision. The Bahá'í process also recognizes the importance of unity of thought and action following a decision. The quality of a decision is only the beginning of a process, a process that usually requires the commitment and understanding of a group of people.

Individuals are elected to Assemblies in secret ballot voting with no campaigning or other forms of self-promotion. Such self-promotion as is the norm in both government and business would disqualify one as a candidate. Rather, one is judged for his spirit of service, for his personal qualities of devotion and competence. Now imagine a corporate structure in which all important decisions are made in groups and the members of those groups are elected by the members of the organization. It is so at variance with current practice that it is rather hard to imagine.

The traditional structure of most organizations looks something like this hierarchical diagram. Given a piece of paper and asked to draw their organization chart, 99 per cent of managers will produce something that looks like this. Images are important. It is clear in this image that up is good. *Moving up* in the organization is what one wants. Power and prestige are at the top. Money is at the top. Being on top is good. Falling down to the bottom is bad. You start at the bottom and move up the organization ladder. All of this language corresponds to the image and has profound implications for motivation and behavior. Much of organizational behavior is driven by this image and the corresponding language of personal ambition and power.

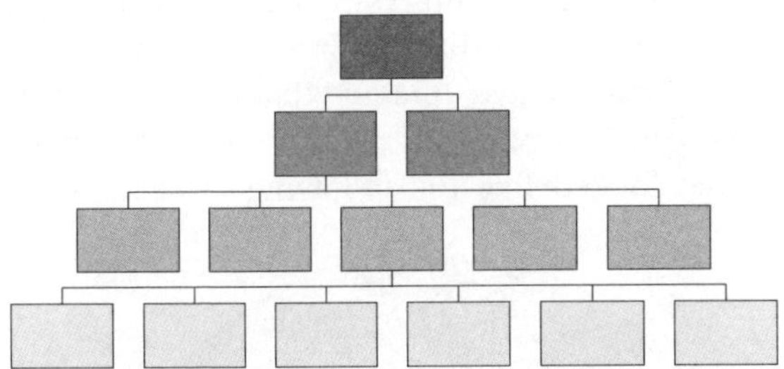

However, there is increasing evidence that the best managers of large organizations are not the much publicized charismatic leaders who relish personal power but rather those who display humility and promote the unity and influence of the group. In the previous chapter on consultation I referred to Jim Collins's description of what he called Level 5 leaders:

> Seemingly ordinary men . . . Level 5 leaders channel their ego needs away from themselves and into the larger goal of building a great company. It is not that Level 5 leaders have no ego or self-interest; indeed, they are incredibly ambitious – but their ambition is first and foremost for the institution, not themselves.

> The great irony is that the animus and personal ambition that often drive people to positions of power stand at odds with the humility required of Level 5 leadership.[6]

And at lower levels of our organizations, the power of teams, small groups of associates or managers who take ownership as a group to manage and improve a process are becoming the most accepted form of organization.

Cultures do not change in a short period of time but if one looks with a historical perspective, one can see a gradual movement towards an organizational form in which the majority of decisions, particularly the important ones, are made in consultative groups, rather than by authoritative individuals. As we move towards more consultative and less egocentric organizations we will conceptualize them in different ways. The images, language and motivations will change. Imagine that if asked to draw a picture of your organization, 99 per cent of the managers produced something that looked like the following circular organization diagram.

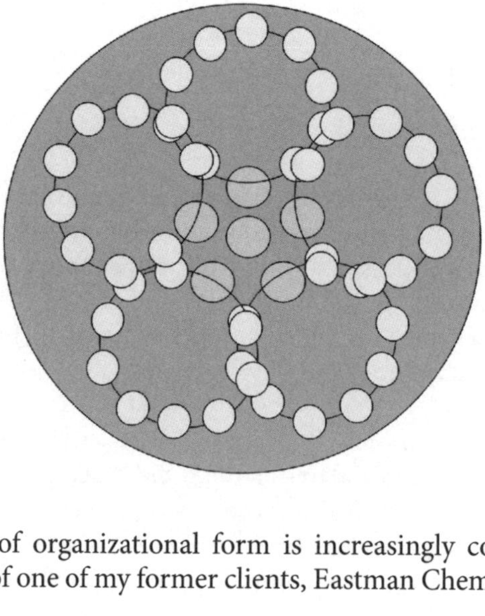

This type of organizational form is increasingly common. The president of one of my former clients, Eastman Chemicals, had an organization chart that he was fond of calling the Pepperoni Pizza diagram. It looked much like this. The person in the center of this diagram, presumably the president, appears to have more of a coordinating role. No one is on 'top'. Who is on the bottom level? No one. Again, both the language and the image have important implications for motivation and behavior. In this model it is not so clear that all rewards and prestige are tied to climbing up the organization chart.

With most of our organizations functioning as a link on a chain of customers and suppliers, all of whom contribute to serving an end-use customer, describing the reality of organizational structures becomes increasingly more complex. Within a large organization there are several operating organizations that may share expertise and have subject-matter experts within them who share expertise across traditional organizational boundaries. For example, quality management experts may network across organizational boundaries. So too may health and safety, training and development, information technology and other experts. Rather than grouping all such experts in one location, they may be spread throughout but formed into a loose, networked organization for the purpose of developing and sharing their competence. This may produce an organization chart the looks something like this.

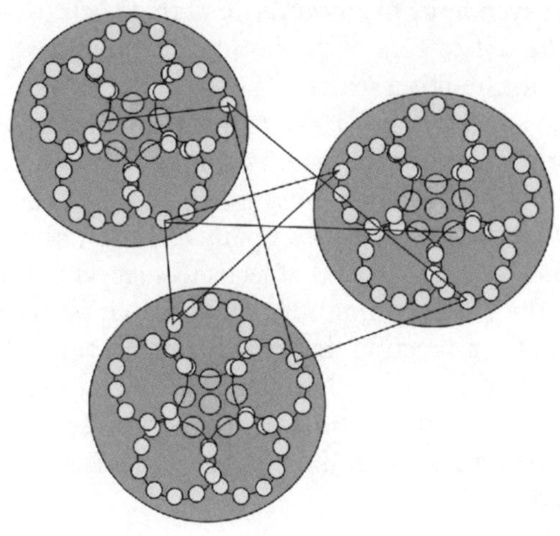

For many years I have been working with major corporations to apply a model of management somewhat resembling the model of the Local Spiritual Assembly. This has been packaged for popular consumption as *Team Management*. The principles must be presented in a language that can be understood and digested by the average business person. What are the essential features of the Assembly model provided in the Bahá'í Faith that can be applied to a secular institution?

First, there is the assumption that members of groups (teams) are of equal status, voice and responsibility. While one member may serve as chairperson or secretary, his voice remains equal to that of others. This understanding is distinctly different from that of virtually every other model of organization. It provides the foundation upon which consultative decision-making can be built. A team in business can be made up of members who have equal status and who may serve different roles without establishing a hierarchy of distinction. Many teams elect a member to act as facilitator or chairperson for some period of time.

Second, there is the process of inclusion and empowerment. A Bahá'í Assembly is elected by the members of the community, serves that community and consults with the members of the community every 19 days. The structure of the Faith is consistent with the psychology of empowerment that leads to motivation and uplifts the self-esteem of the community members. Old hierarchical decision-making structures were built on the assumption that a few had superior knowledge to the many. The realities of the business world today are consistent with the idea that knowledge, creativity and responsibility must be shared among the many, not hoarded by the few. It is a company of smart, involved, creative and dedicated employees that leads to success in the modern economy. In the Bahá'í community, the entire community gathers every 19 days for a meeting that is at once devotional and social and includes a business or administrative function. This process maximizes the opportunity for involvement in decision-making and this can be replicated in the business organization through a team structure.

Teams create unity of thought and action. By sharing common information on performance, analyzing problems and performance together, accepting responsibility for serving their shared customers and designing their common work process, they develop the bond of unity that was present in the earlier work structures of the family farm and craft shop.

The advantage of teams is the acceptance of responsibility by many, the learning that is a natural product of consultative decision-making and the economy that comes from reducing the need for bureaucratic layers of control. The entire structure of the Bahá'í administrative order, with millions of members, is comprised of three levels of group decision-makers: the Local and National Assemblies and the Universal House of Justice. General Motors used to have 16 to 17 levels from the factory worker up to the chief executive. This has been reduced to seven or eight. I was recently in a Ford plant in Mexico with 4,500 employees that is going from five levels to three in the next year. This reduction can only be accomplished by operating on principles of unity and trust, total involvement of employees in the management process and shared rewards and responsibility. This plant will reorganize into a team structure to achieve this sense of ownership and responsibility.

There can be no change in the culture of an organization without a transformation in the decision-making process and understanding of power. The assumption of royalty was the divine authority of kings and upon this was built the authoritarian structure and decision-making process. Democracy is built on a different view of man's relationship to God, power and authority. Democracy was built on the 'natural rights of man', the assumption that God speaks directly to man. The power of government is of limited authority and the individual has rights that are supreme. The Bahá'í system is built on the belief that God has invested responsibility in both the individual and the institutions of governance. This establishes a foundation for decision-making in the Bahá'í administrative order.

The process of consultation, decisions by groups rather than individuals, the creation of unity of thought in place of the exertion of authority and control, will completely change life in the business organization.

> What Bahá'u'lláh is calling for is a consultative process in which the individual participants strive to transcend their respective points of view, in order to function as members of a body with its own interests and goals. In such an atmosphere, characterized by both candor and courtesy, ideas belong not to the individual to whom they occur during the discussion but to the group as a whole, to take up, discard, or revise as seems to best serve the goal pursued . . . Viewed in such a light, consultation is the operating expression of justice in human affairs.[7]

As someone who has worked in what has generally been called the field of *change management* over the past 30 years, it is perfectly clear to me that making significant change in the culture of an organization requires an ability to shift the understanding and use of power. Power is something that men, in particular, have grown addicted to. Every little boy wants to be the quarterback on the football team because the quarterback calls the plays. He is the 'field general' and is therefore awarded the most status. Movement towards a structure and process of group decision-making will require heroic efforts to shift our understanding and use of power.

> . . . power has been largely interpreted as advantage enjoyed by persons or groups . . . This interpretation of power has become an inherent feature of the culture of division and conflict that has characterized the human race during the past several millennia, regardless of the social, religious, or political orientations that have enjoyed ascendancy in given ages, in given parts of the world. In general, power has been an attribute of individuals, factions, peoples, classes, and nations. It has been an attribute especially associated with men rather than women. Its chief effect has been to confer on its beneficiaries the ability to acquire, to surpass, to dominate, to resist, to win.[8]

There is a mystery to the exercise of power in organizations. The more overtly and directly power is exercised, the less effective and fleeting that power is. The more power is exercised to empower others, to include and share, to engage the grass roots of an organization, the more effective and lasting will that power be. The executive who seeks to directly command each decision will soon find her best employees finding other employment and the worst employees entrenching themselves by practicing the art of avoidance – a sure prescription for the loss of competitiveness. On the other hand, the executive who empowers others and shares decision-making will stimulate the creative impulse, establish dedication to the goals of the organization and attract the best talent. The model provided by the Bahá'í Faith of Assembly structures elected from the grass roots, the absence of personal authority or power and the support to those institutions by learned individuals who seek only to advise and encourage is one that can gradually be applied to the business enterprise.

Organization structure sends messages that may uplift or denigrate the individual. The message sent by the structure of the Bahá'í administrative order is one of trust in the individual and the local community; it is one of empowerment, not authoritarian control. This is our model and it is our task to discover its application.

Questions for Discussion and Reflection

1) Reflect on your current organization. Now imagine that it has been agreed that all important decisions, unless they require very specialized knowledge or urgency (like the surgeon in the operating room), will be made in consultation by groups. Draw a new organization chart. One rule – you cannot start at the top. Draw the chart in a way that minimizes the traditional assumptions of 'moving up' and a ladder with power coming from the top.

2) How does the idea of an organization of the 'Learned' apply to the work of your organization? How might a structure of

individual experts, but without the traditional role of authority, be appropriate or useful in your organization? How might this enhance knowledge-sharing and motivation?

3) If you proposed a change in organization such as you proposed from the above questions, what do you think the reaction would be in your organization? If it was proposed by the chief executive, what would the reaction be? What would be required to implement and gain acceptance for such a dramatic change in culture and structure?

Other Quotations and Views on Organization and Structure

The secret of all victory lies in the organization of the non-obvious. *Marcus Aurelius*

The things we fear most in organizations – fluctuations, disturbances, imbalances – are the primary sources of creativity. *Margaret J. Wheatley*

I am personally convinced that one person can be a change catalyst, a 'transformer' in any situation, any organization. Such an individual is yeast that can leaven an entire loaf. It requires vision, initiative, patience, respect, persistence, courage, and faith to be a transforming leader. *Stephen Covey*

Organization doesn't really accomplish anything. Plans don't accomplish anything, either. Theories of management don't much matter. Endeavors succeed or fail because of the people involved. Only by attracting the best people will you accomplish great deeds. *Colin Powell*

Quality is the result of a carefully constructed cultural environment. It has to be the fabric of the organization, not part of the fabric. *Philip Crosby*

Whenever we seek to avoid the responsibility for our own behavior, we do so by attempting to give that responsibility to some other individual or organization or entity. But this means we then give away our power to that entity. *M. Scott Peck*

The trouble with organizing a thing is that pretty soon folks get to paying more attention to the organization than to what they're organized for. *Laura Ingalls Wilder*

Once an organization loses its spirit of pioneering and rests on its early work, its progress stops. *Thomas J. Watson, Sr*

Organization charts and fancy titles count for next to nothing. *Colin Powell*

Leaders must encourage their organizations to dance to forms of music yet to be heard. *Warren G. Bennis*

In any great organization it is far, far safer to be wrong with the majority than to be right alone. *John Kenneth Galbraith*

12

Human Resource Development

All businesses succeed or fail based on the competence, the motivation and the spirit of those who comprise the organization. The development of human competence, motivation and spirit is the fundamental task of all leaders and management systems. There can be no progress without the development of human resources. That development must encompass not only technical skills but also social, spiritual and intellectual ones. The recognition that the whole person and his or her diverse capacities are all employed in the work setting is the foundation of effective human resource development. What is true for companies is also true for society at large.

Economic development and human development are necessarily linked. Human development is limited by economic resources and the efficiency of production that frees time for education. On the other hand, economic systems cannot progress without the development of human capacity and the skills required for the development of technology, science and administration.

There is a necessary and historic evolution of both human and economic development. First, one must eat. If one hundred per cent of the available human resources are devoted to generating food it is impossible to free time for education, manufacturing or technology. Therefore agriculture must first be made more productive.[1] Bahá'u'lláh recognized this when He said,

> Special regard must be paid to agriculture. Although it hath been mentioned in the fifth place, unquestionably it precedeth the

> others. Agriculture is highly developed in foreign lands, however in Persia it hath so far been grievously neglected. It is hoped that His Majesty the Sháh – may God assist him by His grace – will turn his attention to this vital and important matter.[2]

'Abdu'l-Bahá refers to agriculture as the 'foundation of community'[3] and I suspect this is because agriculture must be developed first, it must 'precedeth' other development, just as the foundation of a house must first be well laid before further construction can proceed. Without the investment in the efficiency of agriculture little of social or economic development can take place. Agriculture may also be considered the foundation because it sets the pattern of the family and the interdependency of work.

Much of our relationship to agriculture today is seen through the eyes of a mass production economy in which work processes have resulted in dispiriting work and have been paralleled by the disintegration of the family. Even in American politics the family farm is spoken of in pseudo religious terms, appealing to the longing for that time when the bonds of family and community were strong. However, there will be no going back. Rather we must move forward and bring the lessons of the family system to modern work.

While many in our developed countries look back on agricultural societies with a romanticized nostalgia, they forget that almost all agricultural cultures relied on child labor and routine manual labor. Life expectancy and education were short. Now only a small percentage of the population work in agriculture in western economies (1.5% in the US), precisely because of the efficiencies of the agricultural process made possible by mechanized farming. Perhaps one must experience the drudgery of hoeing rows from early morn till dark and experience the physical and psychological pains associated with this work to appreciate the advantage of tractors, combines and other modern machinery. Those who romanticize the spiritual value of working in the field are likely to be proposing this work for others, not themselves. Perhaps this is why Bahá'u'lláh encouraged the Sháh of Persia to heed the lessons of agricultural efficiency in the West.

Human development was significantly altered by the advent of the mechanization of agriculture and mass production manufacturing. Mass production created efficiency of manufacturing, freeing labor from the manufacturing tasks, following the pattern of agricultural efficiency. No longer did everyone have to work on the production line or in the field. Mandatory education for children and the development of the public education system in the United States emerged only after the mechanization of agriculture when children were freed from the slavery of the field. Some could now pursue additional education, developing specialized technologies, and with these technologies further efficiencies were created, once more expanding leisure or discretionary time. Each of these developments led to greater wealth and increased time for education and leisure.

We are now entering the post-mass production economy in the West, the age of Lean Production[4] and the Intelligent Enterprise,[5] an age in which manufacturing has progressed to the point where there are no 'laborers', only associates and technicians working in teams, controlling large amounts of capital equipment, continuously improving their own work processes, connected to their customers and suppliers, and engaged in the analysis of their work as a business unit. And now the majority of workers are employed in the information economy, engaged in mental activity and working in groups.

Much of the world today is in a struggle to emerge from a subsistence level of economic activity. Many efforts at economic development fail because they attempt to raise economic activity without the necessary attention to human development in all of its aspects.

> It is in the context of raising the level of human capacity through the expansion of knowledge at all levels that the economic issues facing humankind need to be addressed . . . The most important role that economic efforts must play in development lies, therefore, in equipping people and institutions with the means through which they can achieve the real purpose of development: that is,

> laying foundations for a new social order that can cultivate the limitless potentialities latent in human consciousness.[6]

A major issue for those engaged in social and economic development is to determine whether emerging economies must go through the same stages of development as Europe and the United States or whether they can capture the lessons of this history and leapfrog a generation of work systems, thereby avoiding the psychological/social disaster of the mass production era. My view is that a failure to understand this historic process of evolution and to thereby fail to assist developing economies to make the leap from early agricultural production to information economies without the pitfalls experienced in the West would be a tragedy.

The purpose of social and economic development must be first to achieve spiritual human development and the challenge is to merge the benefits of material and spiritual progress, of science and religion. This can be done by designing work organizations that promote spiritual qualities while at the same time gaining efficiency of production and thereby increasing material wealth and freeing human resources for further education.

The Prosperity of Humankind defines an agenda for the development of human resources on a global scale.

> Since, then, the challenge is the empowerment of humankind through a vast increase in access to knowledge, the strategy that can make this possible must be constructed around an ongoing and intensifying dialogue between science and religion. It is – or by now should be – a truism that, in every sphere of human activity and at every level, the insights and skills that represent scientific accomplishment must look to the force of spiritual commitment and moral principle to ensure their appropriate application. People need, for example, to learn how to separate fact from conjecture – indeed to distinguish between subjective views and objective reality; the extent to which individuals and institutions so equipped can contribute to human progress, however, will be determined by their devotion to truth and their detachment from the promptings

> of their own interests and passions. Another capacity that science must cultivate in all people is that of thinking in terms of process, including historical process; however, if this intellectual advancement is to contribute ultimately to promoting development, its perspective must be unclouded by prejudices of race, culture, sex, or sectarian belief. Similarly, the training that can make it possible for the earth's inhabitants to participate in the production of wealth will advance the aims of development only to the extent that such an impulse is illumined by the spiritual insight that service to humankind is the purpose of both individual life and social organization.[7]

While the breadth of this agenda goes beyond the focus of any single enterprise, it nevertheless defines many of the capacities that must be developed by members of every successful enterprise as well. It clearly defines not only technical or functional competencies but general characteristics of intellect, thought and character.

One of the more popular business books of the past few years has been Peter Senge's *Fifth Discipline*[8] in which he articulates the idea of the *learning organization*. A learning organization is simply one in which ongoing human and technical development is an organic process of continual improvement, dialogue, teamwork, shared resources and innovation. In the learning organization there is no formal distinction between teacher and student; rather there is the assumption that a process of sharing knowledge, exploration and honest evaluation leads to the learning of all. This is an organic process. Others have promoted similar philosophies of organic organizational learning and they all agree that it is not only technical learning but development of the social and moral capacities that are essential for organizational success.

The design of the organization's systems contributes to either the advancement or retardation of learning among the organization's members. An organization that is designed on the assumption that team members will be empowered to analyze and improve their work process is more likely to enhance learning and development than one which assumes that managers will define fixed work processes. An organization that has open books, shared financial information with employees and mechanisms for employees to participate in the analysis and decision-making regarding those numbers is likely to lead to greater learning and development than one in which the numbers are hidden from the employees. And constant contact with the customer similarly enhances learning and motivation. The learning organization is not an accident but the result of deliberate architecture.

There are many aspects to human resource development and it is beyond our scope to attempt to explore all of them. However, a brief review may be helpful. Each of these components must incorporate many of the principles previously discussed, such as justice, consultation and honesty. The agreement on clear principles that will guide your relationship to employees in the organization may be the most essential foundation of successful human resource development.

- Defining required and desired skills, knowledge and social characteristics needed by the organization.

- Hiring those who match the desired skills, knowledge and culture.

- Assessing individual and group competencies.

- Training and development.

- Performance management that includes individual appraisal and feedback, reinforcement or recognition of improvement and creating personal development plans.

- Discipline and corrective action.

The planning of human development efforts within an organization, just as within a nation, must take into account issues of diversity of talents and learning styles. This is also an issue of justice. To provide opportunity for learning and development to some and to deny it to others is tantamount to denying those same people economic opportunity. Every organization has limited resources and therefore is in the position of having to allocate resources based on its judgments. It is here that that 'capacity of the soul' is essential.

Still, in most of the world we are far from achieving the equality of men and women. There is a direct link between the education and equality of women and economic development. It is profoundly obvious that if one half of any population is relegated to a status in which they are expected not to develop, not to be heard, not to contribute to productive work and decision-making, that society cannot possibly develop economically to its full capacity. Much of the world, while jealous of the material progress of the West, still seeks to maintain the very characteristics of its culture that have denied its own economic development.

> The effect of the persistent denial to women of full equality with men sharpens still further the challenge to science and religion in the economic life of humankind. To any objective observer the principle of the equality of the sexes is fundamental to all realistic thinking about the future well-being of the earth and its people. It represents a truth about human nature that has waited largely unrecognized throughout the long ages of the race's childhood and adolescence. 'Women and men', is Bahá'u'lláh's emphatic assertion, 'have been and will always be equal in the sight of God.' The rational soul has no sex, and whatever social inequities may have been dictated by the survival requirements of the past, they clearly cannot be justified at a time when humanity stands at the threshold of maturity. A commitment to the establishment of full equality between men and women, in all departments of life and at every level of society, will be central to the success of efforts to conceive and implement a strategy of global development.[9]

Questions for Discussion and Reflection

1) Thinking about your own career, when was the time that you felt that you were developing your own competence and qualities in the most profound way? What conditions led to that development? What are the lessons of that experience for the development of human potential at work, in general?

2) In your organization (or in some other organization) who are the different people responsible for the development of employees? Make a list of them and describe their different responsibilities.

3) How is the process of developing competence managed in your company? What is working well and what could be improved?

4) What are the lessons from human resource development in a company that might be applied to social and economic development on a larger scale?

Other Quotations and Views on Human Resource Development

The aim of life is self-development. To realize one's nature perfectly – that is what each of us is here for. *Oscar Wilde*

All that is valuable in human society depends upon the opportunity for development accorded the individual. *Albert Einstein*

The perfecting of one's self is the fundamental base of all progress and all moral development. *Confucius*

To be thrown upon one's own resources, is to be cast into the very lap of fortune; for our faculties then undergo a development and display an energy of which they were previously unsusceptible. *Benjamin Franklin*

The happiest people are those who think the most interesting thoughts. Those who decide to use leisure as a means of mental development, who love good music, good books, good pictures, good company, good conversation, are the happiest people in the world. And they are not only happy in themselves, they are the cause of happiness in others. *William Lyon Phelps*

I believe that the very purpose of life is to be happy. From the very core of our being, we desire contentment. In my own limited experience I have found that the more we care for the happiness of others, the greater is our own sense of well-being. Cultivating a close, warmhearted feeling for others automatically puts the mind at ease. It helps remove whatever fears or insecurities we may have and gives us the strength to cope with any obstacles we encounter. It is the principal source of success in life. Since we are not solely material creatures, it is a mistake to place all our hopes for happiness on external development alone. The key is to develop inner peace. *Dalai Lama*

The growth and development of people is the highest calling of leadership. *Harvey S. Firestone*

By virtue of being born to humanity, every human being has a right to the development and fulfillment of his potentialities as a human being. *Ashley Montague*

Education is a human right with immense power to transform. On its foundation rest the cornerstones of freedom, democracy and sustainable human development. *Kofi Annan*

Education is the great engine of personal development. It is through education that the daughter of a peasant can become a doctor, that a son of a mineworker can become the head of the mine, that a child of farm workers can become the president. *Nelson Mandela*

13

Information Systems

In the era that recently passed materials management – purchasing and the flow of materials through the organization – was a potential source of competitive advantage and a major issue of concern. To a lesser degree it still is. However, today, it is much more likely that the flow of information will be a source of advantage or disadvantage. The advantages of information flow and management are directly related to the development of the capacity of human resources. The Bahá'í International Community recognized this relationship in its statement that 'the accelerating revolution in communication technologies now brings information and training within reach of vast numbers of people around the globe, wherever they may be, whatever their cultural backgrounds'.[1]

The challenge of information management within the organization is much like that in the larger society: how to design information access to maximize individual performance, the development of human and organizational capacities, and the improvement of those processes that serve the needs of customers. The world is becoming 'webbed' together as groups with almost any common interest self-organize in cyberspace to share information, opinions and even gossip.

It is essential to understand the potential and challenge of the 'Age of Networked Intelligence', as Don Tapscott calls the new era.

> The Age of Networked Intelligence is an age of promise. It is not simply about the networking technology but about the networking

> of humans through technology. It is not an age of smart machines but of humans who through networks can combine their intelligence, knowledge, and creativity for breakthroughs in the creation of wealth and social development. It is not just an age of linking computers but of internet working human ingenuity. It is an age of vast new promise and unimaginable opportunity.[2]

This networking of human intelligence will, inevitably, have revolutionary implications for how people are deepened in the knowledge of God, how they consult and how the affairs of religion are administered.

A critical issue in human development is how to assist in making information access – clearly linked to both empowerment and development of capacity – available to the less fortunate. This task is made easier each day as the cost of information access and processing drops dramatically.

> The tasks entailed in the development of a global society call for levels of capacity far beyond anything the human race has so far been able to muster. Reaching these levels will require an enormous expansion in access to knowledge, on the part of individuals and social organizations alike.[3]

The Bahá'í Faith and its institutions, while strongly asserting that development is not primarily materialistic, in no way shuts itself off from the advantages of science and technology. Many religions have been associated with the rejection of science and the fruits of material and intellectual development. This disconnect between the pursuit of the spiritual and the fruits of reason and science are now ended forever. Rather than religion hovering over science and the technological fruits of science like some overbearing father, 'Abdu'l-Bahá has made it very clear that it is religion that must conform to science:

> Religion must conform to science and reason; otherwise, it is superstition. God has created man in order that he may perceive

the verity of existence and endowed him with mind or reason to discover truth. Therefore, scientific knowledge and religious belief must be conformable to the analysis of this divine faculty in man.[4]

'Abdu'l-Bahá must have been fond of the idea that religion must conform to reason and science because He repeated this principle about a dozen times in different talks given to different audiences. In every case the message is the same – religion that does not conform to science is mere superstition.

Religion must be the cause of affection. It must be a joy-bringer. If it become the cause of difference, it were better to banish it. Should it become the source of hatred, or warfare, it were better that it should not exist. If a remedy produce added illness, it were far better to discard the remedy. A religion which does not conform with the postulates of science is merely superstition.[5]

Third, religion must be conducive to love of all, the cause of fellowship, unity and light. If it be the cause of enmity, bloodshed and hatred, its nonbeing is better than its being, its nonexistence better than its existence. Religion and science conform and agree. If a question of religion violates reason and does not agree with science, it is imagination and not worthy of credence.[6]

And, again:

Furthermore, the teachings of Bahá'u'lláh announce that religion must be in conformity with science and reason; otherwise, it is superstition; for science and reason are realities, and religion itself is the Divine Reality unto which true science and reason must conform. God has bestowed the gift of mind upon man in order that he may weigh every fact or truth presented to him and adjudge whether it be reasonable. That which conforms to his reason he may accept as true, while that which reason and science cannot sanction may be discarded as imagination and superstition, as a phantom and not reality.[7]

You may ask why this relationship between reason and religion is significant to a discussion of information systems. The reason we collect and share information is precisely to enable individuals and institutions to make decisions, to gain understanding, in a manner consistent with reason or science. If decisions are to be made on the basis of dogma, information about current or recent conditions is not important. Dogma changes little over time. A football coach, for example, may go into a season or a game with a belief, a dogmatic assertion, that a certain type of formation is superior. Quickly the other teams will recognize the coach's adherence to this dogma and will, using information and reason, adjust their plays accordingly. If the first coach is unable to process the data, use the mental faculty of science, to adjust his formations and plays, he will quickly be defeated. Dogmatic adherence to a course of action almost inevitably results in defeat in both business and sports. The purpose of information systems in business is precisely as it is in sports: to enable quick, accurate and informed decisions.

It is not our purpose here to delve into any specifics about the technology or format of information systems. However, it is appropriate to identify some principles that may guide the deployment of information systems in a manner that will reinforce a culture of spiritual enterprise.

1) Transparency equals ownership

Twenty years ago it was the norm for managers to assume that employees were either not interested or not capable of understanding financial information or other information on business performance. Information systems were constructed so that the 'decision-makers', the managers, received information and the employees just 'did their own work'. The degree of intelligence and creativity exercised by employees will be directly proportional to the transparency of information provided to them. Almost every business succeeds today because of the motivation of creativity of these employees.

2) Frequency and immediacy equals performance

There are volumes of research documenting the relationship between the immediacy and frequency of feedback with human performance.[8] It is a law of human performance: the more immediate and frequent the feedback related to an individual's performance, the greater the response to that feedback and the greater the increase in performance. Information systems should be designed with the objective of not simply 'controlling' performance but of motivating performance through high rate feedback systems.

3) Information access equals self-respect and dignity

If your manager hides information from you, what is the assumption? Of course, he does not trust you with the information. He assumes that if you had that information you would do something immature, something harmful to the organization. This is a parent–child assumption and reinforces that relationship. We all know of the Pygmalion effect by which individuals adapt their behavior towards the assumptions that others make about them. It is our responsibility to increase human capacity and maturity and the sharing of information contributes to this aspect of human development.

4) Engage the data – engage the mind

If you download an Excel spreadsheet and you stare at the columns of numbers you may be said to have access to information. However, the degree of your knowledge or understanding is likely to be very limited. Now, enable and even encourage the recipient of that spreadsheet to sort the data by different column headings to see the order of entries by different criteria. This ability to be directly engaged, to manipulate the information to discover its meaning, greatly expands its usefulness, its ability to increase knowledge and understanding.

5) A picture is worth a thousand words

I have worked in textile mills where many of the employees cannot read or write. However, put up a graph and explain that the graph is filled out daily and represents that day's production or quality and every employee will be engaged in the 'game' of business. Graphically portrayed data, graphs, are much more easily understood by employees and have a far greater motivational effect than columns of numbers.

Information is a liberating force, whether through the education of women or empowering employees by sharing information on business performance. Information systems are the primary vehicle for this liberation.

> A central challenge, therefore – and an enormous one – is the expansion of scientific and technological activity. Instruments of social and economic change so powerful must cease to be the patrimony of advantaged segments of society, and must be so organized as to permit people everywhere to participate in such activity on the basis of capacity.[9]

Questions for Discussion and Reflection

1) In your own experience, how has the availability (or lack of availability) of information had an impact on your motivation or spirit at work? What lessons do you derive from that experience as you consider how to manage other people?

2) In your organization, have the information systems been designed with the intention of empowering those who do the work or empowering managers to control those who do the work? How would you change these systems?

3) Outside of the workplace, what are some examples of how information increases or decreases motivation? If you transpose those lessons onto the workplace, what changes would you make?

Other Quotations and Views on Information Systems

Know where to find the information and how to use it – That's the secret of success. *Albert Einstein*

We are drowning in information and starved for knowledge. *Anonymous*

One of the great joys of life is creativity. Information goes in, gets shuffled about, and comes out in new and interesting ways. *Peter McWilliams*

True genius resides in the capacity for evaluation of uncertain, hazardous, and conflicting information. *Winston Churchill*

As a general rule, the most successful man in life is the man who has the best information. *Benjamin Disraeli*

Information is the currency of democracy. *Thomas Jefferson*

Data is not information. Information is not knowledge. Knowledge is not understanding. Understanding is not wisdom. *Anonymous*

There is a principle which is a bar against all information, which is proof against all arguments and which cannot fail to keep a man in everlasting ignorance – that principle is contempt prior to investigation. *Herbert Spencer*

Knowing a great deal is not the same as being smart; intelligence is not information alone but also judgment, the manner in which information is collected and used. *Dr Carl Sagan*

14

Reward and Recognition

> In the conduct of life, man is actuated by two main motives: 'The Hope for Reward' and 'The Fear of Punishment'.
>
> This hope and this fear must consequently be greatly taken into account by those in authority who have important posts under Government. Their business in life is to consult together for the framing of laws, and to provide for their just administration.
>
> The tent of the order of the world is raised and established on the two pillars of 'Reward and Retribution'.[1]

The issue of rewards and recognition is one that immediately creates anxieties in western culture. It raises questions of manipulation and behavioral control, of freedom and dignity, of competition and collaboration. Yet every business must make decisions about how to compensate employees, reward innovations and loyalty, and attract the best and brightest employees. The theoretical issues of rewards and recognition may be debated in the university but the business manager has no choice but to get about the task of distributing rewards as best he or she can.

One can think of human performance in terms of strength and direction, the amount of energy and the purpose or activity to which that energy is expended. Decisions, planning, consultation all can provide direction to human performance. However, if there is no energy, no fuel in the tank, no fire, there will be little performance in any direction. It is the job of managers and leaders to both provide direction and to stimulate and reinforce human energy. Encouragement, recognition and reward accomplish both the generation of energy and directing that energy towards activities that are most useful to the organization.

Religion is concerned not only with this life but with the condition of the soul in the next life and many of the teachings of the Bahá'í Faith are about progress in both this world and the next. References to reward and punishment are most often framed in terms of the eternal rewards of the soul.

> Now punishments and rewards are said to be of two kinds. Firstly, the rewards and punishments of this life; secondly, those of the other world. But the paradise and hell of existence are found in all the worlds of God, whether in this world or in the spiritual heavenly worlds. Gaining these rewards is the gaining of eternal life. That is why Christ said, 'Act in such a way that you may find eternal life, and that you may be born of water and the spirit, so that you may enter into the Kingdom.'[2]

When considering the rewards of this life they can be divided into two kinds: those that are intrinsic and those extrinsic. Intrinsic rewards are the pleasures one derives oneself from engaging in an act or from the natural growth and development of newly acquired behavior or virtues. Extrinsic rewards are those we experience from the outer world, the smile of an approving parent, the applause of an audience or a well-earned promotion or increase in pay. Just as organizational psychologists have focused much of their attention on intrinsic rewards by studying how different work patterns and relationships increase or decrease satisfaction, the writings of the Bahá'í Faith also focus more on intrinsic, rather than extrinsic, rewards.

> The rewards of this life are the virtues and perfections which adorn the reality of man. For example, he was dark and becomes luminous, he was ignorant and becomes wise, he was neglectful and becomes vigilant, he was asleep and becomes awakened, he was dead and becomes living, he was blind and becomes a seer,

> he was deaf and becomes a hearer, he was earthly and becomes heavenly, he was material and becomes spiritual. Through these rewards he gains spiritual birth, and becomes a new creature.[3]

It would be a wonderful state of affairs if we could trust that every employee would be energized and motivated in the best direction merely for the sake of gaining spiritual rebirth and for the rewards of the afterlife. These are the motives for religious undertakings, not for writing better software or completing an engineering project. Unfortunately, we are stuck with the job of creating motivating factors for our employees whose work cannot necessarily be linked to the spiritual rewards of the next life or this.

'Abdu'l-Bahá so understood the power of rewards that He even explains that religion must present rewards that will compete with the material rewards of this world.

> Sincerity is the foundation-stone of faith. That is, a religious individual must disregard his personal desires and seek in whatever way he can wholeheartedly to serve the public interest; and it is impossible for a human being to turn aside from his own selfish advantages and sacrifice his own good for the good of the community except through true religious faith. For self-love is kneaded into the very clay of man, and it is not possible that, without any hope of a substantial reward, he should neglect his own present material good. That individual, however, who puts his faith in God and believes in the words of God – because he is promised and certain of a plentiful reward in the next life, and because worldly benefits as compared to the abiding joy and glory of future planes of existence are nothing to him – will for the sake of God abandon his own peace and profit and will freely consecrate his heart and soul to the common good.[4]

Those concerned about the potential for manipulation when discussing rewards need to consider the alternative. Without rewards for desired performance, behavior becomes increasingly random and the consequence is increasingly likely to be the use of punishment. The parents who do not reward the child for a pleasant smile, for sharing toys or for completing homework will increasingly find themselves punishing the opposite behavior. Expending one's energy on the negative forces of motivation, punishment, is far more costly and destructive of the human spirit than any possible concern with an excess of reward. 'Abdu'l-Bahá commented on this cost.

> As to the difference between that material civilization now prevailing, and the divine civilization which will be one of the benefits to derive from the House of Justice, it is this: material civilization, through the power of punitive and retaliatory laws, restraineth the people from criminal acts; and notwithstanding this, while laws to retaliate against and punish a man are continually proliferating, as ye can see, no laws exist to reward him. In all the cities of Europe and America, vast buildings have been erected to serve as jails for the criminals.[5]

The implication of the above passage is that the divine civilization will place more emphasis on the use of positive reinforcement and less on the costly and destructive use of punishment. I am sure that this is just as true in the home and the business as it is in society at large. It is the unfortunate and natural condition of humankind that we are in need of reward and punishment, rather than merely responding to logic and reason. 'The generality of mankind are unable to grasp a sequence of logical arguments. For this reason they stand in need of symbols and parables telling of rewards and punishments in the next world.'[6] And Bahá'u'lláh pointed to the very foundation of order and stability as being based on the awareness of the consequences of our behavior: 'The structure of world stability and order hath been reared upon, and will continue to be sustained by, the twin pillars of reward and punishment.'[7]

'Abdu'l-Bahá further points to the need for training and its outcomes:

> Divine civilization, however, so traineth every member of society that no one, with the exception of a negligible few, will undertake

> to commit a crime. There is thus a great difference between the prevention of crime through measures that are violent and retaliatory, and so training the people, and enlightening them, and spiritualizing them, that without any fear of punishment or vengeance to come, they will shun all criminal acts. They will, indeed, look upon the very commission of a crime as a great disgrace and in itself the harshest of punishments. They will become enamored of human perfections, and will consecrate their lives to whatever will bring light to the world and will further those qualities which are acceptable at the Holy Threshold of God.[8]

The Universal House of Justice recently pointed to the need for 'sustained encouragement'[9] and 'Abdu'l-Bahá constantly encouraged the Bahá'ís, no matter how humble their efforts, with praise and respect. Many of the talks given by the Master begin with praise of those to whom He speaks. The messages of Shoghi Effendi repeatedly point out the glorious nature of our destiny and he frequently expressed gratitude for our efforts when he certainly must have known of our faults and inadequacies. Why this apparently unbalanced emphasis on the good while ignoring the deficiencies?

There are certainly many answers to this. However, you know from your own experience the effect of encouragement and criticism. Try to remember a time when you expended great time and effort on a plan or project and received praise and gratitude. What was the effect on your level of energy and enthusiasm? Do you remember a time when you similarly expended great energies and your effort was followed by criticism? What then was the effect on your energy? Clearly, we are energized by praise and encouragement and our energies are brought down by criticism. Of course, there is a time when we all need criticism offered in a loving and constructive way. But if criticism is more frequent than encouragement it is destructive to performance.

Concerns about rewards in the workplace are often issues around justice. How much compensation is just reward for which job? This is no simple matter and the answer is highly conditioned by local and industry culture. From some cultural perspectives any salary of one hundred thousand dollars may be perceived as an 'extreme of wealth'. However, in many professions it will be impossible to hire a competent employee for under this figure and any such offer would be perceived as an 'injustice'. What then is just? While in the ideal world, and with a global view, a lesser figure may be arguably just, the argument quickly becomes irrelevant as you go out of business owing to the absence of competent employees to serve your clients. Similarly, there are cultures in which offering a person a ten thousand dollar a year salary would be so high relative to local conditions it would create an upsetting 'extreme of wealth'. Until the world is truly merged into a common culture the judgments about just compensation will be conditioned by the industry, location and culture.

The definition of justice, 'That which traineth the world is Justice, for it is upheld by two pillars, reward and punishment. These two pillars are the sources of life to the world'[10] is a significant statement in understanding the role of rewards. The decision regarding rewards is a decision regarding how you wish to train employees. Do you want to train them to focus their energies on serving customers or merely producing quantity of output? Do you want them to work in groups or individually? Do you want them to be concerned about the well-being of the company or only their local work group? Your system of rewards is daily training these responses.

A trend I view as consistent with Bahá'í principles is the movement towards team- or group-based performance rewards. Increasingly, successful performance is not the result of individual effort but of a team or group of teams. In the mass production era incentive systems were commonly individually based. This was consistent with the admonition to 'do your own work'. Now we want our associates to focus on the process, the interaction of activities across a number of individuals, that results in quality production or service. This requires group problem-solving, goal-setting and evaluation. Team-based bonuses or 'gain-sharing' rewards the group for the success of its efforts to enhance performance.

In the United States there is a major problem in the distribution of rewards between the top and bottom of the organization. In Japan the difference between the compensation of the most senior executive and the first level worker is between ten and twenty to one. In the United States there has been a clearly unjust and unnecessary escalation in executive compensation as each board of directors attempts to keep up with the competition in pay. A differential of one hundred to two hundred to one is not unusual in major corporations. Obvious rationalizing takes place around this issue but anyone with eyes to see and ears to hear can clearly perceive that this is a corruption in the system of corporate governance in which boards of directors owe their allegiance to the one whom they must judge. This is a formula for corruption in any system. The system of corporate governance needs to be redesigned. However, who is to provide the mandate for such a redesign?

> A financier with colossal wealth should not exist whilst near him is a poor man in dire necessity. When we see poverty allowed to reach a condition of starvation it is a sure sign that somewhere we shall find tyranny. Men must bestir themselves in this matter, and no longer delay in altering conditions which bring the misery of grinding poverty to a very large number of the people. The rich must give of their abundance, they must soften their hearts and cultivate a compassionate intelligence, taking thought for those sad ones who are suffering from lack of the very necessities of life.[11]

Making Reward and Recognition Effective

While it is not our mission here to focus too specifically on the development of ideal reward systems, a subject worthy of a book in itself, it may be helpful to simply list some of the key ingredients in an effective system of reward at work.

1) Rely on multiple schedules of reinforcement

If employers say that their monthly or weekly pay to their employees is a system of reinforcement, they are mistaken. That is one reward, not a system. One, fixed interval schedule (once a week, month or year) has little effect on performance. The most effective systems combine a fixed and reliable salary with variable compensation based on the amount of work performed. Such systems also do not rely on compensation alone. Rather they include social recognition for improvements, suggestions, outstanding performance for the month, etc., etc. It is the variety and different schedules that together comprise an effective system that actually has a reinforcing effect on performance.

2) Reinforce both individual and group performance

In most work settings the work done by groups is equally or more important than the work of individuals alone. Just as in sports, where there are both individual and team scores, awards and celebrations, the best systems at work celebrate both the achievements of individuals and teams. If there is an emphasis on group consultation, serving the interests of a group, it is particularly important that rewards support that culture.

3) Be both spontaneous and systematic

We often judge the sincerity of appreciation by its spontaneity. It is nice to receive a gift on a birthday or anniversary; it is predictable and systematic. But to receive a gift just because your spouse felt like doing something nice for you is far more appreciated. In the workplace it is important to have systematic forms of recognition but it is equally important that the manager take the time to just stop by an employee's office and say, 'Oh, I just wanted to tell you that the report you handed in last week was really excellent.' That kind of unexpected and spontaneous recognition is one of the most powerful motivators available to a manager . . . and, its free!

4) Reinforcement is contingent on performance

In the literature on behavioral psychology there is a clear distinction between reward and reinforcement. One is an intention; the other is defined by an empirical effect. You may provide an annual bonus to your employees and your intentions are to be encouraging, to reward them for a job well done. But does it actually have any effect on performance? Positive reinforcement is defined as a consequence that results in an increased rate of response of a behavior or performance upon which it was contingent. The contingency, the *if–then* relationship, is critical to effective systems. If you sell *x* number of widgets, you will receive *y* amount of commission or bonus. That is a clear contingency between performance and reward. Even spontaneous recognition should be contingent on specific performance so the individual will know what to do more of in the future. If one says 'You've been doing a great job lately, keep it up!' it is likely that the recipient's behavior will not change. There is no reinforcement because there is no contingency between any known behavior and the consequence. Make the contingency clear.

5) Make it transparent

Employees don't want to guess why some people are being rewarded and others are not. The reward delivered to one person can influence many if the many know why the reward was earned. Mysterious rewards will be the subject of gossip and suspicion. Many reward systems have been designed to be so complex that almost no one understands them. This is a terrible mistake. Make it simple, make it transparent.

6) Make it fun!

'Abdu'l-Bahá was constantly encouraging His followers to be happy. He would ask, 'Are you happy?' A spiritual workplace should be a fun workplace. If there is any time to have fun it is when celebrating victories, celebrating successful performance. When are sports fans and athletes most happy? Of course, after a great victory. And they celebrate. It is part of the normal human experience to work hard, experience anxiety around victory or defeat and then celebrate success. Have great celebrations!

7) Enable peer-to-peer recognition

It is often true that no one knows best who is performing well more than team members or peers. Many companies have encouraged and enabled direct peer-to-peer recognition. Here is a description of one by Steve Kerr at GE:

> At GE we invite employees to assess – and reward – their peers on the spot. A program called Quick Thanks!, used by GE Medical Systems, lets an employee nominate any colleague (even one in another department) to receive a $25 gift certificate from certain restaurants and stores in appreciation of an exemplary job done. (Over the last year GE has given out 10,000 such awards.) The employee himself often hands out the award to his deserving co-worker. And guess what? Peers are often a whole lot tougher than bosses in dishing out praise. For the recipient, it's the approbation of a colleague, not the $25, that matters most.

Questions for Discussion and Reflection

1) Examining the reward systems in your own company and looking at the seven guidelines above – to which of them do they conform? How would you modify them to conform to each of these guidelines?

2) What is the relationship between a 'spiritual' environment at work and the processes of reward and recognition?

3) When did you feel most appreciated at work? What happened to cause you to feel this way and what was the effect on future performance?

4) If you could design the ideal reward system to support the

values discussed in the first section of this book, what would that system include?

Other Quotations and Views on Reward and Recognition

Work is about daily meaning as well as daily bread. For recognition as well as cash; for astonishment rather than torpor; in short, for a sort of life rather than a Monday through Friday sort of dying . . . We have a right to ask of work that it include meaning, recognition, astonishment, and life. *Studs Turkel*

The point is to develop the childlike inclination for play and the childlike desire for recognition and to guide the child over to important fields for society. Such a school demands from the teacher that he be a kind of artist in his province. *Albert Einstein*

People with a scarcity mentality tend to see everything in terms of win–lose. There is only so much; and if someone else has it, that means there will be less for me. The more principle-centered we become, the more we develop an abundance mentality, the more we are genuinely happy for the successes, well-being, achievements, recognition, and good fortune of other people. We believe their success adds to . . . rather than detracts from . . . our lives. *Stephen R. Covey*

Men want recognition of their work, to help them to believe in themselves. *Dorothy Miller Richardson*

When you have success, there is glory for all. With success and glory come great feelings for one another and recognition of one another's contributions. *Jimmy Johnson*

Intellectual 'work' is misnamed; it is a pleasure, a dissipation, and is its own highest reward. *Mark Twain*

The only reward of virtue is virtue; the only way to have a friend is to be one. *Ralph Waldo Emerson*

I believe life is constantly testing us for our level of commitment, and life's greatest rewards are reserved for those who demonstrate a never-ending commitment to act until they achieve. This level of resolve can move mountains, but it must be constant and consistent. As simplistic as this may sound, it is still the common denominator separating those who live their dreams from those who live in regret. *Anthony Robbins*

The journey is the reward. *Chinese proverb*

15

Customers, Suppliers and Community

The corporation is a community member. It benefits from the assets of the community, and contributes to its well-being. Many managers would prefer to ignore this relationship and focus on serving their customers and stockholders and dealing with their internal relationships. The ideology of free enterprise (rather than the facts of an economy based on private ownership) encourages a macho Darwinian view of the corporate role, that of only serving its customers and shareholders and any higher good will derive from doing its job of making money. This is a convenient veil to hide behind while ignoring the generous protections and subsidies provided to numerous industries by even the most conservative governments and ignoring the public funding of roads and ports, universities, healthcare, basic research and the protection provided to patents and other property. No company, in no country, operates in a true free economy. Rather, all business operates in an environment of shared private and public responsibility and cooperation. A healthy attitude is to acknowledge this shared responsibility and cooperation.

Once one acknowledges that one is a member of a community, of a civil society, then one has responsibilities that accompany the benefits provided. This is equally true for a corporation as it is for an individual.

The desire to isolate oneself behind the veil of private enterprise is understandable. Direct business relationships are generally more clear and community interests are often complex, competing and requiring political judgments. These judgments may involve the interests of an environmental group versus a group that wishes to develop property, a group that argues for the quick release of a new drug to save lives versus another that argues for the most thorough testing or a group that wants electric cars for environmental reasons versus another that argues this will require the building of nuclear power plants to generate sufficient electricity. These judgments are often difficult for the most sincere and disinterested party and are very difficult when made within the executive suite. However, most corporations realize that they have little choice but to participate in the complexities of community relations.

Most corporations do the easy things. They give to United Way, support Red Cross campaigns, provide scholarships and internships to youth and give to the arts. Whether these efforts are sincere or merely a public relations campaign depends entirely on the individual company and executive. These are easy, not because of the amount of money involved, but rather because they lack controversy. What bothers executives is becoming embroiled in complexity and controversy that consumes their time and energy away from their primary task.

In recent years there has been a great deal of discussion within corporations regarding the best way to handle relationships with the community, particularly in the case of dangerous or damaging events. Exxon Valdez and the Tylenol incident of Johnson & Johnson present two contrasting cases that have been carefully studied. There is a consensus in the corporate world that the Valdez incident was handled poorly and the Tylenol incident was handled well.

When the Valdez oil spill occurred, Lawrence Rawls, the CEO of Exxon was defensive, denied responsibility and relied on legalistic statements prepared by his legal team. Regardless of actual culpability, the nature of these responses was angering to both public and private individuals and conveyed a sense that Exxon would do the minimum it was required to do to repair the damage. This was a public relations disaster, resulting in picket signs at Exxon gas stations, buttons proclaiming a boycott of Exxon products and a decline in Exxon's stock price. Exxon's intransigence continued, as ten years later they still had not settled the lawsuits filed to recoup damages.

The Tylenol incident was a direct contrast. Someone was inserting poison into containers of Tylenol in drugstores. This could have happened to virtually any consumable product on any store shelf. The problem was never associated with any direct action or failure of the company. Although neither the company nor its employees had anything to do with the actual problem, Johnson & Johnson immediately accepted full public responsibility, acted quickly to remove the product from store shelves, was totally candid and immediately changed its packaging in response to the incident. The appearance of their executives was helpful, sympathetic, open and created trust. The sales of Tylenol were hurt only momentarily and the reputation of the product and the company gained in stature.

The reason these two incidents are important is because they clearly illustrate the business interest in principled behavior. The well-being of the company cannot be separated from its relationship to the larger community. The relationship to the community is much like relationships with individuals. Honesty, helpfulness, empathy and other moral or spiritual qualities are the essence of the relationship.

For a number of years the Chick-fil-A company, a chicken fast food chain headquartered in Atlanta, had been a client of my firm. They are one of the fastest growing food chains and the quality of their product and people are tops. Their unusual character begins with their mission statement, which is carved in the cornerstone of their headquarters building and appears on the first page of their annual report: 'To glorify God by being a faithful steward of all that is entrusted to us, and to have a positive influence on all who come in contact with Chick-fil-A.'

The cynic might suspect that this is merely a good public relations statement designed to appeal to Bible-belt customers. The facts say something else.

Of Chick-fil-A's approximately 600 stores, more than 400 of them are in the food courts of shopping malls. The busiest hours in shopping malls are on Saturday. The second busiest time is Sunday afternoon. The customers are walking by the store and every one of the Chick-fil-A stores is closed! Every other eatery in the mall is open. This makes no business sense. The capital is invested, the marketing is done, the people are trained and the customers are walking by the cash register! Any consultant with an inkling of financial sense would immediately recommend capitalizing on the assets and capture the revenue! It won't be done.

The executives of Chick-fil-A, a family-run company, believe that Sunday is the day of rest and their associates should be home with their families. They will not ask their associates to violate this principle which they believe comes from God. You are certainly welcome to argue with their judgment but they are due respect for placing their faith above their pocketbook.

Chick-fil-A also has one of the most generous scholarship programs for youth who work in their stores, conducts a summer camp through its WinShape Foundation and sponsors foster care programs. They work hard at being good citizens of the community. Does this harm or help their business? They have the highest customer satisfaction of any fast food chain and are one of the fastest growing. Their employees have pride in their company, knowing that they are serving the community's spiritual needs as well as its stomach.

Of course, every company cannot afford to be as generous as Chick-fil-A. However, many corporations and entrepreneurs try in similar ways and many more need to follow this example. Some entrepreneurs have written books about their desire to be of service through their business.[1] Another good source of examples of business efforts to apply moral principles to their organization is the work of the Social Venture Network portrayed in the book *75 Best Business Practices for Socially Responsible Companies.*[2]

Bahá'í principles do not specify the exact behavior of executives and corporations in relation to their communities. However, the examples of Johnson & Johnson, Chick-fil-A, Ben and Jerry's

Ice Cream and others are worth studying in our effort to resolve the struggle to manage both our business and our spiritual life. There is no one right answer as to business practices, just as there is no one right prescription for how individuals should live their lives. There is good judgment, judgment developed through meditation, study of examples and experience.

Customer and Supplier Relations

We are called upon to perform work in the spirit of service to humanity. However, when one is growing food, making furniture or providing a service – the work of the ordinary enterprise – serving humanity may seem rather distant. One serves the cell of the organism called humanity, a single human being, or a particular set of human beings. The focus of service at the enterprise level is the customer, the particular segment of humanity that will receive the output of your work. This principle must be designed into the intrinsic functioning of the systems of the organization so that it becomes an essential component of the fabric of daily life.

American and European understandings of customer relationships have been hindered by an understanding of property ownership and legal relationships that define walls between one company and another. The Japanese and other cultures have entirely different understandings. In the US customers have judged suppliers largely on lowest price with little consideration as to how the low price was achieved. This is changing, largely as a result of the influence of Japanese manufacturers who insist on much different relationships and an emphasis on quality and just-in-time continuous flow through the supplier-to-customer chain.[3]

Inland Steel had for many years supplied Ford, General Motors and Chrysler with sheet metal for their cars. When Honda expanded its manufacturing in Ohio they invited Inland to consider a supplier relationship. However, the nature of the contract caused considerable consternation within the company. Traditionally, the salesmen were the only ones permitted to communicate with the customer, jealously guarding that crucial relationship. The Honda contract specified that Honda engineers would have free access, at any time of day or night, to the Inland plant and the right to speak to any employee. If Honda personnel actually did this, it would completely violate Inland's internal assumptions about communication and responsibility. Needing the business, they agreed.

Somewhat to the surprise of Inland Steel's managers, the Honda engineers did appear, including during night shifts, and did speak directly to front line workers, those who were truly expert in their work. Honda gained direct knowledge of how workers approached their work and the causes of quality problems and offered constructive advice. They were not appearing as detectives to catch problems but to offer counsel and be helpful in achieving both quality and the smooth, timely, flow of materials. Their interest was in the success of the entire process from the beginning of the steel making process to the delivery of the car to the customer. Rather than view the process as fragmented with different companies owning the process within their property lines, Honda views its responsibility as the success of the whole family of suppliers that ultimately produces the car for the final customer. Managing this chain, this family of customers and suppliers, is a critical skill in today's world of business and the principles of unity, honesty and consultation are essential to its success.

Numerous names have been given to the changing relationships between customers and suppliers: the 'Extended Corporation',[4] the 'Boundaryless Organization',[5] or the 'Virtual Organization',[6] all describing the healthy trend towards reducing barriers between organizations and within organizations, uniting interests and efforts for the common benefit of the customer. These relationships, however, require new skills. The skill of consultation, shared decision-making across borders, is essential. I have worked with design teams, designing their future organizations, that included, as full-time members of the team, employees of their customers. We conduct search conferences in which large numbers, one to two hundred employees, gather in a meeting room, first to listen directly to customers explain their requirements and the cause of their satisfaction or dissatisfaction, and then to brainstorm ways to improve the process within the organization. This participation assumes total trust and long-term relationships, rather than short-term self-interest. It assumes that the customer wants the supplier to be profitable, but within a reasoned amount, and it assumes both parties working together to reduce costs with full knowledge of those costs. This requires a maturity that may be absent in many companies. But for those capable of this level of trust and cooperation, it represents a decided competitive advantage.

> To the extent that work is consciously undertaken in a spirit of service to humanity, Bahá'u'lláh says, it is a form of prayer, a means of worshiping God. Every individual has the capacity to see himself or herself in this light, and it is to this inalienable capacity of the self that development strategy must appeal, whatever the nature of the plans being pursued, whatever the rewards they promise. No narrower a perspective will ever call up from the people of the world the magnitude of effort and commitment that the economic tasks ahead will require.[7]

Questions for Discussion and Reflection

1) When considering the customers of your organization, what are the different types of either existing or potential 'walls' that may separate the interest and motivation of the two? For each of these 'walls' what may be done to diminish or eliminate them?

2) Think of one company that you buy from to which you are most loyal and most likely to buy from repeatedly. It may be a store, a car manufacturer or any other company that provides goods or services. Now make a list of all the different experiences, qualities, behaviors or other factors that generate this loyalty within you. Now ask yourself, how does my organization compare or employ those same factors?

3) How is your organization viewed by the community? What do

you do to manage these perceptions? How does this market capital impact the success of your organization?

Other Quotations and Views on Customers, Suppliers and Community

If you work just for money, you'll never make it, but if you love what you're doing and you always put the customer first, success will be yours. *Ray Kroc*

The aim of marketing is to know and understand the customer so well the product or service fits him and sells itself. *Peter F. Drucker*

The purpose of business is to create and keep a customer. *Peter F. Drucker*

I design for real people. I think of our customers all the time. There is no virtue whatsoever in creating clothing or accessories that are not practical. *Giorgio Armani*

Did you ever see the customers in health-food stores? They are pale, skinny people who look half dead. In a steak house, you see robust, ruddy people. They're dying, of course, but they look terrific. *Bill Cosby*

It is not the employer who pays the wages. Employers only handle the money. It is the customer who pays the wages. *Henry Ford*

Profit in business comes from repeat customers, customers that boast about your project or service, and that bring friends with them. *W. Edwards Deming*

The question is, then, do we try to make things easy on ourselves or do we try to make things easy on our customers, whoever they may be? *Niccolo Machiavelli*

Innovation comes from the producer – not from the customer. *W. Edwards Deming*

There is only one boss. The customer. And he can fire everybody in the company from the chairman on down, simply by spending his money somewhere else. *Sam Walton*

Business is not just doing deals; business is having great products, doing great engineering, and providing tremendous service to customers. Finally, business is a cobweb of human relationships. *H. Ross Perot*

In Lowell, Indiana, there was a four-hour hostage standoff in a bank. The bank customers were made to line up and stand still for hours . . . just like in a regular visit. *Bill Maher*

16

On Leadership

A few years back I was conducting a workshop at the annual conference of the European Bahá'í Business Forum (EBBF). While discussing the nature of leadership an older Bahá'í gentleman from Slovakia said with an air of absolute certainty 'Leadership is bad!'

Certain that there must be a translation problem, I attempted to clarify, 'Do you mean that authoritarian leadership is bad?'

Immediately, and with a determined sweep of his hand, he replied, 'No, all leadership is bad. It causes nothing but problems. Look at the world.'

I have no doubt that this gentlemen's experience with leadership supported his statements. He may also have read some of the Bahá'í writings referring to leadership. For example, he may have read one of the following:

> Beware lest Thou become occupied with the mention of those from whom naught save the noisome savors of enmity can be perceived, those who are so enslaved by their lust for leadership that they would not hesitate to destroy themselves in their desire to emblazon their fame and perpetuate their names.[1]

> Leaders of religion, in every age, have hindered their people from attaining the shores of eternal salvation, inasmuch as they held the reins of authority in their mighty grasp. Some for the lust of leadership, others through want of knowledge and understanding, have been the cause of the deprivation of the people.[2]

Or,

> The religious doctors of every age have been the cause of preventing the people from the shore of the Sea of Oneness, for the reins of the people were in their control. Some among them have hindered the people by love of leadership and some by lack of wisdom and knowledge.[3]

Each of these references, and a number of others, refer to the ills of personal leadership, the corruption of power, the self-serving personal ambition that seeks the pride of power and privilege. The above references are all from the pen of Bahá'u'lláh who was exiled, imprisoned, poisoned and conspired against by a long list of individual leaders, religious and secular, who conformed to these descriptions. One may be tempted to assign this illness to the corruption of Middle Eastern cultures of one hundred years ago when there was no other model of leadership than that of authoritarian dictatorships. But as I write, Dennis Koslowski (Tyco) is sentenced to prison to join Bernie Ebbers (WorldCom), who will no doubt be followed by the former executives of Enron. Human nature has not changed. The lust for power and material excess, unchecked by humility and spiritual values, and unchecked by institutional controls, inevitably leads to corruption and tyranny.

From this one might conclude that leadership, *per se*, is an evil. However, for every example of corrupt leadership there is also the leadership of those who have built great companies that have contributed to the well-being of humankind; the leadership of scientists and other leaders of thought who have created new technologies, medicines and knowledge that have saved millions of lives and relieved human suffering; and the leadership of those who have fought for human rights, equality of the races and gender. Without the leadership of high-minded individuals, individuals seeking to better the human condition, we would be without the thousands of advances that have relieved suffering and contributed to the advance of civilization.

Also in the Bahá'í writings, and particularly in those of the

Guardian and the Universal House of Justice, is the recognition of the need for a new type of leadership and for people of capacity who can energize the work of both the Bahá'í Faith itself and other institutions in society.

> Those who wield authority bear a great responsibility to be worthy of public trust. Leaders – including those in government, politics, business, religion, education, the media, the arts and community organizations – must be willing to be held accountable for the manner in which they exercise their authority. Trustworthiness and an active morality must become the foundation for all leadership if true progress is to be achieved. *Moral leadership*, the leadership of the future, will find its highest expression in service to others and to the community as a whole. It will foster collective decision-making and collective action and will be motivated by a commitment to justice, including the equality of women and men, and to the well-being of all humanity. Moral leadership will manifest itself in adherence to a single standard of conduct in both public and private life, for leaders and for citizens alike . . . Three factors that largely determine the state of governance are the quality of leadership, the quality of the governed and the quality of the structures and processes in place.[4]

And, in a statement that may stand as one of the most important and practical for leaders in every form of enterprise, the Guardian of the Bahá'í Faith said,

> The first quality for leadership, both among individuals and Assemblies, is the capacity to use the energy and competence that exists in the rank and file of its followers. Otherwise the more competent members of the group will go at a tangent and try to find elsewhere a field of work and where they could use their energy.
>
> Shoghi Effendi hopes that the Assemblies will do their utmost in planning such teaching activities that every single soul will be kept busy.[5]

Moreover, Bahá'ís are provided with a textbook, a living example, of exactly the type of leadership that is most needed in this age. That leadership is to be found in the example of 'Abdu'l-Bahá:

> The attitude of the individual as a servant, an attitude pre-eminently exemplified in the life and person of 'Abdu'l-Bahá, is a dynamic that permeates the activities of the Faith; it acquires collective, transformative force in the normal functioning of a community. In this regard, the institutions of the Faith stand as channels for the promotion of this salient characteristic. It is in this framework that the concepts of rulership and leadership, authority and power are properly understood and actualized.[6]

What, then, is 'moral leadership'? One could argue that the eight principles described in the first part of this book – honesty, justice, unity, etc. – are as good a definition of moral leadership as any. But what is different in the terms 'leadership' and 'management'? It is the example of personality, the example of another human being doing things, behaving in ways that are admirable and that inspire action in others. Mother Teresa or Nelson Mandela were inspiring examples, provided leadership, precisely because of their selflessness, the long struggle for justice and their dedication to the good of others. It is not just in the systems and structure of the organization, it is in the example of another human being from which we learn and are inspired.

The new world order prescribed by the central figures of the Bahá'í Faith is built on the strength of groups, on the process of creating collective wisdom through consultation. In essence, it acknowledges the limits of individual human virtue by assigning power and authority to groups.

> Naturally, old ways of exercising power and authority must give way to new forms of leadership. Our concept of leadership will need to be recast to include the ability to foster collective decision-making and collective action. It will find its highest expression in service to the community as a whole.[7]

And if our businesses and other organizations are to make the transition from those dominated by a lust for personal power to those that foster collective decision-making and collective action, it will require remaking the mold of leaders, remaking them in a form that is consistent with the principles described in the first part of this book.

It is not unreasonable to ask, 'Why do we need the leadership of individuals at all, now that we have been given a new order in which decisions will be made in consultation by Assemblies and other groups?' It is an important question. Is it not sufficient for an Assembly to meet and consult and then inform the community of plans and encourage them to show up and exert their energies? It is not sufficient.

We need individual leaders because we are human beings! If we were machines, without emotions and only responding to the rationality of a well-designed plan formed by an Assembly in consultation, the power of individual leadership would be unnecessary. Perhaps unfortunately, human beings run on emotion, they are energized by the energy and example of others. An individual speaking with enthusiasm and passion may arouse enthusiasm and passion in others. This is the fuel, this is the energy upon which plans are achieved. Plans are nothing but good intentions. They only become alive when they are combined with the force of human energy and enthusiasm, and generating that energy and enthusiasm is the task of leaders, whether appointed to some official position or individuals acting purely on their own initiative.

A great test for Bahá'ís is to recognize the value of individual initiative and leadership while relying for guidance and decisions, the force of authority, on the consultative institutions. This is a balance that we have just begun to master. The Guardian spoke of this balance when he said,

> The unfettered freedom of the individual should be tempered with mutual consultation and sacrifice, and the spirit of initiative and enterprise should be reinforced by a deeper realization of the

> supreme necessity for concerted action and a fuller devotion to the common weal.[8]

The Universal House of Justice also spoke to this necessary balance between individual initiative and the work of the consultative institutions:

> Within this framework of freedom a pattern is set for institutional and individual behavior which depends for its efficacy not so much on the force of law, which admittedly must be respected, as on the recognition of a mutuality of benefits, and on the spirit of cooperation maintained by the willingness, the courage, the sense of responsibility, and the initiative of individuals – these being expressions of their devotion and submission to the will of God. Thus there is a balance of freedom between the institution, whether national or local, and the individuals who sustain its existence.[9]

In my own experience, looking back on the most exciting accomplishments, whether in business, in the field of social and economic development, or in the building of Bahá'í communities, in every case of significant progress or accomplishment, the initiative and energy was that of individuals who arose and with creativity and dedication determined to make something worthy happen. These initiatives were then sustained and guided by the loving and supportive hand of the institutions.

It is important to recognize that many people, from many different faiths and perspectives, are recognizing the need to remake the concept and quality of leadership. Perhaps foremost among these is the 'Servant Leadership' movement. Robert Greenleaf coined the phrase 'servant-leadership' and described it this way:

> The servant-leader is servant first . . . It begins with the natural feeling that one wants to serve, to serve first. Then conscious choice brings one to aspire to lead. He or she is sharply different from the person who is leader first, perhaps because of the need

> to assuage an unusual power drive or to acquire material possessions. For such it will be a later choice to serve – after leadership is established. The leader-first and the servant-first are two extreme types. Between them there are shadings and blends that are part of the infinite variety of human nature.
>
> The difference manifests itself in the care taken by the servant-first to make sure that other people's highest priority needs are being served. The best test, and difficult to administer, is: do those served grow as persons; do they, while being served, become healthier, wiser, freer, more autonomous, more likely themselves to become servants? And, what is the effect on the least privileged in society; will they benefit, or, at least, will they not be further deprived?[10]

This description of the servant-leader is entirely consistent with the view of Bahá'ís, their priorities and model of behavior.

Accepting Leaders as Mortal Men and Women

Intelligence is the ability to make distinctions, to understand the difference between things that are round and things that are square, between things alive and things dead, and between conduct that is virtuous and conduct that is evil. There can be no understanding or progress without discerning differences. To assign all leaders to one judgment is to engage in a complete failure of intelligence. Leadership is an instrument that may be used for good or evil, that may be asserted with humility and a loving spirit or with a dictatorial and arrogant air. We must learn the difference.

Leaders are not prophets. While we long for moral leaders and are attracted to those who appear to display the qualities that we value, we cannot hold them to standards of perfection. They are mere mortals and we should appreciate them for the contributions they do make, rather than dismiss them for some personal flaw. Leaders are not divine or infallible and should in no wise be confused with the qualities of the divine. Bahá'u'lláh in His own character and life exemplified the qualities of God and His own life was proof of his divine personage.[11] Recognizing our need to witness the example of His teachings in a mortal life Bahá'u'lláh gave us 'Abdu'l-Bahá to serve as the perfect example. Here we must learn to make a distinction if we are to begin to understand leadership and benefit from the energy of those mortal individuals of capacity. From our divine personalities we expect a perfect, God-like, example. We expect them to manifest in their character and behavior the reality of their teachings. Their proof is in the character of their lives, in the consistency of their behavior with the teachings they profess. This is the ultimate standard and one that can be maintained only by those who are given to us by God.

The media casts a spotlight on the sinners but rarely highlights those who are striving to be moral leaders. This creates the perceptual bias that all or most leaders are immoral. It is not true. Those who have not worked in the business world often carry prejudices perpetuated by the media focus and the dramatization of the fat, cigar-smoking, evil tycoon out to conquer and control the world, so powerful and evil that only Spider-Man or Batman are up to the task of combating his evil schemes. This prejudice is no more valid than those held against Jews or those of different races or nationalities. The morality and personality traits of corporate executives are pretty equivalent to the norms in any population. And, there is no doubt that that is not good enough!

Unlike the well-publicized excesses and crimes by the likes of Dennis Koslowski, there are many executives who genuinely pursue the good of the company and group with a sense of humility and even a spirit of service. While you are likely to have seen the former Tyco CEO on television and read repeated articles about his six thousand dollar shower curtains, do you know the name of the current CEO of Tyco who has done much to restore its integrity? This CEO closed down the New York offices, sold the corporate airplanes, entirely replaced the board of directors, lives in the same small house he has for many years, drives an old car, is soft-spoken and prides himself on his humility. On the Tyco website is a letter from this new CEO, Ed Breen, which says in the first paragraph: 'Nothing is more important to a company than its credibility – credibility with investors, customers, government leaders and employees. Since my arrival in July 2002, my biggest challenge has been to begin the process of restoring genuine trust in the leadership of this company.' And the last paragraph ends with 'Tyco's corporate culture today is built on the premise that every employee, without exception, is responsible for the conduct and success of the firm. We are working hard to make ethical business practice and personal integrity an inextricable part of this enterprise and strive to continue to identify, develop and adhere to the highest standards of corporate governance.'[12] Only one out of a million who knows of Koslowski's crimes knows of Ed Breen's integrity. It is therefore no wonder that the public has a skewed view of corporate and other leaders.

Jim Collins, in *Good to Great*, documents leaders who established and led great companies. He describes what he calls Level 5 Leadership:

> We were surprised, shocked really, to discover the type of leadership required for turning a good company into a great one. Compared to high-profile leaders with big personalities who make head-lines and become celebrities, the good-to-great leaders seem to have come from Mars. Self-effacing, quiet, reserved, even shy – these leaders are a paradoxical blend of personal humility and professional will. They are more like Lincoln and Socrates than Patton or Caesar.[13]

I have known many such executives who often consider themselves to be good Christians or Jews and sincerely believe that they have a personal responsibility to live by and instill in their companies the highest values of their faith. Of course, this type of dedication and sincerity never garners the headlines on the nightly news.

The Perversion to Destroy Personalities

While the excessive reliance or worship of personalities is destructive, so too is the reverse: the tendency to tear down anyone who may be held up as a leader.

The perversion of our popular culture is to seek out and magnify any real or imagined blemish, like vultures circling to feed on a corpse. This strikes me as a far greater sin than the failings of men (or women) who were only just that, mortal, fallible, human beings. It is a popular trend in our culture to expose the powerful, to bring down to size anyone, current or historical, who may pose as or be presented as a leader. News has become a primary form of entertainment and the difference between so-called 'reality shows' (which, of course, do not represent reality) and news as education is entirely confused. Like the crowds who gathered in the coliseums to watch their favorite heroic gladiator do battle and kill wild beasts and their fellow men, we cheer at the sight of leaders who have their flaws exposed. Every blemish, every clumsy mistake, is reason enough to dismiss their contribution to the progress of society.

There is no better example than the now assumed-to-be-true pseudo-fact that Thomas Jefferson fathered the children of his young slave Sally Hemings. This pseudo-fact has been used to dismiss Jefferson and all of his writings and contributions to the establishment of democracy. The true facts are that Thomas Jefferson's DNA markers are present in some heirs of Sally Hemings. What is not usually told is that those same DNA markers could have been passed on by any one of two dozen other men related to Jefferson and living at that time, two of whom, his nephews Samuel and Peter Carr, admitted paternity of at least some of Sally Hemings' children.[14] But, of course, it is much more interesting to assume that this 65-year-old statesman who had been so admired did the evil deed. You can almost hear the crowd roar with glee at the sight of the great falling.

Martin Luther King, Jr., along with Mahatma Gandhi and Nelson Mandela all played a historic leadership role in advancing the cause of civil rights, freeing both the white and black races from the degrading conditions of a post-slavery society, and pursuing justice. They were all superlative examples of leadership, not based on position or power, but based on the pursuit of a moral cause. Their words and deeds have inspired thousands of other individuals to pursue their own moral cause. Yet, each was only mortal and surely imperfect. Some have focused on their flaws to dismiss their contributions.

Sometimes it is important to ask 'So what?' It is important to distinguish the trivial from the important. Imagine that a great scientist leads a team of researchers and through his brilliance and dedication he discovers the cure for cancer. Assume also that this scientist abuses his children and is unkind to his wife. I am sorry for his children and wife and I wish he were better behaved, along with the majority of misbehaving mankind. But, so what? If he discovers the cure for cancer he will have made a great contribution to the relief of suffering. Should he not be appreciated for his contribution? Should other researchers not learn from and be inspired by his example. Or would you dismiss his contribution as insignificant because of his personal failures?

This scientist will have engaged in a genuine act of leadership, despite his imperfections. We can be inspired to acts of good ourselves. And this is the purpose of leaders, to inspire others, but we are robbed of this benefit if we only seek to tear them down.

I was at a Bahá'í gathering once and for some reason the subject of Abraham Lincoln came up. A young Bahá'í said 'Well, he didn't want to free the slaves anyway, he was a racist and that's not why he took us into war.' This was said in a dismissive manner as if to say 'So, he isn't worthy of our attention or admiration.' As a student of history I am disappointed at the failure to understand the conditions surrounding Lincoln's inauguration and the causes of the American Civil War. Between the time of Lincoln's election and his inauguration three months later, 13 of the states had already begun the process of separating themselves from the Union, precisely because of Lincoln's well-known opposition to slavery. It is true that his first motive for going to war was to preserve the Union. And of course Lincoln may have held prejudicial views, normal for men of his time and place, although Frederick Douglass said that when he was with Lincoln he felt that he was in the presence of the only man he had ever met who was free of prejudice. But the loss is in the complete failure to appreciate the struggle, the good in the man, and the historic role he played in advancing the cause of human dignity; the great loss of example and learning that comes from failing to understand the struggle and contribution of great men and women.

The Contribution of Leaders is Specific, Not General

The example and lessons from 'Abdu'l-Bahá are general, rather than specific. The example of His kindness to people of all races and economic backgrounds, the example of His concern for the poor and His devotion to God and His faith are all lessons that every one of us can apply throughout our lives.

The examples and lessons to be derived from worldly leaders are entirely different. Their lessons are specific to a time and place or to particular conditions. The examples of both Abraham Lincoln and his most able general, Ulysses S. Grant – two entirely different personalities with entirely different abilities, yet both of whom contributed to advancing the cause of unity and equality – illustrate the specific lessons to be drawn from mortal leaders.

Abraham Lincoln suffered severe and chronic depression, at the time called 'melancholy'. He repeatedly considered suicide, often cried in public and frequently questioned his own ability to continue living with his pain. A colleague at the time, Henry Whitney, said that 'No element of Mr Lincoln's character was so marked, obvious and ingrained as his mysterious and profound melancholy.'[15] Another friend of Lincoln reported that

> Although he appeared to enjoy life rapturously, still he was the victim of terrible melancholy. He sought company and indulged in fun and hilarity without restraint or stint as to time. Still when by himself he told me that he was so overcome with mental depression that he never dared carry a knife in his pocket.[16]

But it is not Lincoln's depression that is a model of leadership. It is his response to this personal plague of personality. Joshua Shenk writes,

> In his mid-forties the dark soil of Lincoln's melancholy began to yield fruit. When he threw himself into the fight against the extension of slavery, the same qualities that had long brought him so much trouble played a defining role. The suffering he had endured lent him clarity and conviction, creative skills in the face of adversity and a faithful humility that helped him guide the nation through its greatest peril.[17]

Many leaders have suffered hubris, the excess of pride, the excessive belief in the correctness of their own course. It is the common downfall of the once great. Lincoln suffered no such pride. His depression gave him a creative realism, an ability to suffer through the process of thinking deeply about the conditions he faced, of listening to others and even to seek God's assistance with humility. Rather than believing that God was on his side and that God was riding in his army and providing him with some supernatural might, a belief held by the Confederate generals Stonewall Jackson and Robert E. Lee, Lincoln said, 'I shall be most happy indeed if I shall be an humble instrument in the hands of the Almighty, and of this, his almost chosen people, for perpetuating the object of that great struggle.'[18] Lincoln prayed that he might be a humble instrument of God's will, rather than praying for God's help in doing his own will. This is not a small distinction and is part of his moral leadership.

After Lincoln's death his secretaries found a note he had written, entitled *Meditations on the Divine Will*:

> The will of God prevails – In great contests each party claims to act in accordance with the will of God. Both may be, and one must be wrong. God can not be for, and against the same thing at the same time. In the present civil war it is quite possible that God's purpose is something different from the purpose of either party – and yet the human instrumentalities, working just as they do, are of the best adaptation to effect this. His purpose. I am almost willing to say this is probably true – that God wills this contest, and wills that it shall not end yet – By his mere quiet

> power, on the minds of the now contestants, He could have either saved or destroyed the Union without a human contest – Yet the contest began – And having begun He could give the final victory to either side any day – Yet the contest proceeds.[19]

These are not the words of an arrogant man set on an egotistical course, rather this and many other evidences of Lincoln's personality are evidence of a man in a great personal struggle, seeking God's guidance, and seeking to do His will. Joshua Shenk's study of Lincoln concludes that 'Lincoln didn't do great work because he solved the problem of his melancholy; the problem of his melancholy was the more fuel for the fire of his great work.' Today Lincoln would be drugged and dismissed. Lincoln was an unlikely leader who would be quickly labeled as 'unmarketable' by today's packagers of political pabulum. He was physically unattractive, clumsy and odd looking. He had no formal schooling. His voice was shrill and high pitched, the opposite of the masculine voice of certainty we expect of our leaders. And unlike the professional smiley faces that make it to the top of today's political waste heap, he suffered the gloomiest of personalities and appearance. Yet the dismissal of such a person, certain today, would be a great loss to the collective progress of the human race.

There are great lessons for us mortals in the leadership of Lincoln. Study Lincoln and deduce your own. But among them I find that great deeds are often done by those who lack any appearance of greatness; personal pain and suffering may lead to the strength and the creative acts that distinguish great leaders from the rest; and, rather than the false confidence so often portrayed, greatness is often accompanied by fear and self doubt. From these lessons and examples we can gain strength and have the humility to recognize that despite our own weaknesses of personality, we too may be capable of arising to do God's will and accomplishing great things.

It may be that God chose Lincoln to be at that place, at that time, precisely because of his very qualities. For the task of leading a country at that most trying of times he was well suited. There are other tasks for which he was not well suited. Lincoln would have made a horrible general and one of his greatest failures was his inability to select the right man to lead his armies. It was only through trial and error, and much more of the latter, that he finally found Ulysses S. Grant and William Tecumseh Sherman. Both, like Lincoln, were extremely mortal in their imperfections of personality, yet perfectly suited to their great challenge.

General Ulysses S. Grant had all the makings of a complete failure. Grant graduated from West Point after being admitted only because of the accidental failure of a Congressman to find a better candidate and left his first tour in the military disappointed and seeing little prospect of success. He then tried his hand at both farming and running a small store, and despite significant assistance from his father-in-law, soon found himself failing at both. Grant's personality, like Lincoln's, can hardly be described as well-balanced and cheery. Throughout his life he also suffered from depression for which he found relief in the excess of alcohol. Sherman had the same problem and at one point a newspaper ran a headline story declaring him 'insane'; his wife frequently referred to the history of insanity in his family. He also struggled with alcohol. Grant was a small, stubby man with little of the physical presence associated with many great generals. He could easily be missed or ignored in a group of other men or on the battlefield. Grant never was successful with money. Even after his mediocre presidency he became involved with friends on Wall Street and, trusting in their judgment, lost everything and was driven near bankruptcy, only to be rescued by admiring friends.

Some men only make significant contributions when crisis demands their action. It is in some personalities that routine conditions drive them towards their worst weakness, while the crisis brings out the sleeping giant within. There was only one thing that Grant was good at and it would emerge from the crisis of war.

George B. McClellan graduated second in his class at West Point, was brilliant, well-loved and looked the part of the handsome general. At the start of the Civil War McClellan was Lincoln's choice to lead the Union Armies after Robert E. Lee turned him down and chose to defend his 'home country', Virginia. McClellan set about recruiting, building and training the army. By every account McClellan was brilliant at preparing for battle. He was a master at training large groups of men. He had deep affection for the army he was creating. However, this may have been his great weakness. During the first year of the war McClellan's army outnumbered the army of northern Virginia by three to one and it had General Lee pinned down in Richmond. Rather than launch an all-out attack, McClellan dithered. He imagined Lee to have twice the forces he had and continually called for additional reinforcements and supplies, although his army sat rotting in the fields around Richmond. McClellan was so proud of his army that he wanted to see no failure, no harm come to his creation. The war could have ended in its first year if McClellan had used his army. His caution and hesitancy, it is generally agreed, resulted in the death of hundreds of thousands unnecessarily.

Grant's personality was almost the opposite of McClellan's. Mark Perry wrote that

> He worked diligently, but without remarkable insight. That perhaps was Grant's most sterling quality. While not the tallest, or strongest, or brightest, or even the most insightful of men or generals, Grant brought a singular concentration to everything he did. When he failed, he would pick himself up and start again, as a child and later as a soldier, he was undeterred, unfazed, and unafraid.[20]

Grant always had the ability to bring order out of chaos, not by the brilliance of his plans but by the single-minded force of his personality. After one day of the bloodiest battles of the war, a day during which there were ten thousand casualties and many thousands fell wounded in woods that were then lit afire, burning the helpless wounded, Grant sat on a stump all day whittling away on a piece of wood while cannon shells burst near by and the screams of broken and dying men could be heard throughout the day and night. His officers around him feared for their own lives and were in a panic that their army was being destroyed. When confronted by his subordinates who demanded some action to extricate them from what appeared to be a calamity, Grant merely looked up and coldly responded that 'tomorrow we will hit them harder'. And, of course, the next day they did and threw the Confederate army into retreat. Repeatedly Grant displayed this quality of iron-willed determination. He appeared to be incapable of either distraction or fear. The sounds of thousands of dying men would have driven the sensitive Lincoln and perhaps McClellan mad with despair, compassion and guilt. And all those emotions would have led to their defeat. If Grant experienced any of these emotions he never gave any indication. He believed that the more ferocious and violent the fight, the sooner it would end and the fewer men would die. Had he been the commander of the forces that surrounded Lee at Richmond in the first year of the war, he surely would have been right.

In Grant, McClellan and Lincoln can be seen the same lesson through different personalities and experiences. All of these men had serious deficiencies in their personalities, yet all of them were perfectly suited to their specific task and were completely incapable of others; and today, in our confused expectations that leaders be exemplars of perfection and virtue, they would all be dismissed, drugged or demeaned. The imperfections of their personalities are the conditions of being human. In examining our own condition and the challenges we face, and as we assess the ability of others in our organizations to lead different functions and to respond to different challenges, it is important to recognize the diversity of human contributions. The ability to place one's own talents in perspective, to humbly recognize one's own strengths and limitations, and the ability to recognize the need for reliance on others who have complementary skills and experience are all hallmarks of personal leadership.

Leadership is the force of personal example. Grant's calm in the face of horror brought calm to his men. His determination and fearlessness emboldened those around him. Grant's single-minded focus and determination gave focus and determination to others. Lincoln's compassion and struggle inspired compassion and struggle in others. Martin Luther King, Jr's and Gandhi's passion for justice and disciplined adherence to the principles of non-violence inspired those same qualities in others. We learn these qualities and emotions only from other human beings whom we see as models. This is the purpose of leadership. It cannot be done by groups who in private consultation make decisions, no matter how perfect those decisions may be.

The Creative Response to Challenge

There are many lessons of history. Arnold Toynbee long ago recognized that 'We have ascertained that civilizations come to birth in environments that are unusually difficult and not unusually easy. The greater the challenge, the greater the stimulus to growth.'[21] He described the role of leaders in the emergence of civilization as those who recognize the challenges presented by their environment and then muster the creative response to that very challenge. This creative response to challenge is the mechanism of growth, both in civilization and corporations. It is not a 'condition of ease' that leads to growth but rather what leads to decline. Lacking the recognition of challenge, leaders lose their creativity and increasingly rely on yesterday's successful response but now in the presence of new challenges. It is this condition of ease and failure of creativity that is the cause of decline.

Toynbee, very much like Shoghi Effendi, described the twin-fold process of integration and disintegration. Civilizations (and companies) when growing, expanding their borders, are integrating different people, ideas and cultures. When they cease the process of integration they start defending their borders, building walls to keep out the energetic barbarians and begin the process of internal disintegration. Toynbee concluded that the decline of every civilization was not at the hands of an external enemy but rather an act of suicide, the loss of will within and the disintegration of the culture. Whether or not you accept Toynbee's analysis of the rise and fall of civilizations – and you should read his work yourself and decide (it is clearly one of the most brilliant works in the English language!) – it is easy to see the parallels to the rise and fall of corporations and organizations.

Some years ago I wrote a book in which I chronicled the rise and fall of companies and drew the parallel to the patterns described by Toynbee.[22] Without restating the premise in its entirety, it is worth a summation here. The key lesson is in the diversity of styles of leadership that are needed at different stages and the qualities that lead to decline.

Most companies appear to be formed by the impetus of a creative personality, the *prophet*, who issues forth the creative response to challenge. The creative personality is almost never a great manager or administrator. The founders of Apple Computer or General Electric were visionaries who were devoted to their technologies, to their research and to the creation of new products. In the latter days the prophets will be crucified or exiled by the bureaucrats and aristocrats who will seek to maintain order. The prophets are inherently disorderly. Disturbing the established order is the business of prophets.

The prophet founders of companies are soon followed, or become themselves, *barbarians*, the commanding generals whose strength of will focuses energy in crisis. The early time of a company's growth is inevitably a time of crisis and what is needed most are leaders capable of acting in crisis, more so than those able to gain broad consensus. While barbarians lead the conquering march, their talents will soon be out of date. They are good when their focus does not require the coordination of complexities or working through the subtleties of political decision-making or power. It is why General Patton was great in combat and a huge bother out of the field of combat. Ray Kroc, the founder of McDonald's, did not create the innovation upon which the company was built. But he did take that innovation and lead it on a conquering march. He was entirely focused on 'quick, clean and courteous', the three simple qualities on which the company was built. He would visit stores and immediately visit the bathroom. As chairman of a company with thousands of restaurants, he would immediately barge through the door to the cleaning supplies and would scrub down the toilets and mop the floor. Insane? Perhaps – but he did it. He built the company with this fierce focus that a General Grant would well understand. The barbarians are always very close to the real work of the organization and are able to understand in simple terms what matters most. This will later be lost.

As organizations grow they become complex. Suddenly there is the need for accounting, legal services, human resource management and development, specialized supply chain management, etc. Suddenly there is a division and the first division is between the *explorers* and *builders*, those who are focused on expanding the territory and those focused on building the factories. Different skills and personalities are required. And in the blink of a historic eye the builder does not just have a factory. He is not just building wheels or chairs or other things required, he has a leg department, a seat department and a back department and a final assembly department; and the process of differentiation organization, skills and focus has begun. Organizations differentiate with growth and each split develops its own priorities, language and culture. This is the building of cities, places of specialization. Increasingly those living in the cities are losing touch with those who are exploring new territory and now the ability of leaders to bring unity out of diverse interests becomes the challenge.

Increasingly the challenge is within, not from the external environment. Increasingly the leaders are seeking to bring order to their diverse groups. And increasingly the processes of administration becomes dominant in their minds and the leaders are drawn from the administrators. Soon, with administrators in charge, counting and recording have become more important than the substance and spirit of creativity, the response to the external challenge that was the source of initial growth. In 30 AD Crassus the moneylender became head of the legions of Rome and, as H. G. Wells, the historian, said,

> After the fall of Carthage the Roman imagination went wild with the hitherto unknown possibilities of finance. Money, like most

> other inventions, had 'happened' to mankind, and men had still to develop – today they have still to perfect – the science of morality and money. What happened to Rome? Various answers are made – a decline of religion, a decline from the virtues of the Roman forefathers, and the like. We, who can look at the problem with a larger perspective, can see that what had happened to Rome was 'money'. Money had floated the Romans off the firm ground.[23]

And 'money happens' to companies as the accountant becomes CEO and the focus and expertise at the top is on counting and recording and the maintenance of order and not on the engineering of the new car or the challenge of conquering a new market. This is the signal of decline in the company. This is the loss of creativity.

As soon as the leader imposes increasing levels of control in his love for order, he has become a *bureaucrat* and fails to understand the original organizing principle that was the energy created by the 'word', the creative act that was the reason to unite and sacrifice. Now the lack of creativity leads to impotence in the marketplace and survival is dependent on cost cutting and control and anyone with the creative spirit, potential prophets who possess the very cure that is so in need, are driven to exile or crucified for their violation of order. The decline will soon lead to death.

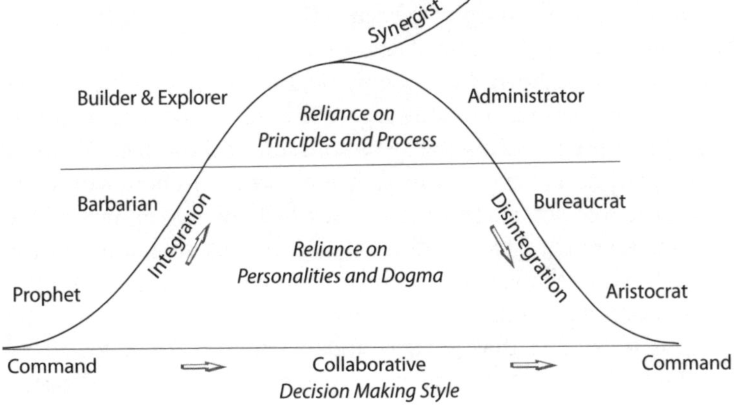

What are the lessons of this story? I think there are several. One is the diversity of leadership styles that are needed to fulfill the potential of any organization. As companies mature, the need for the creative prophet does not disappear; nor does the need for the conquering spirit of the barbarian. But what is needed is balance and the creation of synergy or harmony between the diversity of talents, each put to work on the challenges that match their temperament. The most difficult of all tasks of leadership is to create unity from diversity. It is the purpose of a leadership team. On a leadership team you do not want ten administrators who will create excellent and orderly plans but never have the energy to go anywhere. Nor do you want ten barbarians, each with the strong will and singular focus to fight a battle. You also need the builders, the engineers and specialists who know how to make complex things work and explorers to expand the territory. And you need administrators who bring order to complex organizations and tasks through counting and recording. But you do not need the excess of administration that is bureaucracy. You need leaders, or you need to become a leader, who can bring these personalities together in a harmonious orchestra.

Another lesson regards the role of personalities versus process and principles. The Bahá'í writings repeatedly point to the danger of reliance on personalities. The Bahá'í administrative order is highly reliant on principles and the process of consultation. Civilizations, when they have been at their peak, have had senates, election processes, systems of law, separation of powers, etc. When Rome was being born it was highly reliant on personalities. There was then the period, generally regarded as the peak of the civilization, when the Roman senate was supreme and the acceptance of Roman law and order prevailed. It then was overcome with cults and clashes of personality and the law became subservient to the personalities. The process of disintegration exactly paralleled the decline of the reliance on principles and process and the return of dominance of personalities.

Is it inevitable that growth and expansion are followed by bureaucracy and decline? If you study the course of civilization you might reach that conclusion as the long march of cycles appears as an inevitable pattern. But Arnold Toynbee asked himself this question some years after he wrote *A Study of History*. His answer was 'no'. He said that he believed in free will. He believed that if we understand the causes of integration and disintegration, of emergence and decline, we can alter our behavior and achieve an ever-advancing civilization. It is the failure to recognize and respond to new challenges that leads to a condition of ease, to the loss of muscle and will. But, knowing this, it becomes our job to maintain the energy of creativity, to constantly seek out new challenges and, unifying diverse personalities, maintain integration and avoid disintegration.

The Guardian of the Bahá'í Faith described the same patterns of emergence and decline, of integration and disintegration, as described by Toynbee. He also described the day not to be followed by night, the end of these cycles that have characterized the childhood and adolescence of human history:

> The Revelation of Bahá'u'lláh, whose supreme mission is none other but the achievement of this organic and spiritual unity of the whole body of nations, should, if we be faithful to its implications, be regarded as signalizing through its advent the *coming of age of the entire human race*. It should be viewed not merely as yet another spiritual revival in the ever-changing fortunes of mankind, not only as a further stage in a chain of progressive Revelations, nor even as the culmination of one of a series of recurrent prophetic cycles, but rather as marking the last and highest stage in the stupendous evolution of man's collective life on this planet.[24]

The very purpose of leadership in this age, it seems to me, should be the creation of organic unity, whether among diverse personalities within a business or among diverse groups in society. I use the term 'synergist' simply to represent the type of leader who is able to bring unity to different personalities and to maintain the reliance on principles and process without being overcome by personality. It is the ability not to have one personality or talent or interest win out over another but rather the ability to create unity of interest, of energy and effort that is the primary function of leadership and its most difficult challenge. But this unity cannot be achieved with a blind eye to the diversity inherent in human creation. Just as unity of the races cannot be achieved by ignoring the differing contribution of the races, seeing them all as indistinct, rather it is achieved by appreciating and celebrating their differences and contributions. Similarly, within the management of any company, unity is achieved not by expecting sameness or being blind to the differing talents and personalities but rather by appreciating and valuing those very differences.

The Master and the Force of Example

The Bahá'í Faith is unique in many respects. One of its unique features is the person of 'Abdu'l-Bahá, given to us as the perfect example of the conduct which should characterize Bahá'ís. This gift to us is evidence of our need for leadership. His very life is a testimony to the force of example, the inspiration that one human being can derive from examining the actions and words of another. No book attempting to describe lessons on management and leadership derived from this Faith could fail to include an examination of His life as an example. This is a subject that could fill an entire book by itself, so I am attempting this with some doubt about my ability to do the subject justice. I encourage the reader to investigate the matter in more depth.

Perhaps the overarching lesson of 'Abdu'l-Bahá's life is in the simple spirit of kindness and love for all people, regardless of status, race or religion. Others were attracted to Him and followed His example, not merely because of the brilliance of any teachings or arguments He set forth but rather because of His manner of addressing all those with whom He came in contact. Shoghi Effendi said,

> As the Master so fully and consistently did throughout His lifetime, we must all make a supreme effort to pour out a genuine

> spirit of kindness and hopeful love to peoples of various creeds and classes, and must abstain from all provocative language that may impede the effect of what true and continued kindness can produce.[25]

In His manner of speech, His ability to engage in true dialogue, to become one with another person, His spirit is manifest. The following quotation is attributed to Bahá'u'lláh, describing His son.

> A pleasing, kindly disposition and a display of tolerance towards the people are requisites of teaching the Cause. Whatever a person says, hollow and product of vain imaginings and a parrot-like repetition of somebody else's views though it be, one ought to let it pass. One should not engage in disputation leading to and ending with obstinate refusal and hostility, because the other person would consider himself worsted and defeated. Consequently further veils intervene between him and the Cause, and he becomes more negligent of it. One ought to say: right, admitted, but look at the matter in this other way, and judge for yourself whether it is true or false; of course it should be said with courtesy, with kindliness, with consideration. Then the other person will listen, not seek to answer back and to marshal proofs in repudiation. He will agree, because he comes to realize that the purpose has not been to engage in verbal battle and to gain mastery over him. He sees that the purpose has been to impart the word of truth, to show humanity, to bring forth heavenly qualities. His eyes and his ears are opened, his heart responds, his true nature unfolds, and by the grace of God, he becomes a new creation . . . The Most Great Branch gives a willing ear to any manner of senseless talk, to such an extent that the other person says to himself: He is trying to learn from me. Then, gradually, by such means as the other person cannot perceive, He gives him insight and understanding.[26]

Surely there could be no better description of the power of effective listening, of a true spirit of respect for another person, no matter how humble or incoherent his thoughts might be. If the

Master could deal with others with such respect and love, then surely we can at least attempt to follow in His footsteps.

There is another quality revealed in 'Abdu'l-Bahá's speech that is noteworthy for its spiritualizing effect on others. There is a common pattern in the talks He gave before groups during His travels. Listen for it here:

> I wish to express my gratitude for your hospitality, and my joy that you are spiritually minded. I am happy to be present at a gathering such as this, assembled together to listen to a Divine Message. If you could see with the eye of truth, great waves of spirituality would be visible to you in this place. The power of the Holy Spirit is here for all. Praise be to God that your hearts are inspired with Divine fervor! Your souls are as waves on the sea of the spirit; although each individual is a distinct wave, the ocean is one, all are united in God.
>
> Every heart should radiate unity, so that the Light of the one Divine Source of all may shine forth bright and luminous. We must not consider the separate waves alone, but the entire sea. We should rise from the individual to the whole. The spirit is as one great ocean and the waves thereof are the souls of men.[27]

And again,

> This is in truth a Bahá'í house. Every time such a house or meeting place is founded it becomes one of the greatest aids to the general development of the town and country to which it belongs. It encourages the growth of learning and science and is known for its intense spirituality and for the love it spreads among the peoples.
>
> The foundation of such a meeting-place is always followed by the greatest prosperity.[28]

In almost every talk that 'Abdu'l-Bahá gave He said similar things, expressing His love, His gratitude and appreciation for those to whom He spoke. He uplifted those before Him by pointing to their own nobility, their own dedication to spiritual matters, to their own noble heritage or interests. Their spirit was uplifted merely by the assertion that they possessed noble qualities. They were drawn to Him because He saw the good in them. In the first sentence above He says that He wishes to express His joy that you are spiritually minded. Imagine that your presence brought joy to His heart because He saw in you the quality of being spiritually minded.

This ability to see the good in others is an essential quality of leadership. No one leads others by tearing them down and demeaning them. We follow those who love us, who have faith in us, and 'Abdu'l-Bahá attracted us to follow Him by His appreciation of our good qualities, no matter how humble they might be and no matter how unapparent to our own eyes.

How any individual approaches his work and his relations with others is conditioned by what might be called a world view, a prism through which one evaluates actions and opportunities. From the study of the Master we learn a world view and seek to adopt it in our own lives. This view will determine any individual's ability to be an example to others.

> All humanity are the children of God; they belong to the same family, to the same original race. There can be no multiplicity of races, since all are the descendants of Adam. This signifies that racial assumptions and distinctions are nothing but superstition. In the estimate of God there are no English, French, Germans, Turkish or Persians. All these in the presence of God are equal; they are one race and creation; God did not make these divisions. These distinctions have had their origin in man himself. Therefore, as they are against the plan and purpose of reality, they are false and imaginary. We are of one physical race, even as we are of one physical plan of material body – each endowed with two eyes, two ears, one head, two feet.[29]

This simple statement concerning the oneness of the human race permeated every action that 'Abdu'l-Bahá took.

All leaders project their beliefs about others and their view of the world. In so many subtle ways this view is an influence, whether intentional or not, on those who look to the individual for leadership. In the ideal world one would say, 'Yes, but they shouldn't look to me for leadership. They should simply respond to my views, they should study matters, they should study the Master and develop their own views.' And, yes, of course this is true. But it also does not matter that it is true. It is simply a statement of reality, that if you become the owner of a business, if you hire others or teach others, those others will look to your example and may know little or nothing of the Master and may not be either capable or motivated to the degree of independent investigation you may wish of them. It is therefore incumbent upon us to look in the mirror and study our own behavior and the views we project and inquire as to whether they are those that we wish to be models for others.

> 'Abdu'l-Bahá's whole life contradicted this assumption that He was a visionary, an impractical idealist. When He addressed the student body at Leland Stanford University He was introduced by its president, David Starr Jordan, in these words: "Abdu'l-Bahá will surely unite the East and the West for *He treads the mystical way with practical feet*.' He was a successful business man and was often consulted by other men, not believers by the way, as to the conduct of their businesses. One of His outstanding characteristics was a calm judgment in all material affairs; a poise in dealing with men and occasions of all kinds unrivaled by the most astute of captains of industry. He has been known to go into the kitchen and prepare a meal for His guests. He never failed in such small attentions as seeing that the room where His visitors were entertained contained every possible comfort, though He paid no attention to His own comfort.
>
> In short, the slightest investigation into the facts will force the conclusion that our first hypothesis is untenable.[30]

An important quality of 'Abdu'l-Bahá that should be a model

for all who pursue a career in business and for all those who are fortunate enough to achieve some degree of wealth was His constant attention to the poor. When some people enter a city they immediately want to be become associated with those of wealth and power. 'Abdu'l-Bahá's attention was constantly focused in the other direction and He encouraged all in the virtue of voluntarily helping those in need.

> Man reacheth perfection through good deeds, voluntarily performed, not through good deeds the doing of which was forced upon him. And sharing is a personally chosen righteous act: that is, the rich should extend assistance to the poor, they should expend their substance for the poor, but of their own free will, and not because the poor have gained this end by force. For the harvest of force is turmoil and the ruin of the social order. On the other hand voluntary sharing, the freely-chosen expending of one's substance, leadeth to society's comfort and peace. It lighteth up the world; it bestoweth honor upon humankind.[31]

There are many other qualities of 'Abdu'l-Bahá that are worthy of consideration for anyone concerned with the subject of leadership. He had a unique ability to live in both the practical and spiritual worlds at the same time. This is a struggle for many in the world of business. While always maintaining a spiritual perspective, He did the very practical things such as anticipating the possibility of famine during World War I and storing grain for distribution when the need came. He gave practical advice on investing in businesses and real estate and demonstrated an appreciation for different talents and abilities in those who served Him. It is such a temptation to choose either the spiritual or the practical path and to leave the other behind. It is clear in the Master's life that it is entirely possible to find the balance, to excel at both.

For those of us who have pursued a career in business there is no choice as to whether one will be asked to serve in a leadership role. Leadership is not something one seeks for the egotistic satisfaction of ruling over others. It is the natural consequence of becoming successful in any field of endeavor. If you are a successful scientist, engineer, teacher or manager, you are automatically in a position of leadership, a position (formal or informal) in which others will respond to your example. It is important that we develop our sensibilities about how we influence others and how we discern and judge the qualities of others. The fact that human beings respond to the influence of other human beings is one that will not disappear any time in our lifetime, no matter how mature and well functioning our decision-making groups may become.

Questions for Discussion and Reflection

1) Looking back on your experience at work, what is the best example you have seen of leadership in action. What did the leader do that caused this to be a positive experience? How did this action(s) or the qualities of this leader correspond to the eight principles in the first part of this book?

2) When there is a group decision-making process, what are some of the key factors that inhibit successful leadership and some of the factors that enable successful leadership? How can the inhibiting factors be reduced and the enabling factors increased?

3) We are told that the leadership of the future will be 'moral leadership'. What do you think this means in practice? Have you seen examples of moral leadership?

Other Quotations and Views on Leadership

> Perhaps the most central characteristic of authentic leadership is the relinquishing of the impulse to dominate others. *David Cooper*

> Leadership is a privilege to better the lives of others. It is not an opportunity to satisfy personal greed. *Mwai Kibaki*

Management is about arranging and telling. Leadership is about nurturing and enhancing. *Thomas J. Peters*

The day soldiers stop bringing you their problems is the day you have stopped leading them. They have either lost confidence that you can help them or concluded that you do not care. Either case is a failure of leadership. *Colin Powell*

True leadership must be for the benefit of the followers, not the enrichment of the leaders. *Robert Townsend*

Leadership and learning are indispensable to each other. *John Fitzgerald Kennedy*

No institution can possibly survive if it needs geniuses or supermen to manage it. It must be organized in such a way as to be able to get along under a leadership composed of average human beings. *Peter F. Drucker*

The test of leadership is not to put greatness into humanity, but to elicit it, for the greatness is already there. *James Buchanan*

Leadership is a potent combination of strategy and character. But if you must be without one, be without the strategy. *Norman Schwarzkopf*

We know that leadership is very much related to change. As the pace of change accelerates, there is naturally a greater need for effective leadership. *John Kotter*

The most dangerous leadership myth is that leaders are born – that there is a genetic factor to leadership. This myth asserts that people simply either have certain charismatic qualities or not. That's nonsense; in fact, the opposite is true. Leaders are made rather than born. *Warren G. Bennis*

You don't lead by hitting people over the head – that's assault, not leadership. *Dwight David Eisenhower*

Leadership should be born out of the understanding of the needs of those who would be affected by it. *Marian Anderson*

The supreme quality for leadership is unquestionably integrity. Without it, no real success is possible, no matter whether it is on a section gang, a football field, in an army, or in an office. *Dwight David Eisenhower*

If we ever pass out as a great nation we ought to put on our tombstone 'America died from a delusion that she had moral leadership'. *Will Rogers*

Appendix A

The Evolution of Authority and Organization

The evolving nature of organizations is a small act in a larger play. It cannot be understood without some historical context.

Not only the nature of organization but the values, structures and habits of society have been in transition from the beginning of time, now at an accelerating rate. There are many ways to describe these transitions. They have been described by Arnold Toynbee as the cycles of civilizations and by Alvin Toffler as the march of technology. Another way to describe them is simply in regard to the maturing of the human race and the nature of authority and decision-making appropriate at each stage.

For the sake of simplicity I will briefly describe four stages of human social evolution, the nature of authority and how decision-making has shifted at each stage, affecting all forms of governance.

There can be no order without the acceptance of authority by the people. Government, the authority of administration, must be viewed as legitimate in the eyes of the people or anarchy will prevail. It is the loss of legitimacy on the part of government and other institutions that is the catalyst for the destruction of a civilization. How authority is defined, how an order is established, can be described in four stages of maturity representing the historic progress of the human race.

Stage One: Pre-Historic Society

Our known history essentially begins with the early history revealed in the Old Testament, the history of Egypt and the Jewish people in the West. The period before this can loosely be referred to as pre-historic. We know little of that period but there is probably little to know. Life was a simple process of the struggle for survival, living in caves or huts and hunting in small groups or gathering fruits and vegetables. Work was that of the hunter–gatherer.

The work organization was the family structure and authority or decision-making must have been the province of the stronger or older family member.

Stage Two: Traditional Society

Traditional society can be said to have begun with the age of Moses and the revelation of divine law. Divine law was bestowed, not through a separate clergy but through the singular leader, Moses. The source of knowledge flowed from God to ruler to man; whether the ruler was king or clergy, his authority was derived from his connection to God. No other form of governance, other than an authoritarian one, had any legitimacy.

The divine right of kings is expressed in some manner in all traditional societies. In Europe it was assumed that the king was the leader of the Church because the king derived his authority from a divine relationship. The Japanese emperor, the shah of Persia, and the pharaohs of Egypt claimed similar divine connection. To oppose the king was to oppose God. For hundreds of years in Europe there was a struggle for power as the connection between king and God came into question. The trauma caused by Henry VIII as he split from the Church of Rome and by Philip III (last emperor of the Holy Roman Empire) as he launched the Spanish Armada in his attempt to regain England for the 'one true Church' represents the struggle to preserve this assumption.

This hierarchical model separates man from God. The idea of clergy is consistent with the idea that people need an interpreter, someone between them and the direct word of God. Royalty served as the intermediary for matters of governance and the clergy for matters of the soul.

This model is also consistent with the idea of obedience, rather than independent investigation of truth. If the king was close to God, who were you to question the king? If the clergy was God's intermediary, you need not directly read the word of God or independently investigate. In early traditional societies there was no printing press and therefore only the few of wealth and leisure could learn to read or afford the written word.

The Old Testament teaches, first and foremost, obedience to authority. The story of Abraham and Sarah, and Abraham's test of obedience to God, is symbolic of the authoritarian age. God did not impel Abraham to reason. Nor did He implore Abraham to consult with his wife Sarah regarding the guidance he had received from God. It is likely that Sarah would have asked some serious questions about her husband's sanity. Rather, in Genesis Abraham was instructed to 'Take now thy son, thine only son, Isaac, whom thou lovest, and get thee into the land of Moriah; and offer him there for a burnt offering upon one of the mountains which I will tell thee of'.[1] Of course the story continues that Abraham obeys and takes his son to the mountain, lying to both of his two companions and his own son by telling them that they will offer a lamb that God will provide. Honesty takes a back seat to obedience at this stage. At the last moment, as Abraham raises his knife to slay his son, God speaks and tells Abraham 'Lay not thy hand upon the lad, neither do thou any thing unto him: for now I know that thou fearest God . . .'[2]

There could be no more unreasonable act than to murder your own son. Yet in the days of the Old Testament here is the test of faith and faith is held in esteem above Abraham's deceit and attempted murder. Never is it revealed how Isaac felt about his father afterwards but it is a sound bet he never went to a mountaintop with him alone again! This is the cultural tale at the beginning of our historic tradition that establishes the primacy of obedience and faith over reason. Do what the ruler says and put your own reason aside.

In all traditional societies there can be only one legitimate faith. There is one, and only one, path to God. Pluralism is impossible. If there were more than one legitimate path to God, then the legitimacy of both secular and ecclesiastic institutions could be questioned. Anarchy would result. Heretics must, therefore, be burned at the stake! The very existence of order depends upon it. It was for this reason that religions and their governments conducted crusades against one another. If Christendom were to accept the legitimacy of Islamic nations, then the very source of legitimacy of the Christian Church and kings would be undermined.

The concept of a single path to God was acceptable as long as people did not travel or attempt to expand their borders, physically or mentally. But once people increasingly came into contact with one another it was inevitable that there must be either acceptance of multiple paths to God, therefore multiple sources of legitimacy, or one must dominate and crush the other. Unfortunately, for most of mankind's childhood, the latter course of action was preferred.

Stage Three: Democratic Pluralism

Philosophies and patterns of logic that form the basis of governance, both in larger society and in the corporation, take hold gradually, but then there comes a 'tipping point' when suddenly their supremacy is apparent and the tide of the culture turns. The philosophies that emerged from the Enlightenment and were developing in Europe through Charles de Montesquieu and John Locke were institutionalized in the American system of government. The Enlightenment philosophers, particularly Michel de Montaigne and René Descartes, dared to place man's capacity to reason above superstition, tradition and religious dogma. This freed the chains of men's minds to allow them to question the nature of authority.

John Locke said that 'The end of law is not to abolish or restrain, but to preserve and enlarge freedom. For in all the states of created beings capable of law, where there is no law, there is no freedom.' Today this may seem an unremarkable statement. However, the

Stages of Maturity

	Traditional Society (Childhood)	Democratic Pluralism (Adolescence)	Spiritual/Global (Maturity)
Source of Authority	From God to king or clergy to man	From God to man empowered to choose govenance	From God to man & God to divine institutions; elections plus divine guidance
Breadth of Religion	Single religious path and authority	Acceptance of diversity of religion	Belief in complete unity of religion & acceptance of diverse beliefs
Freedom & Responsibility	Responsibility of obedience	Primacy of personal freedom & liberty	A golden mean Moderation in all things
Science & Religion	Faith over science or reason	Reason & science over faith	Unity of science and faith
Decision-Making	Command authority and obedience	Representative democracy & individual authority	Consultative decision-making informed by spiritual teachings
Racial View	One chosen people	Racial tolerance and diversity	Unity of the one human race
Class Distinction	Inherited class superiority & rule	Mobility of class according to wealth & education	One class of servants to God and humankind

very idea that the purpose of law is to preserve and enlarge freedom was a radical departure from the assumption of traditional societies ruled by a king. Montesquieu, thinking many of the same thoughts as Locke, even dared to say , 'If I knew something that would serve my country but would harm mankind, I would never reveal it; for I am a citizen of humanity first and by necessity, and a citizen of France second, and only by accident.' This statement breaks with all of the assumptions of traditional society. Imagine – loyalty to humanity before one's country. How could one be loyal and subservient to a king if this rebellious notion became predominant? Both Locke and Montesquieu would die before they would see a government founded on their thoughts.

The significance of the American Revolution and its core documents is that they made real, put into working form, a complete break with traditional society. And this break was more than a rebellion against the authority of a foreign king; it was a rebellion against thousands of years of hierarchical assumptions, destroying the connection between kings, clergy and God, and the genie would never be put back into the bottle. This changed all assumptions about the legitimacy and source of authority.

The most important document in American history is the Declaration of Independence. The following is the first paragraph and part of the second. Consider the source of legitimacy assumed by these writings:

> When in the Course of human events, it becomes necessary for one people to dissolve the political bands which have connected them with another, and to assume among the powers of the earth, the separate and equal station to which the *Laws of Nature and of Nature's God entitle them,* a decent respect to the opinions of mankind requires that they should declare the causes which impel them to the separation.
>
> We hold these truths to be self-evident, that all men are created equal, that they are endowed by their Creator with certain unalienable Rights, that among these are Life, Liberty and the pursuit of Happiness.[3]

The Constitution of the United States begins with the phrase 'We the people of the United States, in order to form a more perfect union . . . do ordain and establish this Constitution . . . '[4]

These writings and many others clearly define a new basis for the legitimacy of government. Now God has directly endowed to the people inalienable rights, which no king or government can deny, and the people, based on their endowment by God, are seeking to create a more perfect union. To proclaim that God speaks directly to man, circumventing the king and church, breaks the mold that has been the basis for authoritarian rule.

Alexander Hamilton made this new relationship clear when he said,

> Good and wise men, in all ages, have embraced a very dissimilar theory. They have supposed, that the deity, from the relations, we stand in, to himself and to each other, has constituted an eternal and immutable law, which is, indispensably, and obligatory upon all mankind, prior to any human institution whatever.
>
> This is what is called the law of nature . . .
>
> Upon this law depend the natural rights of mankind, the supreme being gave existence to man, together with the means of preserving and beautifying that existence.[5]

The correlation between the break with England and changes in religious thought did not escape the American founding fathers. Thomas Paine said,

> I saw the exceeding probability that a revolution in the system of government would be followed by a revolution in the system of religion . . . until the system of government should be changed, those subjects could not be brought fairly and openly before the world; but that whenever this should be done, a revolution in the system of religion would follow. Human inventions and priestcraft would be detected; and man would return to the pure, unmixed and unadulterated belief of one God, and no more.[6]

And John Adams said,

> The Revolution was effected before the War commenced. The Revolution was in the minds and hearts of the people; a change in their religious sentiments of their duties and obligations . . . This radical change in the principles, opinions, sentiments, and affections of the people, was the real American Revolution.

The real American Revolution of which Adams spoke was not only an American revolution. It was British, French, and would, in time, permeate the 'opinions, sentiments and affections' of all humankind. It was a revolution against authoritarian rule and against the claim by rulers, including clergy, of any exclusive connection to God. This was the real declaration of independence. And could authoritarian rule long last in any institution, education, government or commerce as these ideas spread?

This independence could not logically be restricted to independence from England or kings. It also implied independence of thought and religious views and therefore required plurality of religion, rather than dominance of any single religious path. George Washington said that 'The establishment of Civil and Religious Liberty was the Motive which induced me to the Field'.[7] And contrary to the hopes of some current fundamentalists to claim the founding fathers as their own, the founding founders made clear that their views were even more liberal than any politician today would dare admit. 'I never told my own religion, nor scrutinized that of another. I never attempted to make a convert, nor wished to change another's creed. I have ever judged of the religion of others by their lives . . .' declared Thomas Jefferson.[8] Jefferson was so independent in his thought and beliefs that he literally created his own Bible by going through the Bible with a scissors and cutting out every statement he felt represented superstition. And Benjamin Franklin, expressing a view that was not uncommon among these revolutionaries, said in a letter to a clergyman who wrote questioning his faith,

> You desire to know something of my religion. It is the first time I have been questioned upon it. But I cannot take your curiosity amiss, and shall endeavor in a few words to gratify it. Here is my creed. I believe in one God, the creator of the universe. That he governs by his providence. That he ought to be worshiped. That the most acceptable service we render to him is doing good to his other children. That the soul of man is immortal, and will be treated with justice in another life respecting its conduct in this. These I take to be the fundamental points in all sound religion, and I regard them as you do in whatever sect I meet with them.
>
> As to Jesus of Nazareth, my opinion of whom you particularly desire, I think his system of morals and his religion, as he left them to us, the best the world ever saw or is likely to see; but I apprehend it has received various corrupting changes, and I have, with most of the present dissenters in England, some doubts as to his divinity; though it is a question I do not dogmatize upon, having never studied it, and think it needless to busy myself with it now, when I expect soon an opportunity of knowing the truth with less trouble. I see no harm, however, in its being believed, if that belief has the good consequences, as probably it has, of making his doctrines more respected and more observed . . .[9]

This independence of faith was essential to enter into an age of reason. Traditionally, faith was dominant over reason. Jefferson called on all men to assert the power of their intellect over the dogmas of faith:

> I very much suspect that if thinking men would have the courage to think for themselves, and to speak what they think, it would be found they do not differ in religious opinions as much as is supposed. I remember to have heard Dr Priestley say, that if all England would candidly examine themselves, and confess, they would find that Unitarianism was really the religion of all . . .[10]

The Declaration of Independence was a declaration for independence of thought and religion. It was a declaration against dogma.

Its authors clearly stated their understanding that you could not have democratic government side by side with dogmatic and single religious conformity. They understood the historic relationship between the authority of God and the authority of rulers and they knew that these relationships had to be unchained.

Stage Four: Spiritual Society – Global Commerce, Culture and Faith

The adolescent seeks independence of parental authority. But neither the age of adolescence nor the age of independence can be considered maturity. Is it wise for one to marry and form a family when one's priority is 'doing my own thing'? Or does maturity require another stage, that of interdependence, an age when we are willing to sacrifice the satisfactions of self to the satisfactions of a group? Family life, marriage, requires sacrifice of the self to the institution of family. Unity, or interdependence, requires willingness to sacrifice what may be perceived as selfish or immediate needs.

The Declaration of Independence by the thirteen colonies was not a declaration of interdependence. Many in the United States view American democracy as an end-state, a final chapter in history, the ultimate form of government. They are wrong. It has been a necessary period of experimentation and maturing, breaking away from the parent–child paradigm of authority. But now there is a new challenge.

It requires no genius to see that the mechanisms of global culture, global commerce and global institutions are rapidly taking hold. The emergence of global culture, contrary to the views of some conservative thinkers, is not a liberal theory. In my view it is God's plan for His people. It is a historic inevitability.

With each stage of history a new religion provides both renewal of eternal spiritual truths accompanied by a set of social teachings, a perfect prescription for life and organization on the planet at that time. When God declared to Moses 'eye for eye'[11] it was no doubt a social law needed at that time. When Jesus said, 'But I say unto you, Love your enemies, bless them that curse you, do good to them that hate you, and pray for them which despitefully use you, and persecute you',[12] He was completely altering the social order. This was a new social teaching for a new age. And now, as we enter into a global society, I believe it is time for a new social order. This is the very purpose of the Bahá'í Faith and its intention is to remake all institutions and relationships in society.

In its 1988 letter concerning individual rights and freedoms, the Universal House of Justice, the international governing body of the Bahá'í Faith, referred to the current stage of maturity:

> How significant is the difference between infancy and childhood, adolescence and adulthood! In a period of history dominated by the surging energy, the rebellious spirit and frenetic activity of adolescence, it is difficult to grasp the distinguishing elements of the mature society to which Bahá'u'lláh beckons all humanity. The models of the old world order blur vision of that which must be perceived; for these models were, in many instances, conceived in rebellion and retain the characteristics of the revolutions peculiar to an adolescent, albeit necessary, period in the evolution of human society.[13]

The revolutionary change in society proposed by Bahá'u'lláh, the founder of the Bahá'í Faith, is not simply another competing hierarchy of religion, a simple addition to the choices offered by the hundreds of religious options. Rather it proclaims God's will to create a fundamental transformation in society:

> . . . Bahá'u'lláh, referring to the transformation effected by every Revelation in the ways, thoughts and manners of the people, reveals these words: 'Is not the object of every Revelation to effect a transformation in the whole character of mankind, a transformation that shall manifest itself, both outwardly and inwardly, that shall affect both its inner life and external conditions? For if the character of mankind be not changed, the futility of God's universal Manifestation would be apparent.'[14]

And, if mankind's character is to be transformed, then surely all of the institutions he creates must also be fundamentally transformed.

In the Bahá'í view, complete independence from the authority of God, or from religion, is not the course most likely to bring maturity to the planet. The great challenge now facing society is how to bring together the authority and wisdom of religion without destroying the fundamentals of freedom and democracy. Unlike earlier religions, the Bahá'í Faith very directly proposes a system of governance that incorporates the best of democracy (I would actually suggest that it is a higher form of democracy) along with the provision for divine guidance and authority. Within the Bahá'í Faith, these two previously competing sources of authority become married in interdependence.

In the Bahá'í system of governance there is a duality of assumptions. On the one hand God does speak directly to humankind, insisting on the independent investigation of truth. Through Bahá'u'lláh, God tells us 'Noble have I created thee'[15] and He has endowed the individual with both the rights and responsibilities of self-governance through a system of democratic elections and decision-making bodies that one can argue are more democratically based than the current system of American government. However, he has also recognized the limitations of 'self' governance by providing laws and ordinances with great clarity and by establishing perpetual infallibility and authority in the establishment of the Universal House of Justice.

This duality assumes that we are mature enough to think two thoughts at once: obedience and independent judgment. These two patterns of thought have, until now, been assumed to be in contradiction. They are contrary only if one is unable to create balance and make wise judgments. As with the assumptions about the material and spiritual worlds, this age creates a new unity: the unity of obedience and self-governance.

But this balance requires moderation. In so many of the problems in the world can be seen the illness of extremism and fundamentalism that inhibits compromise, reflection or the ability of diverse people to consult together. In the West we have asserted personal liberty and freedom without moderation. In some parts of the East the dogma of religion has been asserted in extreme, crushing personal liberty. In the Bahá'í Faith the golden mean is struck. All of the following passages from the letter of the Universal House of Justice on individual rights and freedoms illustrate this principle:

> . . . the moderate freedom which guarantees the welfare of the world of mankind and maintains and preserves the universal relationships is found in its fullest power and extension in the teaching of Bahá'u'lláh.[16]

> The fundamental attitude of the Faith in this respect is best demonstrated by statements of 'Abdu'l-Bahá concerning the family. 'The integrity of the family bond', He says, 'must be constantly considered, and the rights of the individual members must not be transgressed . . . All these rights and prerogatives must be conserved, yet the unity of the family must be sustained. The injury of one shall be considered the injury of all; the comfort of each, the comfort of all; the honor of one, the honor of all.'[17]

> The Bahá'í conception of social life is essentially based on the principle of the subordination of the individual will to that of society. It neither suppresses the individual nor does it exalt him to the point of making him an antisocial creature, a menace to society. As in everything, it follows the 'golden mean'.[18]

In traditional societies, people served the king, who in turn was to serve God. In the American system, the government was to serve the people who possessed natural rights. In the Bahá'í system both individuals and government serve God directly. When one sits on a Local Spiritual Assembly, the first level of governance in the Bahá'í system, one is not a 'servant of the people' whose duty is to represent their will but is rather one who is serving the will of God and thereby serving the people. It is this attitude of both independence from interest groups and respect for divine teachings and authority that will enable the transition to a mature society.

The most important principle of governance that will transform the institutions of society is that which Bahá'ís call *consultation*. This is the process of decision-making that allows participation without competition, that creates collective wisdom by assuring the contribution of all in the group, and it is this principle that creates unity of action and commitment that can energize an organization or community. The spirit of consultation perhaps best describes the spirit of the new age that can bring about global cooperation, respect for the values and interests of the most humble on the planet, while creating an efficiency of organization that will fuel the creation of wealth. The Guardian of the Bahá'í Faith, Shoghi Effendi, said,

> Let us also bear in mind that the keynote of the Cause of God is not dictatorial authority but humble fellowship, not arbitrary power, but the spirit of frank and loving consultation. Nothing short of the spirit of a true Bahá'í can hope to reconcile the principles of mercy and justice, of freedom and submission, of the sanctity of the right of the individual and of self-surrender, of vigilance, discretion and prudence on the one hand, and fellowship, candor, and courage on the other.[19]

Appendix B

A Recent History of Management Theory

The nature of families and the nature of organizations have undergone many changes from their conception many millennia ago. However, I doubt that there has ever been a time when change has occurred more rapidly than today and the demand to adjust has so shocked the social systems in which we live. It may have been a million years over which the transition from single family units to tribal structures occurred. And how many millions of years were consumed in the transition to larger and more diverse cultures built around a city state? The transition from agricultural economies to industrial economies was one of a couple hundred years. And now we are being thrown forward at light speed into a global economy in which national boundaries mean little, place is of less significance and most work is being done within a digital framework and communicated instantaneously over the Internet. The nature of work groups is just as likely to be one of Internet conferences, chat rooms and on-line libraries as it is likely to be a work team in a manufacturing setting. We have not yet mastered human relations in a group that works together in a single location and we have little idea how to do the same in cyberspace.

What is clear is that the pace of change and the constant reorganization of work processes and systems make rule-based management impossible. You can't make and change the rules fast enough! Only principle-based management can compete, in which self-organization and self-management, by both individuals and groups, will be able to move with sufficient speed. It is also principle-based management rather than rule-based management that will gain the cooperation and discretionary effort that is the margin of competitive success in the new economy.

In order to understand where we are going, it is helpful to know where we have been. How have work structures and processes evolved? Most of the evolution has happened within the small period of the past one hundred years. For thousands, if not millions, of years the nature of work systems was relatively stable. The work system was the family system. The vast majority of people in every society, in every corner of the globe, worked at home or very close to it. They worked on the family farm or in the small craft shop and they worked for their parents or a craftsman who acted as like a parent. The family farm and small craft shops making furniture or metal tools for use on the farm, was the essential work structure and it met the material, psychological and

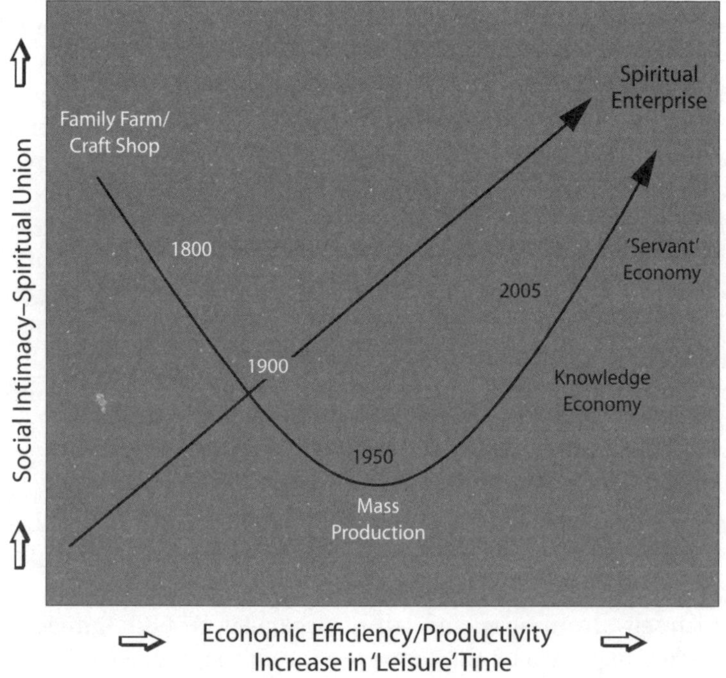

spiritual needs of its members. The work could be brutally hard, sometimes dangerous, and often monotonous, but you knew and trusted those with whom you worked.

The family farm and small craft shop were intimate environments, mother and father working together and the children an essential part of the work unit. Both the small craft shop and family farm provided low efficiency (equals little 'leisure' time) but high intimacy or social bonding.

One might speculate, if one accepts that evolutionary biology and socio-biology have some credence, that the adaptive behavior required for success in this small group setting became, over millions of years, that which is 'natural' for our species.[1] The need for social interaction, for working with people you trust, the desire to be part of a small, intimate group, may have become imprinted in our genetic code as the expected behavior and environment. Without entering into the debate about evolution and particularly the possibility of psychological and social evolution, it is simply logical that any system that was part of our being for the vast majority of human life on this planet might be difficult to leave behind. What is certainly true is that when human beings are placed into systems that turn these characteristics on their head, when people are denied a work group with whom they can have social and intimate interaction, when they have no control over their own work and when the system is one in which there is no expression of emotional support or concern, the consequences are disastrous.

Infants die of Marasmus[2] when they are deprived of social interaction, the holding and cuddling that is the expression of parental love. Prisoners of war have gone into severe anaclitic depression and die – essentially give up on life – when isolated from other prisoners of war. Workers in a manufacturing plant who are told to 'do your own work' and are isolated from other workers in a mechanized system suffer depression and are likely to engage in some form of rebellion, essentially to save themselves from death by induced helplessness.

The great transformation of work systems began with the invention of the combine and other mechanical aids to agriculture. A good thing happened. Productivity, output per acre of land and per hour of work, went up. This is the essential mechanism of wealth creation. Societies become wealthier by achieving greater productivity that then frees human capital to be employed in the creation of new goods and services. The excess labor from the farm moved to the town and city and was employed in the manufacture of industrial and consumer goods. Over the course of one hundred years the population working on the family farm went from 65 per cent down to 1.5 per cent. At the same time our cities grew. Cities and factories are places of specialization.

In the small craft shop, like on the family farm, the worker made a 'whole' product and followed the complete process of production. Furniture manufactured in a craft shop was entirely made by one person who signed his name to the chair or table, indicating his intimate connection to the product. In the new factory workers only made parts and no one could feel any intimate relationship to the product. Efficiency was gained but intimacy was lost. Intimacy, the close social interaction of a group, and the feeling of ownership of one's work, that once was the bedrock of motivation, was destroyed by the mechanical system that was the factory.

Because the increase in productivity was, in many respects a good thing, we came to believe in the value of production efficiency as an essential value over all other values in the work place. Henry Ford believed that he was on a mission to build cars for the 'common man', which meant driving down costs to the lowest possible level. And he succeeded. Now the common man could buy a car and house and even expect a higher standard of living. This new system of mass production also created sufficient leisure time (time not required for work) so children could be freed from their required manual labor and now could be required to attend school. The entire public school movement in the United States emerged exactly parallel to the development of mass production. It was good. But how this material success was achieved denied the entire previous human history of work and social systems. There was a huge spiritual cost, a Faustian bargain made, to achieve this new wealth.

Management Theories: An Attempt to Repair the Social System

Each management theory or practice over the past one hundred years has contributed to either achieving greater efficiency or attempting to repair the damage of a fractured social system.

Henry Ford and Frederick Taylor are the two giant figures of mass production and scientific management. In the early part of the last century the development of *scientific management* was viewed as 'modern'. Rather than simply relying on the personality of a supervisor and the individual craft skills of a worker, Taylor's methods of engineering work (measuring the time required for the different movements or operations within a job, seeking to rearrange those in the ideal way and establishing measurable standards) created an entirely new method of management. The fathers of modern quality management, both in the United States and Japan, were students of Taylor and developed his emphasis on measurement to what became known as statistical process control and process management.

Taylor's methods, which emphasized the definition of one 'right way' to perform a job, led to a top-down rigidity that prohibited worker input, decision-making or flexibility. It was the lack of moderation in the application of these methods that contributed to dehumanizing the workplace and a counter reaction. One counter reaction to the industrial system of Taylor and Ford was the rise of the union movement, a rebellion not just for wages but for dignity, a voice, a recognition that the human beings employed in the factory were not just subjects of engineering or a scientific method. The development of humanistic management practices was the reaction from the academic universe.

The field of organization development (OD) emerged primarily from the work of social psychologists. Social psychology focused on human needs and feelings and the dynamics between people in groups. Researchers and writers such as Kurt Lewin and Carl Rogers developed models to describe the interaction within groups and the patterns of communication between individuals.

In 1954 Maslow defined seven stages of human motivation or

needs. This structure was useful in helping managers understand the significance of motivational influences beyond the simple need for survival and money. Maslow's work and the work of Herzberg[3] and McGregor[4] further developed the understanding of the relationship between organizational systems, management styles (Theory X and Theory Y) and employee motivation. This work became the foundation upon which numerous management and organization development practices were built. Job enrichment,[5] Blake and Mouton's Managerial Grid and various forms of group training and team building all have their foundation in the principles and values promoted by social and humanistic psychology. Each of these theories and practices were simply efforts to recreate some of the same dynamics that had met human needs for millennia in the family farm and craft shop. They were efforts to repair the spiritual and social damage done by the system of mass production.

Humanistic psychology had its competitor for the attention of psychologists trying to improve the workplace in the 1960s and 70s. Applied behavior analysis is the application in the natural environment of experimental psychology, the scientific exploration of Dr B. F. Skinner and his followers. Dr Deming said that managers must 'know the facts', look at the data. If one has respect for the scientific method, for statistics and true knowledge versus superstition, one cannot ignore the vast body of scientific research on the analysis of behavior. While human beings are all unique creatures they do have tendencies to respond to the consequences of their behavior.

All organizational systems are systems that modify behavior. All organizations create reinforcement schedules that reinforce behavior and create habits. It is an inevitable and essential aspect of all organizations. Just as the family system rewards children for desired behavior, all work organizations incorporate reward systems as part of their efforts to both attract employees and to reinforce the behavior they value. Knowledge of behavior analysis can be helpful in designing organizational systems that develop habits that are both important for the work system and the human system.

The next major wave of change was brought about by the sudden emergence of Japanese electronics and automobile companies. Overnight Toyota was producing not only inexpensive cars but cars that were more reliable than those from Europe or the United States. A flurry of books and theories emerged to explain this commercial success. One of the first was the infatuation with Quality Circles.

The development of Quality Circles in Japan can be traced back to the research in group dynamics and decision-making conducted in the 1950s in the United States. Somewhat strangely, group problem-solving and team development have returned to the US through efforts to emulate Japanese problem-solving and decision-making.

After World War II several Americans were invited to Japan to assist in the rebuilding of Japanese industry and their teachings, filtered through the prism of Japanese culture, led to much of modern *total quality management*. Among these were W. Edwards Deming,

Walter A. Shewhart and Joseph Juran. Shewhart's *Economic Control of Quality of Manufactured Products* may be the most important book on quality or manufacturing ever written and the seminars of these three fathers of modern quality management created much of the foundation of what is now regarded as Japanese management.

From Dr Deming and Dr Juran we learned to place emphasis on the performance to customer requirements, to define performance in terms of customer satisfaction and to provide feedback to suppliers.[6] Dr Deming and his disciples emphasized the importance of variability in manufacturing processes and of gaining statistical knowledge and control of the process. These views complemented the emphasis on teamwork and employee satisfaction that was emerging from the humanistic school of management.

Dr Deming repeatedly emphasized the power of the system and the importance of managing it. Unfortunately, Dr Deming and the quality advocates provided no method for analyzing and changing the system. They were unaware of the work going on in a parallel universe at the Tavistock Institute.

Forty years ago Eric Trist and others at the Tavistock Institute[7] in London began studying the environment of organizations and the interaction of the technical system of work with the social systems. The foundation study of *socio-technical systems design* was conducted by Trist in British coal mines. He found that the traditional culture of the mines was one of small, self-selected and highly interdependent groups of workers. When new technology was introduced into the mines, workers were assigned to single tasks controlled by external supervisors. The reactions of workers were negative and led to high absenteeism and low productivity. When workers were allowed to design their own organization, they duplicated their traditional cultural arrangements. Each person performed a number of different jobs as a member of a self-supervising work group. Productivity went up and absenteeism went down.

There are two major precepts to socio-technical design theory. The first is *how well the social and technical systems are designed with respect to one another and with respect to the demands of the external environment determines how effective the organization will be.* The second is that *the organization is an open system.* This simple idea is that the organization, like every living organism, depends upon interaction with its environment to maintain energy and avoid entropy. No organization is right or wrong, effective or ineffective, because of its own qualities alone. Rather, it is effective or ineffective depending on how it meets the demands and utilizes the resources of the external environment. Because the external environment is constantly changing, the organization must remain an 'open system', open to constant change and responsive to environmental needs. This ability to adapt, to learn, will determine its survival.

The idea of the organization as a system made up of interacting technical and social components is consistent with Dr Deming's view of the system and the need to improve the process of work. The open-systems concept is another way of arriving at the conclusion that the organization must be 'customer focused' and must engage in continuous improvement to meet ever-changing customer needs.

Perhaps the strongest force influencing change in corporations over the past 30 years has been the competitive pressure and example of the Japanese manufacturing processes. While Japan has suffered from a bureaucratic financial system, its production system is now the prototype adopted from Dearborn to Stuttgart. Globally, Ford is implementing the 'Ford Production System', an admitted adaptation of the Toyota Production System. Even Mercedes Benz and Porsche have adopted the basic design of work process that was derived from Toyota.

The evolution of production systems can be seen in three stages (which have been well-described in *The Machine that Changed the World*, the result of a five-year MIT comparative study of the global auto industry).[8] These stages are 1) craft production, 2) mass production and 3) lean production. James P. Womack and Daniel T. Jones have recently described their view of how to implement lean production systems in their *Lean Thinking*.[9]

The third stage of production began in post-World War II Japan and Eiji Toyoda and Taiichi Ohno must be credited with its development. Contrary to the belief of many in the quality profession, it is this different system of production and organization that is the primary determinant of quality, not statistical methods or Quality Circles, despite their obvious value.

In 1949 Toyota's sales collapsed and they were forced to lay off large numbers of workers. This collapse followed a lengthy and bitter strike by their union. By 1950 Toyota was producing a total of only 2,685 cars a year, compared to one Ford plant that produced more than 7,000 each day. Eiji Toyoda made many trips to Ford's River Rouge plant in Dearborn to study the most efficient production system in the world. He concluded that the Ford system could not succeed in Japan.

The environment in Japan was different. First, the market was small and required a wide variety of different types of vehicles. Long production runs of identical cars and parts was not possible. Second, the workforce and their unions would no longer accept being treated as insignificant interchangeable parts. Labor laws introduced by the American occupational forces had so strengthened the unions that they represented everyone, eliminating the distinction between white and blue collar workers. They had also negotiated a share of the profits. Third, capital was scarce, making heavy expenditures for the latest technology impossible.

The development of 'lean production' methods by Toyota's production chief Taiichi Ohno was a response to this environment. It began with the stamping of body parts.

In the craft shop, body panels were hammered by hand into shape. The metal sheet was laid over a die and gradually shaped by hammering the metal. Aston Martin and Morgan still use this method. Contrary to myth, this step does not produce a superior product to mass production methods; it is simply more expensive. In Ford's factory the production of body parts was based on large quantities of identical metal sheets being placed in a die and stamped into shape. The quantities of identical parts required in Ford's factories allowed for die presses to be dedicated to single parts. There were die change engineers who supervised the die change process. Changing a die usually required one or two days of machine downtime. Ohno concluded that this second method was impossible owing to the quantities required for efficient operation. Toyota could not afford dedicated die presses. If they used this method to change dies, the stamping presses would be inoperative half of the time. Ohno had to develop a system whereby dies could be changed every couple of hours. This meant that the die change process had to be reduced from days to minutes.[10]

Ohno developed a system of rollers that allowed dies to be quickly moved in and out of place by the workers themselves. He concluded after experimentation that the requirement of specialists slowed the process down. It could be accomplished quickly only if the workers working as a team had the knowledge and skills to perform the task themselves. In order to do this they not only had to have the necessary skills, they had to have knowledge of the larger production process to know when to change dies. They had to accept full responsibility for their own work.

In accomplishing this quick die change process Taiichi Ohno had established a pattern that would be replicated throughout the factory. Small groups of workers would be treated as full partners in the process, responsible for their own work, able to improve and modify their process, and having knowledge of the previous and next stages of production (their internal customers and suppliers) so that they would understand the requirements and effect of their work. Ohno found that these work groups, given the necessary information, worked to continuously improve their work process.

On the assembly line Ohno formed workers into teams with a working team leader rather than a foreman. Teams were given a set of assembly steps and told to work together to devise the best possible ways to accomplish the assembly. The team leader would participate in the work, stepping in to help where needed. These teams soon accepted responsibility for housekeeping, small machine repair, maintenance and checking their own quality. The teams would meet periodically to find ways to continuously improve (Kaizen) their process.

The total system in the Toyota plants became distinctly different from those in American auto plants. Lots were small and quick change-to-order was a priority. They achieved the combination of efficiency and small production runs which American producers assumed to be contradictory. This was accomplished only by completely redefining the system of work and worker responsibility. It was a whole new system.

Ohno's system had implications for all areas of the business and organization. Engineering and design teams now functioned in a fast-cycle process. The need for quick response, quick change and just-in-time was extended to supplier relations. These processes produced a different type of organization than was developing in Detroit. Toyota required few layers of management with less distinction in function, pay and status between workers and managers while Detroit was increasing layers and distinctions.

Business process reengineering was one of the hottest buzz words of the 1990s. Michael Hammer and James Champy[11] define reengineering as 'starting over'. It means abandoning long-established procedures and looking afresh at the work required to create a company's product or service and deliver value to the customer. It means asking the question, 'If I were recreating this company today, given what I know and given current technology, what would it look like?' Reengineering a company means tossing aside old systems and starting over.

The emphasis of reengineering has been to study the flow of the work process and seek to redesign that work process to eliminate cycle time, unnecessary steps and, particularly, apply the capabilities of information technology to that process. Toyota, socio-technical systems and quality management also employed process analysis and redesign. The strength of reengineering was the application of information technology; the weakness was the frequent failure to take into account the social system or culture of the organization.

Chaos theory may be one step beyond useful to most managers. However, for those struggling with the transformation of their organizations, understanding complex systems may be the key to creating order from apparent chaos. Complexity matters. It defines the difference between successfully managing a McDonald's restaurant and a pharmaceutical research lab and why the misapplication of management techniques, such as reengineering and performance measurement, can stifle the productivity of knowledge work. The high-performance organization must include an understanding of the dynamics of complex systems since most organizations are no longer makers of 'things' but makers of 'knowledge'.

As knowledge work expands, as work increasingly becomes shared across companies and nations, as place becomes less important and connections and interaction become more important, as the Internet becomes the factory, we are working in a complex system in which trust and relationships are the keys to success. We are also gaining efficiency. Just as the transition from manual and animal labor on the farm to machine labor freed time, created 'leisure' time that could be employed in other ways, we are again engaged in a process of freeing time. How will this be employed? I believe that it will be increasingly employed in acts of service, time spent in efforts to live one's values.

What is next? How will the evolution of the work place proceed to both improve economic efficiency and to create social systems that lead to human and spiritual development? Many authors are now exploring the principles of religion and spirituality in the workplace. Dorothy Marcic and her *Managing with the Wisdom of Love* was one of the first to be so bold as to suggest that a spiritual principle such as love had relevance in the work place. But in the past few years authors have become increasingly bold, coming out of the religious closet, to write about the connection between faith, spirituality and work.

Stephen Covey, a devote Mormon with whom I have had the pleasure of working, has followed up his extremely successful *Seven Habits of Highly Effective People* with *The 8th Habit*. What is the 8th Habit?

> The 8th Habit represents the pathway to the enormously promising side of today's reality . . . It is the voice of the human spirit

> – full of hope and intelligence, resilient by nature, boundless in its potential to serve the common good. This voice also encompasses the soul of the organization that will survive, thrive and profoundly impact the future of the world.[12]

'Voice' Covey says, 'is unique personal significance – significance that is revealed as we face our greatest challenges and which makes us equal to them.'[13] There is no doubt that throughout the book Covey is exploring spiritual reality and seeking its application to the corporate setting.

Peter Senge, the author of the influential *Fifth Discipline*, in his recent book, *Presence: Human Purpose and the Field of the Future*, takes the reader on a spiritual search, a journey to find the inner voice. While Senge is not as clearly religious as Covey, nevertheless he is seeking to express, in his own way, a spiritual path. Dennis W. Bakke's *Joy at Work* is a very overt effort to apply Christian teachings to the corporate setting. And Marc Gunther's *Faith and Fortune* is essentially a book of case studies, each one an attempt to discover the application of spiritual teachings in the workplace.

I have no doubt that this conversation will go on for many years. People of all faiths want to reconcile the world of material pursuit with the world of faith and spirit. It is my hope that this book can make a small contribution in this direction. I also hope that Bahá'ís will be examples, in every respect, of spiritual principles in every aspect of their lives. I hope that by exploring the ideas and the references in this book, Bahá'ís will find ways to advance this dialogue in their own workplace and community.

Appendix C

References from the Bahá'í Writings on Management and Economics[1]

Honesty: The Foundation of All Virtues

Beautify your tongues, O people, with truthfulness, and adorn your souls with the ornament of honesty. Beware, O people, that ye deal not treacherously with any one. Be ye the trustees of God amongst His creatures, and the emblems of His generosity amidst His people. They that follow their lusts and corrupt inclinations, have erred and dissipated their efforts. They, indeed, are of the lost. Strive, O people, that your eyes may be directed towards the mercy of God, that your hearts may be attuned to His wondrous remembrance, that your souls may rest confidently upon His grace and bounty, that your feet may tread the path of His good-pleasure. Such are the counsels which I bequeath unto you. Would that ye might follow My counsels![2]

The fifth Glad-Tidings: In every country where any of this people reside, they must behave towards the government of that country with loyalty, honesty and truthfulness. This is that which hath been revealed at the behest of Him Who is the Ordainer, the Ancient of Days.[3]

O Ḥaydar-'Alí! Upon thee be the praise of God and His glory. Say: Honesty, virtue, wisdom and a saintly character redound to the exaltation of man, while dishonesty, imposture, ignorance and hypocrisy lead to his abasement. By My life! Man's distinction lieth not in ornaments or wealth, but rather in virtuous behavior and true understanding. Most of the people in Persia are steeped in deception and idle fancy. How great the difference between the condition of these people and the station of such valiant souls as have passed beyond the sea of names and pitched their tents upon the shores of the ocean of detachment.[4]

Trustworthiness, wisdom and honesty are, of a truth, God's beauteous adornments for His creatures. These fair garments are a befitting vesture for every temple. Happy are those that comprehend, and well is it with them that acquire such virtues.[5]

Commerce is as a heaven, whose sun is trustworthiness and whose moon is truthfulness. The most precious of all things in the estimation of Him Who is the Sovereign Truth is trustworthiness . . .[6]

Furthermore, any agency whatever, though it be the instrument of mankind's greatest good, is capable of misuse. Its proper use or abuse depends on the varying degrees of enlightenment, capacity, faith, honesty, devotion and highmindedness of the leaders of public opinion.[7]

Another friend asked, 'In the Tablets it is stated that we must be severed and detached. In another place it is stated that we must learn a trade or profession. Do not these two statements contradict each other?' 'Abdu'l-Bahá replied, 'In the Cause of Bahá'u'lláh, it is incumbent upon every soul to acquire a trade and an occupation. For example, I know how to weave or make a mat, and you know some other trade. This, in itself is an act of worship, provided that it is conducted on the basis of utmost honesty and faithfulness.

'And this is the cause of prosperity. Yet, in spite of being so occupied, if the heart is not chained and tied to this world, and is not troubled by current events, neither hindered by wealth from rendering service to mankind, nor grieved because of poverty, – then this is human perfection. Otherwise in a state of poverty, to manifest generosity and in a state of weakness to claim justice

– this can easily be said, but it is not a proof of man's attainments and alertness.'[8]

If any of the friends should enter into the service of the government, they should make their occupation a means of drawing nearer to the divine Threshold: they should act with probity and uprightness, rigorously shun all forms of venality and corruption, and content themselves with the salaries they are receiving, taking pride, rather, in the degree of sagacity, competence and judgment that they can bring to their work. If a person content himself with a single loaf of bread, and perform his duties with as much justice and fair-mindedness as lieth within his power, he will be the prince of mortals, and the most praiseworthy of men. Noble and distinguished will he be, despite his empty purse! Pre-eminent will he rank among the free, although his garb be old and worn! For man, praise and glory reside in virtuous and noble qualities; honor and distinction in nearness to the divine Threshold. The world's wealth is, by contrast, the stuff of illusion. Those who lust after it are the followers of evil and, erelong, they shall be plunged into confusion and despair. Which is better – that a man should be thus, or that he should comport himself with consecration and sanctity of purpose and stand out conspicuously for his integrity, uprightness and honesty? Nay, such qualities are better than the riches of Korah, and dearer than all the treasures of existence.[9]

Truthfulness is the foundation of all human virtues. Without truthfulness progress and success, in all the worlds of God, are impossible for any soul. When this holy attribute is established in man, all the divine qualities will also be acquired.[10]

The Spirit of Service

To the extent that work is consciously undertaken in a spirit of service to humanity, Bahá'u'lláh says, it is a form of prayer, a means of worshiping God. Every individual has the capacity to see himself or herself in this light, and it is to this inalienable capacity of the self that development strategy must appeal, whatever the nature of the plans being pursued, whatever the rewards they promise. No narrower a perspective will ever call up from the people of the world the magnitude of effort and commitment that the economic tasks ahead will require.[11]

It is obligatory for men and women to engage in a trade or profession. Bahá'u'lláh exalts 'engagement in such work' to the 'rank of worship' of God. The spiritual and practical significance of this law, and the mutual responsibility of the individual and society for its implementation are explained in a letter written on behalf of Shoghi Effendi:

> With reference to Bahá'u'lláh's command concerning the engagement of the believers in some sort of profession: the Teachings are most emphatic on this matter, particularly the statement in the Aqdas to this effect which makes it quite clear that idle people who lack the desire to work can have no place in the new World Order. As a corollary of this principle, Bahá'u'lláh further states that mendicity should not only be discouraged but entirely wiped out from the face of society. It is the duty of those who are in charge of the organization of society to give every individual the opportunity of acquiring the necessary talent in some kind of profession, and also the means of utilizing such a talent, both for its own sake and for the sake of earning the means of his livelihood. Every individual, no matter how handicapped and limited he may be, is under the obligation of engaging in some work or profession, for work, especially when performed in the spirit of service, is according to Bahá'u'lláh a form of worship. It has not only a utilitarian purpose, but has a value in itself, because it draws us nearer to God, and enables us to better grasp His purpose for us in this world. It is obvious, therefore, that the inheritance of wealth cannot make anyone immune from daily work.[13]

'Abdu'l-Bahá describes the Mashriqu'l-Adhkár as 'one of the most vital institutions in the world', and Shoghi Effendi indicates that it exemplifies in tangible form the integration of 'Bahá'í worship and service'. Anticipating the future development of this institution, Shoghi Effendi envisages that the House of Worship and its dependencies 'shall afford relief to the suffering, sustenance to the poor, shelter to the wayfarer, solace to the bereaved, and education to the ignorant'. In the future, Bahá'í Houses of Worship will be constructed in every town and village.[14]

It is incumbent upon every man of insight and understanding to strive to translate that which hath been written into reality and action . . . That one indeed is a man who, today, dedicateth himself to the service of the entire human race. The Great Being saith: Blessed and happy is he that ariseth to promote the best interests of the peoples and kindreds of the earth. In another passage He hath proclaimed: It is not for him to pride himself who loveth his own country, but rather for him who loveth the whole world.[15]

Justice: The Trainer of the World

The best beloved of all things in My sight is Justice; turn not away therefrom if thou desirest Me, and neglect it not that I may confide in thee. By its aid thou shalt see with thine own eyes and not through the eyes of others, and shalt know of thine own knowledge and not through the knowledge of thy neighbor. Ponder this in thy heart; how it behooveth thee to be. Verily justice is My gift to thee and the sign of My loving-kindness. Set it then before thine eyes.[16]

We have decreed that a third part of all fines shall go to the Seat of Justice, and We admonish its men to observe pure justice, that they may expend what is thus accumulated for such purposes as have been enjoined upon them by Him Who is the All-Knowing, the All-Wise. O ye Men of Justice! Be ye, in the realm of God, shepherds unto His sheep and guard them from the ravening wolves that have appeared in disguise, even as ye would guard your own sons. Thus exhorteth you the Counselor, the Faithful.[17]

Justice is the one power that can translate the dawning consciousness of humanity's oneness into a collective will through which the necessary structures of global community life can be confidently erected. An age that sees the people of the world increasingly gaining access to information of every kind and to a diversity of ideas will find justice asserting itself as the ruling principle of successful social organization.[18]

And now concerning thy question regarding the nature of religion. Know thou that they who are truly wise have likened the world unto the human temple. As the body of man needeth a garment to clothe it, so the body of mankind must needs be adorned with the mantle of justice and wisdom. Its robe is the Revelation vouchsafed unto it by God. Whenever this robe hath fulfilled its purpose, the Almighty will assuredly renew it. For every age requireth a fresh measure of the light of God. Every Divine Revelation hath been sent down in a manner that befitted the circumstances of the age in which it hath appeared.[19]

Know verily that the essence of justice and the source thereof are both embodied in the ordinances prescribed by Him Who is the Manifestation of the Self of God amongst men, if ye be of them that recognize this truth. He doth verily incarnate the highest, the infallible standard of justice unto all creation. Were His law to be such as to strike terror into the hearts of all that are in heaven and on earth, that law is naught but manifest justice. The fears and agitation which the revelation of this law provokes in men's hearts should indeed be likened to the cries of the suckling babe weaned from his mother's milk, if ye be of them that perceive. Were men to discover the motivating purpose of God's Revelation, they would assuredly cast away their fears, and, with hearts filled with gratitude, rejoice with exceeding gladness.[20]

The Great Being saith: O well-beloved ones! The tabernacle of unity hath been raised; regard ye not one another as strangers. Ye are the fruits of one tree, and the leaves of one branch. We cherish the hope that the light of justice may shine upon the world and sanctify it from tyranny. If the rulers and kings of the earth, the symbols of the power of God, exalted be His glory, arise and resolve to dedicate themselves to whatever will promote the highest interests of the whole of humanity, the reign of justice will assuredly be established amongst the children of men, and the effulgence of its light will envelop the whole earth. The Great Being saith: The structure of world stability and order hath been reared upon, and will continue to be sustained by, the twin pillars of reward and punishment . . . In another passage He hath written: Take heed, O concourse of the rulers of the world! There is no force on earth that can equal in its conquering power the force of justice and wisdom . . . Blessed is the king who marcheth with the ensign of wisdom unfurled before him, and the battalions of justice massed in his rear. He verily is the ornament that adorneth the brow of peace and the countenance of security. There can be no doubt whatever that if the day star of justice, which the clouds of tyranny have obscured, were to shed its light upon men, the face of the earth would be completely transformed.[21]

Overstep not the bounds of moderation, and deal justly with them that serve thee. Bestow upon them according to their needs, and not to the extent that will enable them to lay up riches for themselves, to deck their persons, to embellish their homes, to acquire the things that are of no benefit unto them, and to be numbered with the extravagant. Deal with them with undeviating justice, so that none among them may either suffer want, or be pampered with luxuries. This is but manifest justice.

Allow not the abject to rule over and dominate them who are noble and worthy of honor, and suffer not the high-minded to be at the mercy of the contemptible and worthless, for this is what We observed upon Our arrival in the City (Constantinople), and to it We bear witness. We found among its inhabitants some who were possessed of an affluent fortune and lived in the midst of excessive riches, whilst others were in dire want and abject poverty. This ill beseemeth thy sovereignty, and is unworthy of thy rank.[22]

The sixth leaf of the Most Exalted Paradise is the following: The light of men is Justice. Quench it not with the contrary winds of oppression and tyranny. The purpose of justice is the appearance of unity among men. The ocean of divine wisdom surgeth within this exalted word, while the books of the world cannot contain its inner significance. Were mankind to be adorned with this raiment, they would behold the daystar of the utterance, 'On that day God will satisfy everyone out of His abundance', shining resplendent above the horizon of the world. Appreciate ye the value of this utterance; it is a noble fruit that the Tree of the Pen of Glory hath yielded. Happy is the man that giveth ear unto it and observeth its precepts. Verily I say, whatever is sent down from the heaven of the Will of God is the means for the establishment of order in the world and the instrument for promoting unity and fellowship among its peoples.[23]

Know that to do justice is to give to everyone according to his deserts. For example, when a workman labors from morning until evening, justice requires that he shall be paid his wages; but when he has done no work and taken no trouble, he is given a gift: this is bounty. If you give alms and gifts to a poor man although he has taken no trouble for you, nor done anything to deserve it, this is bounty. So Christ besought forgiveness for his murderers: this is called bounty.[24]

Consultation: Decision-making in the Knowledge World

O people of God! Give ear unto that which, if heeded, will ensure the freedom, well-being, tranquillity, exaltation and advancement of all men. Certain laws and principles are necessary and indispensable for Persia. However, it is fitting that these measures should be adopted in conformity with the considered views of His Majesty – may God aid him through His grace – and of the learned divines and of the high-ranking rulers. Subject to their approval a place should be fixed where they would meet. There they should hold fast to the cord of consultation and adopt and enforce that which is conducive to the security, prosperity, wealth and tranquillity of the people. For were any measure other than this to be adopted, it could not but result in chaos and commotion.[25]

Question: Concerning consultation.
Answer: If consultation among the first group of people assembled endeth in disagreement, new people should be added, after which persons to the number of the Greatest Name, or fewer or more, shall be chosen by lot. Whereupon the consultation shall be renewed, and the outcome, whatever it is, shall be obeyed. If, however, there is still disagreement, the same procedure should be repeated once more, and the decision of the majority shall prevail. He, verily, guideth whomsoever He pleaseth to the right way.[26]

Bahá'u'lláh has established consultation as one of the fundamental principles of His Faith and has exhorted the believers to 'take counsel together in all matters'. He describes consultation as 'the lamp of guidance which leadeth the way' and as 'the bestower of understanding'. Shoghi Effendi states that the 'principle of consultation . . . constitutes one of the basic laws' of the Bahá'í Administrative Order.

In Questions and Answers, number 99, Bahá'u'lláh outlines an approach to consultation and stresses the importance of achieving unanimity in decision-making, failing which the majority decision must prevail. The Universal House of Justice has clarified that this guidance concerning consultation was revealed before Spiritual Assemblies had been established and was in answer to a question about the Bahá'í teachings on consultation. The House of Justice affirms that the emergence of Spiritual Assemblies, to which the friends may always turn for assistance, in no way prohibits them from following the procedure outlined in Questions and Answers. This approach may be used by the friends, should they wish, when they desire to consult on their personal problems.[27]

Central to the task of reconceptualizing the system of human relationships is the process that Bahá'u'lláh refers to as consultation. 'In all things it is necessary to consult,' is His advice. 'The maturity of the gift of understanding is made manifest through consultation.'[28]

What Bahá'u'lláh is calling for is a consultative process in which the individual participants strive to transcend their respective points of view, in order to function as members of a body with its own interests and goals. In such an atmosphere, characterized by both candor and courtesy, ideas belong not to the individual to whom they occur during the discussion but to the group as a whole, to take up, discard, or revise as seems to best serve the goal pursued . . . Viewed in such a light, consultation is the operating expression of justice in human affairs. So vital is it . . . that it must constitute a basic feature of a viable strategy of social and economic development . . . [and] made the organizing principle of every project.[29]

. . . power has been largely interpreted as advantage enjoyed by persons or groups . . . This interpretation of power has become an inherent feature of the *culture of division* and conflict that has characterized the human race during the past several millennia, regardless of the social, religious, or political orientations that have enjoyed ascendancy in given ages, in given parts of the world. In general, power has been an *attribute of individuals, factions, peoples, classes, and nations.* It has been an attribute especially associated with *men rather than women.* Its chief effect has been to confer on its beneficiaries the ability to acquire, to surpass, to dominate, to resist, to win.[30]

The standard of truth seeking this process demands is far beyond the patterns of negotiation and compromise that tend to characterize the present-day discussion of human affairs. It cannot be achieved – indeed, its attainment is severely handicapped – by the *culture of protest* that is another widely prevailing feature of contemporary society. Debate, propaganda, the adversarial method, the entire apparatus of partisanship that have long been such familiar features of collective action are all fundamentally harmful to its purpose: that is, arriving at a consensus about the truth of a given situation and the wisest choice of action among the options open at any given moment.[31]

Unity: The Circle of Commitment

Unity is the expression of the loving power of God and reflects the reality of divinity. It is resplendent in this day through the bestowals of light upon humanity.[32]

This means the oneness of the world of humanity. That is to say, when this human body-politic reaches a state of absolute unity, the effulgence of the eternal Sun will make its fullest light and heat manifest. Therefore we must not make distinctions between individual members of the human family. We must not consider any soul as barren or deprived. Our duty lies in educating souls so that the Sun of the bestowals of God shall become resplendent in them, and this is possible through the power of the oneness of humanity. The more love is expressed among mankind and the stronger the power of unity, the greater will be this reflection and revelation, for the greatest bestowal of God is love. Love is the source of all the bestowals of God. Until love takes possession of the heart no other divine bounty can be revealed in it.[33]

Therefore it is our duty to put forth our greatest efforts and summon all our energies in order that the bonds of unity and accord may be established among mankind. For thousands of years we have had bloodshed and strife. It is enough; it is sufficient. Now is the time to associate together in love and harmony . . . Therefore unity is the essential truth of religion and when so understood embraces all the virtues of the human world. Praise be to God! this knowledge has been spread, eyes have been opened and ears have become attentive. Therefore we must endeavor to promulgate and practice the religion of God which has been founded by all the prophets. And the religion of God is absolute love and unity.[34]

The divine Manifestations since the day of Adam have striven to unite humanity so that all may be accounted as one soul. The function and purpose of a shepherd is to gather and not disperse his flock. The prophets of God have been divine shepherds of humanity. They have established a bond of love and unity among mankind, made scattered peoples one nation and wandering tribes a mighty kingdom. They have laid the foundation of the oneness of God and summoned all to universal peace. All these holy, divine Manifestations are one.[35]

Another unity is the spiritual unity which emanates from the breaths of the Holy Spirit. This is greater than the unity of mankind. Human unity or solidarity may be likened to the body whereas unity from the breaths of the Holy Spirit is the spirit animating the body. This is a perfect unity. It creates such a condition in mankind that each one will make sacrifices for the other and the utmost desire will be to forfeit life and all that pertains to it in behalf of another's good. This is the unity which existed among the disciples of His Holiness Jesus Christ and bound together the prophets and holy souls of the past. It is the unity which through the influence of the divine spirit is permeating the Bahá'ís so that each offers his life for the other and strives with all sincerity to attain his good-pleasure. This is the unity which caused twenty thousand people in Persia to give their lives in love and devotion to it. It made the Báb the target of a thousand arrows and caused Bahá'u'lláh to suffer exile and imprisonment forty years. This unity is the very spirit of the body of the world. It is impossible for the body of the world to become quickened with life without its vivification. His Holiness Jesus Christ – may my life be a sacrifice to him! – promulgated this unity among mankind. Every soul who believed in Jesus Christ became revivified and resuscitated through this spirit, attained to the zenith of eternal glory, realized the life everlasting, experienced the second birth and rose to the acme of good fortune.[36]

. . . Bahá'u'lláh compared the world to the human body . . . Paradoxically, it is precisely the wholeness and complexity of the order constituting the human body – and the perfect integration . . . that permit the full realization of the distinctive capacities inherent in each . . .[37]

Clearly, the advancement of the race has not occurred at the expense of human individuality. As social organization has increased, the scope for the expression of the capacities latent in each human being has correspondingly expanded. Because the relationships between the individual and society is a reciprocal one, the transformation now required must occur simultaneously within human consciousness and the structure of social institutions . . . that purpose must be to establish enduring foundations on which planetary civilization can gradually take shape.[38]

Moderation: Abolish Extremes of Wealth and Poverty

Put away all covetousness and seek contentment; for the covetous hath ever been deprived and the contented hath ever been loved and praised.[39]

It is quite otherwise with the human species, which persists in the greatest error, and in absolute iniquity. Consider an individual who has amassed treasures by colonizing a country for his profit: he has obtained an incomparable fortune and has secured profits and incomes which flow like a river, while a hundred thousand unfortunate people, weak and powerless, are in need of a mouthful of bread. There is neither equality nor benevolence. So you see that general peace and joy are destroyed, and the welfare of humanity is negated to such an extent as to make fruitless the lives of many. For fortune, honors, commerce, industry are in the hands of some industrialists, while other people are submitted to quite a series of difficulties and to limitless troubles: they have neither advantages, nor profits, nor comforts, nor peace.

Then rules and laws should be established to regulate the excessive fortunes of certain private individuals and meet the needs of millions of the poor masses; thus a certain moderation would be obtained. However, absolute equality is just as impossible, for absolute equality in fortunes, honors, commerce, agriculture, industry would end in disorderliness, in chaos, in disorganization of the means of existence, and in universal disappointment: the order of the community would be quite destroyed. Thus difficulties will also arise when unjustified equality is imposed. It is, therefore, preferable for moderation to be established by means of laws and regulations to hinder the constitution of the excessive fortunes of certain individuals, and to protect the essential needs of the masses. For instance, the manufacturers and the industrialists heap up a treasure each day, and the poor artisans do not gain their daily sustenance: that is the height of iniquity, and no just man can accept it. Therefore, laws and regulations should be established which would permit the workmen to receive from the factory owner their wages and a share in the fourth or the fifth part of the profits, according to the capacity of the factory; or in some other way the body of workmen and the manufacturers should share equitably the profits and advantages. Indeed, the capital and management come from the owner of the factory, and the work and labor, from the body of the workmen. Either the workmen should receive wages which assure them an adequate support and, when they cease work, becoming feeble or helpless, they should have sufficient benefits from the income of the industry; or the wages should be high enough to satisfy the workmen with the amount they receive so that they may themselves be able to put a little aside for days of want and helplessness.[40]

We see amongst us men who are overburdened with riches on the one hand, and on the other those unfortunate ones who starve with nothing; those who possess several stately palaces, and those who have not where to lay their head. Some we find with numerous courses of costly and dainty food; whilst others can scarce find sufficient crusts to keep them alive. Whilst some are clothed in velvets, furs and fine linen, others have insufficient, poor and thin garments with which to protect them from the cold.

This condition of affairs is wrong, and must be remedied. Now the remedy must be carefully undertaken. It cannot be done by bringing to pass absolute equality between men.

Equality is a chimera! It is entirely impracticable! Even if equality could be achieved it could not continue – and if its existence were possible, the whole order of the world would be destroyed. The law of order must always obtain in the world of humanity. Heaven has so decreed in the creation of man.

Some are full of intelligence, others have an ordinary amount of it, and others again are devoid of intellect. In these three classes of men there is order but not equality. How could it be possible that wisdom and stupidity should be equal? Humanity, like a great army, requires a general, captains, under-officers in their degree, and soldiers, each with their own appointed duties. Degrees are absolutely necessary to ensure an orderly organization. An army could not be composed of generals alone, or of captains only, or of nothing but soldiers without one in authority. The certain result of such a plan would be that disorder and demoralization would overtake the whole army.

King Lycurgus, the philosopher, made a great plan to equalize the subjects of Sparta; with self-sacrifice and wisdom was the experiment begun. Then the king called the people of his kingdom, and made them swear a great oath to maintain the same order of government if he should leave the country, also that nothing should make them alter it until his return. Having secured this oath, he left his kingdom of Sparta and never returned. Lycurgus abandoned the situation, renouncing his high position, thinking to achieve the permanent good of his country by the equalization of the property and of the conditions of life in his kingdom. All the self-sacrifice of the king was in vain. The great experiment failed. After a time all was destroyed; his carefully thought-out constitution came to an end.

The futility of attempting such a scheme was shown and the impossibility of attaining equal conditions of existence was proclaimed in the ancient kingdom of Sparta. In our day any such attempt would be equally doomed to failure.

Certainly, some being enormously rich and others lamentably poor, an organization is necessary to control and improve this state of affairs. It is important to limit riches, as it is also of importance to limit poverty. Either extreme is not good. To be seated in the mean is most desirable. If it be right for a capitalist to possess a large fortune, it is equally just that his workman should have a sufficient means of existence.

A financier with colossal wealth should not exist whilst near him is a poor man in dire necessity. When we see poverty allowed to reach a condition of starvation it is a sure sign that somewhere we shall find tyranny. Men must bestir themselves in this matter, and no longer delay in altering conditions which bring the misery of grinding poverty to a very large number of the people. The rich must give of their abundance, they must soften their hearts and cultivate a compassionate intelligence, taking thought for those sad ones who are suffering from lack of the very necessities of life.

There must be special laws made, dealing with these extremes of riches and of want. The members of the Government should consider the laws of God when they are framing plans for the ruling of the people. The general rights of mankind must be guarded and preserved.

The government of the countries should conform to the Divine Law which gives equal justice to all. This is the only way in which the deplorable superfluity of great wealth and miserable, demoralizing, degrading poverty can be abolished. Not until this is done will the Law of God be obeyed.[41]

But if conditions are such that some are happy and comfortable and some in misery; some are accumulating exorbitant wealth and others are in dire want – under such a system it is impossible for man to be happy and impossible for him to win the good pleasure of God. God is kind to all. The good pleasure of God consists in the welfare of all the individual members of mankind.[42]

As to the first, the tenths or tithes: we will consider a farmer, one of the peasants. We will look into his income. We will find out, for instance, what is his annual revenue and also what are his expenditures. Now, if his income be equal to his expenditures, from such a farmer nothing whatever will be taken. That is, he will not be subjected to taxation of any sort, needing as he does all his income. Another farmer may have expenses running up to one thousand dollars we will say, and his income is two thousand dollars. From such an one a tenth will be required, because he has a surplus. But if his income be ten thousand dollars and his expenses one thousand dollars or his income twenty thousand dollars, he will have to pay as taxes, one-fourth. If his income be one hundred thousand dollars and his expenses five thousand, one-third will he have to pay because he has still a surplus since his expenses are five thousand and his income one hundred thousand. If he pays, say, thirty-five thousand dollars, in addition to the expenditure of five thousand he still has sixty thousand left. But if his expenses be ten thousand and his income two hundred thousand then he must give an even half because ninety thousand will be in that case the sum remaining. Such a scale as this will determine allotment of taxes. All the income from such revenues will go to this general storehouse.[43]

World Citizenship: The Field of Action

The Revelation of Bahá'u'lláh, whose supreme mission is none other but the achievement of this organic and spiritual unity of the whole body of nations, should, if we be faithful to its implications, be regarded as signalizing through its advent the *coming of age of the entire human race*. It should be viewed not merely as yet another spiritual revival in the ever-changing fortunes of mankind, not only as a further stage in a chain of progressive Revelations, nor even as the culmination of one of a series of recurrent prophetic cycles, but rather as marking the last and highest stage in the stupendous evolution of man's collective life on this planet. The emergence of a world community, the consciousness of world citizenship, the founding of a world civilization and culture – all of which must synchronize with the initial stages in the unfoldment of the Golden Age of the Bahá'í Era – should, by their very nature, be regarded, as far as this planetary life is concerned, as the furthermost limits in the organization of human society, though man, as an individual, will, nay must indeed as a result of such a consummation, continue indefinitely to progress and develop.[44]

The decision-making agencies involved would do well to consider giving first priority to the education of women and girls, since it is through educated mothers that the benefits of knowledge can be most effectively and rapidly diffused throughout society. In keeping with the requirements of the times, consideration should also be given to teaching the concept of world citizenship as part of the standard education of every child.[45]

Some form of a world Super-State must needs be evolved, in whose favor all the nations of the world will have willingly ceded every claim to make war, certain rights to impose taxation and all rights to maintain armaments, except for purposes of maintaining internal order within their respective dominions. Such a state will have to include within its orbit an International Executive adequate to enforce supreme and unchallengeable authority on every recalcitrant member of the commonwealth; a World Parliament whose members shall be elected by the people in their respective countries and whose election shall be confirmed by their respective governments; and a Supreme Tribunal whose judgment will have a binding effect even in such cases where the parties concerned did not voluntarily agree to submit their case to its consideration. A world community in which all economic barriers will have been permanently demolished and the interdependence of Capital and Labor definitely recognized; in which the clamor of religious fanaticism and strife will have been forever stilled; in which the flame of racial animosity will have been finally extinguished; in which a single code of international law – the product of the considered judgment of the world's federated representatives – shall have as its sanction the instant and coercive intervention of the combined forces of the federated units; and finally a world community in which the fury of a capricious and militant nationalism will have been transmuted into an abiding consciousness of world citizenship – such indeed, appears, in its broadest outline, the

Order anticipated by Bahá'u'lláh, an Order that shall come to be regarded as the fairest fruit of a slowly maturing age.[46]

Universal Education: Building Social Capital

The tasks entailed in the development of a global society call for levels of capacity far beyond anything the human race has so far been able to muster. Reaching these levels will require an enormous expansion in access to knowledge, on the part of individuals and social organizations alike.[47]

Therefore, surely, God is not pleased that so important an instrument as woman should suffer from want of training in order to attain the perfections desirable and necessary for her great life's work! Divine Justice demands that the rights of both sexes should be equally respected since neither is superior to the other in the eyes of Heaven. Dignity before God depends, not on sex, but on purity and luminosity of heart. Human virtues belong equally to all!

Woman must endeavor then to attain greater perfection, to be man's equal in every respect, to make progress in all in which she has been backward, so that man will be compelled to acknowledge her equality of capacity and attainment.

In Europe women have made greater progress than in the East, but there is still much to be done! When students have arrived at the end of their school term an examination takes place, and the result thereof determines the knowledge and capacity of each student. So will it be with woman; her actions will show her power, there will no longer be any need to proclaim it by words.

It is my hope that women of the East, as well as their Western sisters, will progress rapidly until humanity shall reach perfection.

God's Bounty is for all and gives power for all progress. When men own the equality of women there will be no need for them to struggle for their rights! One of the principles then of Bahá'u'lláh is the equality of sex.

Women must make the greatest effort to acquire spiritual power and to increase in the virtue of wisdom and holiness until their enlightenment and striving succeeds in bringing about the unity of mankind. They must work with a burning enthusiasm to spread the Teaching of Bahá'u'lláh among the peoples, so that the radiant light of the Divine Bounty may envelop the souls of all the nations of the world![48]

The Function and Use of Money

His means of livelihood was his business partnership with me. That is, I provided him with a capital of three krans; with it he bought needles, and this was his stock-in-trade. The women of Nazareth gave him eggs in exchange for his needles and in this way he would obtain thirty or forty eggs a day: three needles per egg. Then he would sell the eggs and live on the proceeds. Since there was a daily caravan between 'Akká and Nazareth, he would refer to Áqá Riḍá each day, for more needles. Glory be to God! He survived two years on that initial outlay of capital; and he returned thanks at all times.[49]

Some years ago the following passage was revealed from the heaven of the All-Merciful in honor of the one who beareth the name of God, entitled Zaynu'l-Muqarrabín – upon him be the glory of the Most Glorious. He – exalted be His Word – saith: Many people stand in need of this. Because if there were no prospect for gaining interest, the affairs of men would suffer collapse or dislocation. One can seldom find a person who would manifest such consideration towards his fellow-man, his countryman or towards his own brother and would show such tender solicitude for him as to be well-disposed to grant him a loan on benevolent terms. Therefore as a token of favor towards men We have prescribed that interest on money should be treated like other business transactions that are current amongst men. Thus, now that this lucid commandment hath descended from the heaven of the Will of God, it is lawful and proper to charge interest on money, that the people of the world may, in a spirit of amity and fellowship and with joy and gladness, devotedly engage themselves in magnifying the Name of Him Who is the Well-Beloved of all mankind. Verily He ordaineth according to His Own choosing. He hath now made interest on money lawful, even as He had made it unlawful in the past. Within His grasp He holdeth the kingdom of authority. He doeth and ordaineth. He is in truth the Ordainer, the All-Knowing.[50]

No more trusts will remain in the future. The question of the trusts will be wiped away entirely. Also, every factory that has ten thousand shares will give two thousand shares of these ten thousand to its employees and will write the shares in their names, so that they may have them, and the rest will belong to the capitalists. Then at the end of the month or year whatever they may earn after the expenses and wages are paid, according to the number of shares, should be divided among both.[51]

In His later writings Bahá'u'lláh made explicit the implications of this principle for the age of humanity's maturity. 'Women and men have been and will always be equal in the sight of God,' He asserts, and the advancement of civilization requires that society so organize its affairs as to give full expression to this fact. The earth's resources are the property of all humanity, not of any one people. Different contributions to the common economic welfare deserve and should receive different measures of reward and recognition, but the extremes of wealth and poverty which afflict most nations on earth, regardless of the socio-economic philosophies they profess, must be abolished.[52]

For instance, the owners of properties, mines and factories should share their incomes with their employees and give a fairly certain percentage of their products to their workingmen in order that the employees may receive, beside their wages, some of the general income of the factory so that the employee may strive with his soul in the work.[53]

Since the body of humankind is one and indivisible, each member of the race is born into the world as a trust of the whole. This trusteeship constitutes the moral foundation of most of the other rights – principally economic and social . . . The security of the family and the home, the ownership of property, and the right to privacy are all implied in such a trusteeship. The obligations on the part of the community extend to the provision of employment, mental and physical health care, social security, fair wages, rest and recreation, and a host of other reasonable expectations on the part of the individual members of society.[54]

Therefore, laws and regulations should be established which would permit the workmen to receive from the factory owner their wages and a share in the fourth or the fifth part of the profits, according to the capacity of the factory; or in some other way the body of workmen and the manufacturers should share equitably the profits and advantages. Indeed, the capital and management come from the owner of the factory, and the work and labor, from the body of the workmen. Either the workmen should receive wages which assure them an adequate support and, when they cease work, becoming feeble or helpless, they should have sufficient benefits from the income of the industry; or the wages should be high enough to satisfy the workmen with the amount they receive so that they may themselves be able to put a little aside for days of want and helplessness.[55]

When matters will be thus fixed, the owner of the factory will no longer put aside daily a treasure which he has absolutely no need of (for, if the fortune is disproportionate, the capitalist succumbs under a formidable burden and gets into the greatest difficulties and troubles; the administration of an excessive fortune is very difficult and exhausts man's natural strength). And the workmen and artisans will no longer be in the greatest misery and want; they will no longer be submitted to the worst privations at the end of their life.[56]

It would be well, with regard to the common rights of manufacturers, workmen and artisans, that laws be established, giving moderate profits to manufacturers, and to workmen the necessary means of existence and security for the future. Thus when they become feeble and cease working, get old and helpless, or leave behind children under age, they and their children will not be annihilated by excess of poverty. And it is from the income of the factory itself, to which they have a right, that they will derive a share, however small, toward their livelihood.[57]

The Design of Work

Armed with the strength of action and the cooperation of the individual believers composing it, the community as a whole should endeavor to establish greater stability in the patterns of its development, locally and nationally, through sound, systematic planning and execution of its work – and this, in striking contrast to the short-lived enthusiasms and frenetic superficialities so characteristic of present-day American life. A Bahá'í community which is consistent in its fundamental life-giving, life-sustaining activities will at its heart be serene and confident; it will resonate with spiritual dynamism, will exert irresistible influence, will set a new course in social evolution, enabling it to win the respect and eventually the allegiance of admirers and critics alike.[58]

The eagerness of the friends to serve often carries them away, and they forget that a sound sense of business management is also much needed, if we are to harbor our resources and accomplish all our goals.[59]

Projects should be properly organized from the outset with the participants' roles, responsibilities and lines of authority clearly understood by all. The work to be done should be broken down into activities with schedules and, where necessary, estimated resources required. The level of detail should be commensurate with the complexity of the project, and should be as simple as possible.

The aim of community self-reliance should be kept constantly in mind and care should be taken to ensure that projects do not become self-serving. Local authorities should be kept informed, all local labor regulations and other laws observed, and permits and permissions obtained where required.

A project record should be kept so that important events, decisions and actions taken are recorded promptly and accurately. Finances should be handled with scrupulous attention to accuracy, and financial records kept in a manner that will facilitate subsequent auditing.

Regular project reviews should be held at which the progress of the work and expenditures are discussed and compared with planned schedules and cash flows. Future plans and schedules should be adjusted where necessary through experience gained.

Where resources from outside the community are used in a project, the supporting agency (Bahá'í or non-Bahá'í) should receive regular reports according to procedures agreed upon at the outset.

Some projects may have a short-term objective and should be brought to a clear termination point. All records should be brought up to date, any material and equipment properly disposed of and care taken of project records. Local authorities should be notified and thanked where appropriate. A factual project report should be written recording significant events and deviations from the original plans, to provide data for the project evaluation.[60]

It is also worth remembering that projects may need amendment to or alteration of their objectives as operational experience may show. The need for such changes can only be realized if constant monitoring is carried out and is accepted as a component part of the project.[61]

Organization Structure

As a national community grows, the activities undertaken by its members also increase in number and diversity. Some of these activities will be initiated and administered by the Bahá'í institutions. Others will fall in the realm of private initiative. When an initiative is in the form of a private business venture undertaken by an individual or a group, the institutions of the Faith have little reason to interfere with its daily affairs. In general, only if difficulties arise among the friends involved in such an enterprise, if their activities could damage the good name of the Faith, or if they misrepresent their relationship to the Faith, would a Local or National Spiritual Assembly intervene. Bahá'í institutions should, of course, welcome any effort by such private ventures to apply the Teachings to their operations and to use their position in society to further the interests of the Faith. Spiritual Assemblies would do well to offer them guidance as requested or as circumstances require, and to help them develop their potential for the advancement of the Cause . . .[62]

Human Resource Systems

It is in the context of raising the level of human capacity through the expansion of knowledge at all levels that the economic issues facing humankind need to be addressed . . . The most important role that economic efforts must play in development lies, therefore, in equipping people and institutions with the means through which they can achieve the real purpose of development: that is, laying foundations for a new social order that can cultivate the limitless potentialities latent in human consciousness.[63]

A central challenge, therefore – and an enormous one – is the expansion of scientific and technological activity. Instruments of social and economic change so powerful must cease to be the patrimony of advantaged segments of society, and must be so organized as to permit people everywhere to participate in such activity on the basis of capacity.[64]

The third requirement of perfection is to arise with complete sincerity and purity of purpose to educate the masses: to exert the utmost effort to instruct them in the various branches and useful sciences, to encourage the development of modern progress, to *widen the scope of commerce, industry and the arts, to further such measures as will increase the people's wealth.* For the mass of the population is uninformed as to these *vital agencies which would constitute an immediate remedy for society's chronic ills.*[65]

In the Bolshevistic principles equality is effected through force. The masses who are opposed to the people of rank and to the wealthy class desire to partake of their advantages.

But in the divine teachings equality is brought about through a ready willingness to share. It is commanded as regards wealth that the rich among the people, and the aristocrats should, by their own free will and for the sake of their own happiness, concern themselves with and care for the poor. This equality is the result of the lofty characteristics and noble attributes of mankind.[66]

Information Systems

Since, then, the challenge is the empowerment of humankind through a vast increase in access to knowledge, the strategy that can make this possible must be constructed around an ongoing and intensifying dialogue between science and religion. It is – or by now should be – a truism that, in every sphere of human activity and at every level, the insights and skills that represent scientific accomplishment must look to the force of spiritual commitment and moral principle to ensure their appropriate application. People need, for example, to learn how to separate fact from conjecture – indeed to distinguish between subjective views and objective reality; the extent to which individuals and institutions so equipped can contribute to human progress, however, will be determined by their devotion to truth and their detachment from the promptings of their own interests and passions. Another capacity that science must cultivate in all people is that of thinking in terms of process, including historical process; however, if this intellectual advancement is to contribute ultimately to promoting development, its perspective must be unclouded by prejudices of race, culture, sex, or sectarian belief. Similarly, the training that can make it possible for the earth's inhabitants to participate in the production of wealth will advance the aims of development only to the extent that such an impulse is illumined by the spiritual insight that service to humankind is the purpose of both individual life and social organization.[67]

. . . the accelerating revolution in communication technologies now brings information and training within reach of vast numbers of people around the globe, wherever they may be, whatever their cultural backgrounds.[68]

Reward and Recognition

In the conduct of life, man is actuated by two main motives: 'The Hope for Reward' and 'The Fear of Punishment'.

This hope and this fear must consequently be greatly taken into account by those in authority who have important posts under Government. Their business in life is to consult together for the framing of laws, and to provide for their just administration.

The tent of the order of the world is raised and established on the two pillars of 'Reward and Retribution'.[69]

Now punishments and rewards are said to be of two kinds. Firstly, the rewards and punishments of this life; secondly, those of the other world. But the paradise and hell of existence are found in all the worlds of God, whether in this world or in the spiritual heavenly worlds. Gaining these rewards is the gaining of eternal life. That is why Christ said, 'Act in such a way that you may find eternal life, and that you may be born of water and the spirit, so that you may enter into the Kingdom.'[70]

The rewards of this life are the virtues and perfections which adorn the reality of man. For example, he was dark and becomes luminous, he was ignorant and becomes wise, he was neglectful and becomes vigilant, he was asleep and becomes awakened, he was dead and becomes living, he was blind and becomes a seer, he was deaf and becomes a hearer, he was earthly and becomes heavenly, he was material and becomes spiritual. Through these rewards he gains spiritual birth, and becomes a new creature.[71]

Sincerity is the foundation-stone of faith. That is, a religious individual must disregard his personal desires and seek in whatever way he can wholeheartedly to serve the public interest; and it is impossible for a human being to turn aside from his own selfish advantages and sacrifice his own good for the good of the community except through true religious faith. For self-love is kneaded into the very clay of man, and it is not possible that, without any hope of a substantial reward, he should neglect his own present material good. That individual, however, who puts his faith in God and believes in the words of God – because he is promised and certain of a plentiful reward in the next life, and because worldly benefits as compared to the abiding joy and glory of future planes of existence are nothing to him – will for the sake of God abandon his own peace and profit and will freely consecrate his heart and soul to the common good.[72]

The generality of mankind are unable to grasp a sequence of logical arguments. For this reason they stand in need of symbols and parables telling of rewards and punishments in the next world.[73]

On Leadership

Now some of the mischief-makers, with many stratagems, are seeking leadership, and in order to reach this position they instill doubts among the friends that they may cause differences, and that these differences may result in their drawing a party to themselves. But the friends of God must be awake and must know that the scattering of these doubts hath as its motive personal desires and the achievement of leadership.[74]

Consider these martyrs of unquestionable sincerity, to whose truthfulness testifieth the explicit text of the Book, and all of whom, as thou hast witnessed, have sacrificed their life, their substance, their wives, their children, their all, and ascended unto the loftiest chambers of Paradise. Is it fair to reject the testimony of these detached and exalted beings to the truth of this pre-eminent and Glorious Revelation, and to regard as acceptable the denunciations which have been uttered against this resplendent Light by this faithless people, who for gold have forsaken their faith, and who for the sake of leadership have repudiated Him Who is the First Leader of all mankind?[75]

Behold how the divine Touchstone hath, according to the explicit text of the Book, separated and distinguished the true from the false. Notwithstanding, they are still oblivious of this truth, and in the sleep of heedlessness, are pursuing the vanities of the world, and are occupied with thoughts of vain and earthly leadership.[76]

Beware lest Thou become occupied with the mention of those from whom naught save the noisome savors of enmity can be perceived, those who are so enslaved by their lust for leadership that they would not hesitate to destroy themselves in their desire to emblazon their fame and perpetuate their names.[77]

Leaders of religion, in every age, have hindered their people from attaining the shores of eternal salvation, inasmuch as they held the reins of authority in their mighty grasp. Some for the lust of leadership, others through want of knowledge and understanding, have been the cause of the deprivation of the people.[78]

The religious doctors of every age have been the cause of preventing the people from the shore of the Sea of Oneness, for the reins of the people were in their control. Some among them have hindered the people by love of leadership and some by lack of wisdom and knowledge.[79]

The Bahá'í community has entered a new stage in its external affairs work with an impressive record of success at a time when widespread disorder has thrust society into a worsening disequilibrium. A feeling of rudderless-ness looms as world leaders seem unable to provide coherent answers to the questions of the times. There is a sense of a vacuum in the absence of any moral leadership. Despite all this, or because of it, people in various countries are increasingly seeking alternative means of asserting themselves.[80]

The Lesser Peace anticipated by Bahá'u'lláh will, of course, be established by the nations themselves. It seems clear that two entities will push for its realization: the governments of the world, and the peoples of the world through the instrumentality of the organizations of civil society. But to lend spiritual impetus to the momentum which that grand attainment will generate, the need for a Bahá'í strategy is evident. One of its expressions should be the exertion of a kind of leadership, principally a moral leadership, by coherently, comprehensively and continually imparting our ideas for the advancement of civilization, and this through a unified voice that because of the diverse composition of our community could come to be regarded as representative of the aspirations of the peoples of the world.[81]

Basically, 'people of capacity' are those individuals, no matter in what walk of life they are found, and no matter what their level of education, who demonstrate capacity in various ways. For example, among any group of people there are those who are outstanding because they show a capacity for understanding, for work, for efficient action, for leadership, for drawing other people together, for self-sacrificing and devoted service – for any number of qualities which enable them to respond actively to the needs of their environment and make a difference to it.[82]

The first quality for leadership, both among individuals and Assemblies, is the capacity to use the energy and competence that exists in the rank and file of its followers. Otherwise the more competent members of the group will go at a tangent and try to find elsewhere a field of work and where they could use their energy.

Shoghi Effendi hopes that the Assemblies will do their utmost in planning such teaching activities that every single soul will be kept busy.[83]

There is certainly a place in the Cause for outstanding people, and we need more of them. But the administration must function on a consultative basis, not leadership.[84]

He feels the importance of young believers taking an active part in every field of service cannot be overestimated, for they must carry on the great work of reconstruction into the future, which will be in dire need of spiritual example and leadership.[85]

These same fiery tribulations will not only firmly weld the American nation to its sister nations in both hemispheres, but will through their cleansing effect, purge it thoroughly of the accumulated dross which ingrained racial prejudice, rampant materialism, widespread ungodliness and moral laxity have combined, in the course of successive generations, to produce, and which have prevented her thus far from assuming the role of world spiritual leadership forecast by 'Abdu'l-Bahá's unerring pen – a role which she is bound to fulfill through travail and sorrow.[86]

Naturally, old ways of exercising power and authority must give way to new forms of leadership. Our concept of leadership will need to be recast to include the ability to foster collective decision-making and collective action. It will find its highest expression in service to the community as a whole.[87]

Those who wield authority bear a great responsibility to be worthy of public trust. Leaders – including those in government, politics, business, religion, education, the media, the arts and community organizations – must be willing to be held accountable for the manner in which they exercise their authority. Trustworthiness and an active morality must become the foundation for all leadership if true progress is to be achieved. *Moral leadership*, the leadership of the future, will find its highest expression in service to others and to the community as a whole. It will foster collective decision-making and collective action and will be motivated by a commitment to justice, including the equality of women and men, and to the well-being of all humanity. Moral leadership will manifest itself in adherence to a single standard of conduct in both public and private life, for leaders and for citizens alike.[88]

Good governance is essential to social progress. While governance is often equated with government, it in fact involves much more. Governance occurs on all levels and encompasses the ways that formal government, non-governmental groups, community organizations and the private sector manage resources and affairs. Good governance is necessary if communities are to maintain their equilibrium, steer themselves through difficulties, and respond creatively to the challenges and opportunities ahead. Three factors that largely determine the state of governance are the quality of leadership, the quality of the governed and the quality of the structures and processes in place.[89]

The attitude of the individual as a servant, an attitude pre-eminently exemplified in the life and person of 'Abdu'l-Bahá, is a dynamic that permeates the activities of the Faith; it acquires collective, transformative force in the normal functioning of a community. In this regard, the institutions of the Faith stand as channels for the promotion of this salient characteristic. It is in this framework that the concepts of rulership and leadership, authority and power are properly understood and actualized.[90]

In your openness and candor you will, no doubt, avoid ineptitudes that pass as norms in the freedom of speech practiced in your nation. In a society where 'telling it like it is' employs a style of expression which robs language of its decorum, and in a time when stridency is commonly presumed to be a quality of leadership, candor is crass, and authority speaks in a loud and vulgar voice. People are frequently obliged to receive direction from their leaders in such disrespectful modes; this is a reason for resentment and suspicion towards those in authority. By contrast, Bahá'í institutions have the task of accustoming the friends to recognizing the expression of authority in language at a moderate pitch.[91]

With regard to the harmony of science and religion, the Writings of the Central Figures and the commentaries of the Guardian make abundantly clear that the task of humanity, including the Bahá'í community that serves as the 'leaven' within it, is to create a global civilization which embodies both the spiritual and material dimensions of existence. The nature and scope of such a civilization are still beyond anything the present generation can conceive. The prosecution of this vast enterprise will depend on a progressive interaction between the truths and principles of religion and the discoveries and insights of scientific inquiry. This entails living with ambiguities as a natural and inescapable feature of the process of exploring reality. It also requires us not to limit science to any particular school of thought or methodological approach postulated in the course of its development. The challenge facing Bahá'í thinkers is to provide responsible leadership in this endeavor, since it is they who have both the priceless insights of the Revelation and the advantages conferred by scientific investigation.[92]

Bibliography

'Abdu'l-Bahá. *Foundations of World Unity*. Wilmette, IL: Bahá'í Publishing Trust, 1945.

— *Memorials of the Faithful*. Wilmette, IL: Bahá'í Publishing Trust, 1971.

— *Paris Talks*. London: Bahá'í Publishing Trust, 1967.

— *The Promulgation of Universal Peace*. Wilmette, IL: Bahá'í Publishing Trust, 1982.

— *The Secret of Divine Civilization*. Wilmette, IL: Bahá'í Publishing Trust, 1990.

— *Selections from the Writings of 'Abdu'l-Bahá*. Haifa: Bahá'í World Centre, 1978.

— *Some Answered Questions*. Wilmette, IL: Bahá'í Publishing Trust, 1981.

Abdul Baha on Divine Philosophy. Boston: The Tudor Press, 1918.

'Abdu'l-Bahá in London. London: Bahá'í Publishing Trust, 1987.

Albrecht, Karl and Lawrence J. Bradford. *The Service Advantage: How to Identify and Fulfill Customer Needs*. New York: Dow Jones Irwin, 1990.

Ashkenas, Ron, Dave Ulrich, Todd Jick and Steve Kerr. *The Boundaryless Organization: Breaking the Chains of Organizational Structure*. New York: Jossey-Bass, 1995.

Bahá'í International Community. *Bahá'u'lláh*. New York: Bahá'í International Community Office of Public Information, 1991 (this edition London: Bahá'í Publishing Trust, 1991).

— *The Prosperity of Humankind*. London: Bahá'í Publishing Trust, 1995.

— *Sustainable Communities in an Integrating World*. A statement presented to the United Nations Conference on Human Settlements (Habitat II), Istanbul, Turkey, 3–14 June 1996, BIC Document no. 96–0530.

— *Valuing Spirituality in Development: Initial Considerations Regarding the Creation of Spiritually Based Indicators for Development*. London: Bahá'í Publishing Trust, 1998. A concept paper presented to the 'World Faiths and Development Dialogue' hosted by the President of the World Bank and the Archbishop of Canterbury at Lambeth Palace, London, 18–19 February 1998.

— *World Citizenship: A Global Ethic for Sustainable Development*. Based on a concept paper shared at the 1st session of the United Nations Commission on Sustainable Development, New York, 14–25 June 1993.

Bahai Scriptures. New York: Brentano's, 1923.

Bahá'í World Faith. Wilmette, IL: Bahá'í Publishing Trust, 2nd edn. 1976.

Bahá'u'lláh. *Gleanings from the Writings of Bahá'u'lláh*. Wilmette, IL: Bahá'í Publishing Trust, 1983.

— *The Hidden Words*. Wilmette, IL: Bahá'í Publishing Trust, 1990.

— *The Kitáb-i-Aqdas*. Haifa: Bahá'í World Centre, 1992.

— *Kitáb-i-Íqán*. Wilmette, IL: Bahá'í Publishing Trust, 1989.

— *The Summons of the Lord of Hosts: Tablets of Bahá'u'lláh*. Haifa: Bahá'í World Centre, 2002.

— *Tablets of Bahá'u'lláh*. Wilmette, IL: Bahá'í Publishing Trust, 1988.

Bakke, Dennis W. *Joy at Work: A Revolutionary Approach to Fun on the Job*. Seattle: PVG, 2005.

Balyuzi, H. M. *'Abdu'l-Bahá: The Centre of the Covenant of Bahá'u'lláh*. Oxford: George Ronald, 2nd edn. with minor corr. 1987.

Chappell, Tom. *The Soul of a Business: Managing for Profit and the Common Good*. New York: Bantam Books, 1993.

Collins, Jim. *Good to Great: Why Some Companies Make the Leap . . . and Others Don't*. New York: Harper Business, 2001.

The Compilation of Compilations. Prepared by the Universal House of Justice 1963–1990. 2 vols. [Mona Vale NSW]: Bahá'í Publications Australia, 1991.

Covey, Stephen R. *The 7 Habits of Highly Successful People*. New York, Free Press, 1990.

— *The 8th Habit: From Effectiveness to Greatness*. New York: Free Press, 2004.

Csikszentmihalyi, Mihaly. *Flow: The Psychology of Optimal Experience*. New York: Harper & Row, 1990.

Davidow, William H. and Michael S. Malone. *The Virtual Corporation*. New York: Harper Business, 1992.

Deming, W. Edwards. *Out of the Crisis*. Cambridge, MA: MIT Center for Advanced Engineering Studies, 1986.

Drucker, Peter. *Post-Capitalist Society*. New York: Harper Business, 1993.
— *The Unseen Revolution: How Pension Fund Socialism Came to America*. New York: Harper & Row, 1976.

Final Report of the Scholars Commission on the Jefferson-Hemings Matter, 12 April 2001.

Franklin, Benjamin. Letter to Ezra Stiles, 9 March 1790.

Fukuyama, Francis. *Trust: The Social Virtues & the Creation of Prosperity*. New York: Free Press, 1995.

Greenleaf, Robert K. *Servant as Leader*. Indianapolis, IN: Robert K. Greenleaf Center, 1982.
— *Servant Leadership: A Journey into the Nature of Legitimate Power and Greatness*. New York: Paulist Press, 1977.

Gunther, Marc. *Faith and Fortune: The Quiet Revolution to Reform American Business*. New York: Crown Business, 2004.

Hamilton, Alexander. 'The Farmer Refuted' (23 February 1775), in Syrett, Harold C. et al. (eds.). *The Papers of Alexander Hamilton*. 26 vols. New York and London: Columbia University Press, 1961–79.

Hammer, Michael and James Champy. *Reeingineering the Corporation: A Manifesto for Business Revolution*. New York: Harper Business, 1993.

Herzberg, Frederick. *Work and the Nature of Man*. New York: World Publishing, 1966.

Holy Bible. King James Version. London: Collins, 1839.

Ives, Howard Colby. *Portals to Freedom*. Oxford: George Ronald, 1973.

Jefferson, Thomas. Letter to John Adams, 22 August 1813.
— Letter to Mrs Samuel H. Smith, 6 August 1816.

Journal of Organizational Behavior Management. The official journal of the OBM Network, a Special Interest Group of the Association for Behavior Analysis.

Lights of Guidance: A Bahá'í Reference File. Compiled by Helen Hornby. New Delhi: Bahá'í Publishing Trust, 2nd edn. 1988.

Marcic, Dorothy. *Managing with the Wisdom of Love: Uncovering Virtue in People and Organizations*. San Francisco, CA: Jossey-Bass, 1997.

McGregor, Douglas M. *The Human Side of Enterprise*. New York: McGraw-Hill, 1960.

Meyer, M. Scott. *Every Employee a Manager*. New York: McGraw-Hill, 1970.

Miller, Lawrence M. *Barbarians to Bureaucrats: Corporate Life Cycle Strategies*. New York: Clarkson Potter, 1989.

Naisbitt, John. *Global Paradox*. New York: William Morrow, 1994.

Needleman, Jacob. *Money and the Meaning of Life*. New York: Currency-Doubleday, 1991.

Office of Social and Economic Development. 'The Evolution of Institutional Capacity for Social and Economic Development'. Prepared by the Office of Social and Economic Development, Bahá'í World Centre, 28 August 1994.

— 'Some Guidelines for SED Projects'. Bahá'í World Centre, December 1985.

Ohmae, Kenichi. *The End of the Nation State*. New York: Free Press, 1995.

Ohno, Taiichi and Setsuo Mito. *Just-In-Time for Today and Tomorrow.* Cambridge, MA: Productivity Press, 1986.

Paine, Thomas. *The Age of Reason*. Mineola, NY: Dover Publications, 2004.

Pande, Peter S., Robert P. Newman and Roland R. Cavanagh, *The Six Sigma Way Team Fieldbook: An Implementation Guide for Process Improvement Teams*. New York: McGraw-Hill, 2001.

Perry, Mark. *Grant and Twain: The Story of an American Friendship*. New York: Random House, 2005.

Quinn, James Brian. *The Intelligent Enterprise*. New York: Free Press, 1992.

Reder, Alan. *75 Best Business Practices for Socially Responsible Companies*. New York: G.P. Putnam & Sons, 1995.

Schonberger, Richard J. *Building a Chain of Customers*. New York: Free Press, 1990.

Seligman, Martin E.P. *Authentic Happiness*. New York: Free Press, 2002.

Senge, Peter. *Fifth Discipline: The Art & Practice of the Learning*

Organization. New York: Currency–Doubleday, 1990.
— C. Otto Scharmer, Joseph Jaworski, Betty Sue Flowers. *Presence: Human Purpose and the Field of the Future*. Cambridge, MA: SOL, 2004.

Shenk, Joshua Wolf. 'Lincoln's Great Depression'. *The Atlantic Monthly*, October 2005.

Shewhart, W.A. *Economic Control of Quality of Manufactured Product*. New York: D. Van Nostrand, 1931.

Shoghi Effendi. *The Advent of Divine Justice*. Wilmette, IL: Bahá'í Publishing Trust, 1990.
— *Bahá'í Administration*. Wilmette, IL: Bahá'í Publishing Trust, 1968.
— *Citadel of Faith: Messages to America 1947–1957*. Wilmette, IL: Bahá'í Publishing Trust, 1965.
— *The Light of Divine Guidance: The Messages from the Guardian of the Bahá'í Faith to the Bahá'ís of Germany and Austria*. 2 vols. Hofheim-Langenhain: Bahá'í-Verlag, 1982.
— *The World Order of Bahá'u'lláh*. Wilmette, IL: Bahá'í Publishing Trust, 1991.

Smith, Adam. *The Wealth of Nations*. New York: Pelican Books, 1970. First published 1776.

Stack, Jack. *The Great Game of Business*. New York: Doubleday, 1992.

Tapscott, Don. *The Digital Economy*. New York: McGraw-Hill, 1998.

Toynbee, Arnold. *A Study of History*, vol.11. London: Oxford University Press, 1947–57.

Trist, E. and C. Higgins, H. Murray and A. Pollock. *Organizational Choice*. London: Tavistock Institute, 1963.

The Universal of Justice. *Individual Rights and Freedoms in the World Order of Bahá'u'lláh*. Wilmette IL: Bahá'í Publishing Trust, 1989.
— *The Promise of World Peace*. London: Bahá'í Publishing Trust, 1985.
— *Scholarship and Related Subjects*, 20 July 1997.
— *A Wider Horizon: Selected Messages of the Universal House of Justice 1983–1992*. Riviera Beach, FL: Palabra Publications, 1992.

Letters of the Universal House of Justice to:
National Spiritual Assemblies, Naw-Rúz 1974.
National Spiritual Assemblies, 10 October 1994.
The Conference of the Continental Boards of Counsellors, 9 January 2001.

Washington, George. Letter to the Ministers, Elders, Deacons, and Members of the Reformed German Congregation of New York, 27 November 1783.

Wells, H.G. *The Outline of History*. Garden City, NY: Doubleday, 1971.

Wilson, Edward O. *On Human Nature*. Cambridge, MA: Harvard University Press, 1978.

Womack, James P. and Daniel T. Jones. *Lean Thinking: Banishing Waste and Create Wealth in Your Corporation*. New York: Simon & Schuster, 1996.

— Daniel T. Jones and Daniel Roos. *The Machine that Changed the World*. New York: Rawson Associates, 1990.

Wright, Robert. *Nonzero – The Logic of Human Destiny*. New York: Vintage Books, 2000.

www.esopassociation.org (accessed 1 September 2006).

www.greenleaf.org/leadership/servant-leadership/What-is-Servant-Leadership.html (accessed 1 September 2006).

www.nationmaster.com/graph-T/eco_pat_gra

www.nceo.org/library (accessed 1 September 2006).

www.tyco.com/livesite/Page/Tyco/Our+Commitment/Governance/Letter+from+Ed+Breen/ (accessed 1 September 2006).

References and Notes

Preface

1. www.nationmaster.com/graph-T/eco_pat_gra
2. Throughout this book you will see many quotations taken from the writings of Bahá'u'lláh (founder of the Bahá'í Faith), 'Abdu'l-Bahá (son of Bahá'u'lláh and the Interpreter of His teachings), Shoghi Effendi (Guardian of the Bahá'í Faith) and the Universal House of Justice (the supreme governing body of the religion). All of these are considered 'authoritative' by members of the Bahá'í Faith. Collectively they are given the same authority of divine guidance that is given to the Bible and the Qur'án. If the reader is not familiar with the central figures and institutions of the Bahá'í Faith it would be helpful to refer to www.bahai.org where you will find a reliable description of each of these figures, the teachings of the Faith and an overview of its administration, laws and institutions.

Chapter 1

1. Bahá'u'lláh, *Gleanings*, pp. 165–6.
2. Wright, *Nonzero – The Logic of Human Destiny*.
3. Bahá'í International Community, *Prosperity of Humankind*, p. 25.
4. http://www.rim.edu.bt/rigphel/rigphel2/gnh.htm. From Bhutan 2020: 'A Vision for Peace, Prosperity and Happiness – Central Development Concept: Maximizing Gross National Happiness. The concept of Gross National Happiness was articulated by His Majesty to indicate that development has many more dimensions than those associated with Gross Domestic Product, and that development should be understood as a process that seeks to maximize happiness rather than economic growth. The concept places the individual at the center of all development efforts, and it recognizes that the individual has material, spiritual and emotional needs. It asserts that spiritual development cannot and should not be defined exclusively in material terms of the increased consumption of goods and services.

   'GNH is founded in the belief that human happiness is a composite satisfaction of both the material and the non-material needs.

It rejects the view that there is a direct and unambiguous relationship between human happiness and economic growth. Blind consumption and wealth accumulation do not necessarily enhance happiness.

'One of the prime focuses of Bhutanese culture is spiritual development. Bhutanese culture would constitute the external manifestations as well as the conscious refinement of the mind, which is the essence of spiritual development. Hence culture promotion is an expansive concept inasmuch as it includes spiritual development. Lyonpo Jigmi alludes to this relationship of the culture and spiritual development when he says, "Within Bhutanese culture, inner spiritual development is as prominent a focus as external material development."'

5. Bahá'u'lláh, *Gleanings*, p. 297.
6. Fukuyama, *Trust*.
7. ibid. p. 7.
8. ibid. p. 47.
9. Shoghi Effendi, in *Compilation*, vol. 1, p. 174, no. 342.
10. 'Abdu'l-Bahá. quoted in Shoghi Effendi, *Advent of Divine Justice*, p. 26.
11. At the end of each chapter there will be a series of questions that ask the reader to apply the principle discussed in that chapter to some management functions or practices. These questions are not ones with simple right/wrong answers. It is not a test. Rather, they are intended to exercise the muscle of judgment, wisdom and intellectual inquiry. Each of the questions represents real world situations that the author has encountered, or is very similar to ones he has encountered. It is hoped that these may be used in a form of study circle established to assist those who work in organizations to explore the principles as they may apply to their own organizations. If in any case you find that there is a quick and simple right or wrong answer, you have probably not understood the question.

Chapter 2

1. 'Abdu'l-Bahá, *Promulgation*, p. 465.
2. Bahá'u'lláh, *Gleanings*, p. 92.
3. ibid. p. 250.
4. Bahá'u'lláh, *Hidden Words*, Arabic no. 3.
5. From a letter written on behalf of Shoghi Effendi, in Bahá'u'lláh, *Kitáb-i-Aqdas*, Notes, no. 56, p. 192.
6. Greenleaf, *Servant Leadership*.
7. Albrecht and Bradford, *The Service Advantage*.

8. 'Abdu'l-Bahá, *Promulgation*, pp. 238–9.
9. Covey, *The 8th Habit*, p. 117.

Chapter 3

1. Bahá'u'llah, *Hidden Words*, Arabic no. 2.
2. Bahá'í International Community, *Prosperity of Humankind*, p. 9.
3. Smith, *Wealth of Nations*. First published in 1776.
4. 'Abdu'l-Bahá, *Some Answered Questions*, p. 273.
5. ibid. p. 276.
6. 'Abdu'l-Bahá, *Selections*, p. 158.
7. Bahá'í International Community, *Prosperity of Humankind*, p. 9.
8. Bahá'u'lláh, *Kitáb-i-Aqdas*, p. 91.
9. 'Abdu'l-Bahá, *Promulgation*, p. 217.
10. Note that before considering what you 'should' do or what is wise to do, you may want to consider that, depending on your location, there may be legal requirements. Many countries have created laws to protect employees from unjust termination or other unjust treatment. You should, of course, be familiar with and comply with those laws.
11. 'Abdu'l-Bahá, *Promulgation*, p. 108.
12. Wright, *Nonzero – The Logic of Human Destiny*.
13. 'Abdu'l-Bahá, *Promulgation*, p. 132.
14. Seligman, *Authentic Happiness*.
15. 'Abdu'l-Bahá, *Promulgation*, p. 132.

Chapter 4

1. Bahá'í International Community, *Prosperity of Humankind*, p. 15.
2. 'Abdu'l-Bahá, *Promulgation*, pp. 72–3.
3. Bahá'í International Community, *Prosperity of Humankind*, pp. 15–16.
4. Collins, *Good to Great*, p. 21.
5. There are many books on quality management or team problem-solving. A good starting point might be *The Six Sigma Way Team Fieldbook* by Peter S. Pande, Robert P. Newman and Roland R. Cavanagh, published by McGraw-Hill.
6. Bahá'í International Community, *Prosperity of Humankind*, pp. 15–16.
7. Balyuzi, *'Abdu'l-Bahá*, p. 27.

Chapter 5

1. *'Abdu'l-Bahá in London*, p. 28.
2. 'Abdu'l-Bahá, in *Bahá'í World Faith*, pp. 284–5.

3. From an interview with 'Abdu'l-Bahá, in *'Abdu'l-Bahá in London*, p. 114.
4. 'Abdu'l-Bahá , in ibid. p. 19.
5. 'Abdu'l-Bahá, in *Bahá'í World Faith*, p. 233.
6. Stack, *Great Game of Business*.
7. Bahá'í International Community, *Prosperity of Humankind*, pp. 6–7.
8. ibid. pp. 7–8.
9. Miller, *Wisdom of One*.
10. Wright, *Nonzero*, p. 19.
11. Csikszentmihalyi, *Flow*, p. 3.

Chapter 6

1. Bahá'u'lláh, *Gleanings*, p. 251.
2. 'Abdu'l-Bahá, *Selections*, p. 88.
3. Abdu'l-Bahá, *Foundations of World Unity*, p. 41.
4. Drucker, *Post-Capitalist Society*, p. 8.
5. Abdu'l-Bahá, *Foundations of World Unity*, pp. 39–41.
6. 'Abdu'l-Bahá, *Some Answered Questions*, p. 274.
7. The Universal House of Justice, *Individual Rights and Freedoms*, para. 13.
8. ibid. paras. 55-6.

Chapter 7

1. Ohmae, *End of the Nation State*, p. 11.
2. Naisbitt, *Global Paradox*, p. 14.
3. Shoghi Effendi, *World Order*, p. 41.
4. ibid. pp. 41–2.
5. Bahá'u'lláh, *Tablets*, p. 167.
6. Bahá'í International Community, *Prosperity of Humankind*, p. 2.
7. Bahá'í International Community, *World Citizenship*, para. 5.

Chapter 8

1. 'Abdu'l-Bahá, *Promulgation*, pp. 165–6.
2. Seligman, *Authentic Happiness*, p. 59.
3. 'Abdu'l-Bahá, *Bahá'í World Faith*, p. 244.
4. Bahá'í International Community, *Prosperity of Humankind*, p. 21.
5. 'Abdu'l-Bahá, *Some Answered Questions*, p. 9.

Chapter 9

1. From a letter written on behalf of Shoghi Effendi to an individual, 19 November 1945, in *Lights of Guidance*, p. 550, no. 1869.

2. 'Abdu'l-Bahá, *Memorials of the Faithful*, p. 53.
3. 'Abdu'l-Bahá, in *Bahai Scriptures*, pp. 340–1.
4. Shoghi Effendi, *God Passes By*, p. 204.
5. Shoghi Effendi, *Promised Day is Come*, p. 113.
6. 'Abdu'l-Bahá, in *Bahá'í World Faith*, p. 281.
7. Drucker, *Unseen Revolution*.
8. 'Abdu'l-Bahá, *Foundations of World Unity*, p. 43.
9. Bahá'í International Community, *Bahá'u'lláh*, p. 32.
10. 'Abdu'l-Bahá, *Foundations of World Unity*, p. 43.
11. Bahá'í International Community, *Prosperity of Humankind*, p. 12.
12. 'Abdu'l-Bahá, *Some Answered Questions*, pp. 274–5.
13. The Scanlon Plan was developed from the innovative work of Joseph Scanlon during the 1940s and 1950s. Joe's experience as a steelworker and union leader during the Depression prompted him to conclude that a company's health, indeed its very survival, required a climate of cooperation rather than competition between labor and management. As a staff member of the United Steelworkers of America, he used his ideas to improve productivity thereby saving many organizations and jobs. Joe's work came to the attention of Dr Douglas McGregor at the Massachusetts Institute of Technology, where he was invited to join the faculty. Together, McGregor and Scanlon pioneered the concept of employee involvement. The early 'Scanlon Plans', as they were labeled by Joe's clients, included a monthly cash bonus to all employees when labor costs were reduced below historical base periods. So Scanlon not only pioneered employee involvement but was one of the early developers of 'gainsharing'. Unfortunately, Joe Scanlon's premature death in 1956 denied him the opportunity to fully realize the impact he had on world industry. It is a tribute to Scanlon's genius that interest in participative management and productivity 'gainsharing' have reached international proportions.
14. For information on ESOP plans see www.esopassociation.org
15. See the National Center for Employee Ownership (www.nceo.org/library) for several studies and details regarding ESOPs and other forms of employee ownership.
16. 'Abdu'l-Bahá, *Some Answered Questions*, p. 275.
17. ibid. pp. 275–6.
18. Needleman, *Money and the Meaning of Life*, p. 53.
19. Seligman, *Authentic Happiness*, p. 53.
20. 'Abdu'l-Bahá, *Foundations of World Unity*, p. 41.
21. ibid. p. 44.

Chapter 10

1. 'Abdu'l-Bahá, in *Bahá'í World Faith*, p. 377.
2. ibid. pp. 377–8.
3. 'Abdu'l-Bahá, *Bahá'í World Faith*, pp. 371–2.

Chapter 11

1. 'Abdu'l-Bahá, in *Bahá'í World Faith*, pp. 247–8.
2. Shoghi Effendi, *World Order*, p. 162.
3. ibid. p. 163. (Emphasis in the original.)
4. Bahá'u'lláh, *Kitáb-i-Aqdas*, para. 30.
5. 'Abdu'l-Bahá, quoted in Shoghi Effendi, *Bahá'í Administration*, pp. 21–2.
6. Collins, *Good to Great*.
7. Bahá'í International Community, *Prosperity of Humankind*, pp. 15–16.
8. ibid. p. 28.

Chapter 12

1. It is important to understand *productivity* as the ratio of output to input. In other words, if it requires one full day of labor to produce a bushel of corn, that is a measure of labor productivity – input to output. If the same one day of work can produce two bushels of corn, you have then doubled productivity and freed labor for other activities. Historically, there is a necessary and direct link between increased labor productivity in both agriculture and manufacturing and the number of years spent in education.
2. Bahá'u'lláh, *Tablets*, p. 90.
3. 'Abdu'l-Bahá, *Foundations of World Unity*, p. 37: 'The fundamental basis of the community is agriculture, tillage of the soil.'
4. Womack, Jones and Roos, *The Machine that Changed the World*.
5. Quinn, *Intelligent Enterprise*.
6. Bahá'í International Community, *Prosperity of Humankind*, p. 22.
7. Bahá'í International Community, *Prosperity of Humankind*, p. 21.
8. Senge, *Fifth Discipline*.
9. Bahá'í International Community, *Prosperity of Humankind*, pp. 25–6.

Chapter 13

1. Bahá'í International Community, *Prosperity of Humankind*, p. 18.
2. Tapscott, *Digital Economy*. p. xiv.
3. Bahá'í International Community, *Prosperity of Humankind*, p. 17.

4. 'Abdu'l-Bahá, *Promulgation*, p. 287.
5. Attributed to 'Abdu'l-Bahá, in *Divine Philosophy*, p. 82.
6. 'Abdu'l-Bahá, *Promulgation*, p. 170.
7. ibid. pp. 373–4.
8. See the *Journal of Organizational Behavior Management*.
9. Bahá'í International Community, *Prosperity of Humankind*, p. 18.

Chapter 14

1. 'Abdu'l-Bahá, *Paris Talks*, p. 157.
2. Abdu'l-Bahá, in *Bahá'í World Faith*, pp. 323–4.
3. ibid. p. 324.
4. 'Abdu'l-Bahá, *Secret of Divine Civilization*, pp. 96–7.
5. 'Abdu'l-Bahá, *Selections*, p. 132.
6. 'Abdu'l-Bahá, *Secret of Divine Civilization*, p. 84.
7. Bahá'u'lláh, *Gleanings*, p. 219.
8. 'Abdu'l-Bahá, *Selections*, pp. 132–3.
9. Letter of the Universal House of Justice to the Conference of the Continental Boards of Counsellors, 9 January 2001, p. 3.
10. Bahá'u'lláh, *Tablets*, p. 27.
11. 'Abdu'l-Bahá, *Paris Talks*, p. 153.

Chapter 15

1. Chappell, *The Soul of a Business*.
2. Reder, *75 Best Business Practices for Socially Responsible Companies*.
3. See Schonberger, *Building a Chain of Customers* and Womack, Jones and Roos, *The Machine that Changed the World*.
4. Tapscott, *Paradigm Shifts*.
5. Ashkenas, *The Boundaryless Organization*.
6. Davidow and Malone, *The Virtual Corporation*.
7. Bahá'í International Community, *Prosperity of Humankind*, p. 24.

Chapter 16

1. Bahá'u'lláh, *Summons*, p. 17.
2. Bahá'u'lláh, *Kitáb-i-Íqán*, p. 15.
3. Bahá'u'lláh, in *Bahai Scriptures*, pp. 6–7.
4. Bahá'í International Community, *Valuing Spirituality in Development*, pp. 17–18, 23–4. (Emphasis in the original.)
5. From a letter written on behalf of Shoghi Effendi to the National Spiritual Assembly of the United States and Canada, 30 August 1930, in *Compilation*, vol. 2, p. 54, no. 1389.
6. Letter of the Universal House of Justice to the National Spiritual

Assembly of the United States, 19 May 1994.

7. Bahá'í International Community, *Sustainable Communities in an Integrating World.*
8. Shoghi Effendi, *Bahá'í Administration*, p. 87.
9. The Universal House of Justice, *Individual Rights and Freedoms*, para. 18.
10. Greenleaf, *Servant As Leader*. Posted on www.greenleaf.org/leadership/servant-leadership/What-is-Servant-Leadership.html (accessed 1 September 2006). See www.greenleaf.org for further information about Servant Leadership (accessed 1 September 2006).
11. 'He was most generous, giving abundantly to the poor. None who came to Him were turned away. The doors of His house were open to all. He always had many guests. This unbounded generosity was conducive to greater astonishment from the fact that He sought neither position nor prominence. In commenting upon this His friends said He would become impoverished, for His expenses were many and His wealth becoming more and more limited. "Why is he not thinking of his own affairs?" they inquired of each other; but some who were wise declared, "This personage is connected with another world; he has something sublime within him that is not evident now; the day is coming when it will be manifested." In truth, the Blessed Perfection was a refuge for every weak one, a shelter for every fearing one, kind to every indigent one, lenient and loving to all creatures' ('Abdu'l-Bahá, *Promulgation*, pp. 25–6).
12. See www.tyco.com/livesite/Page/Tyco/Our+Commitment/Governance/Letter+from+Ed+Breen/ (accessed 1 September 2006).
13. Collins, *Good to Great*, pp. 12–13.
14. Final Report of the Scholars Commission on the Jefferson-Hemings Matter, 12 April 2001.
15. Shenk, 'Lincoln's Great Depression', *The Atlantic Monthly*, October 2005.
16. ibid.
17. ibid.
18. Quoted in ibid.
19. Quoted in ibid.
20. Perry, *Grant and Twain*, p. 7.
21. Toynbee, *Study of History*, vol. 11, p. 259.
22. Miller, *Barbarians to Bureaucrats.*
23. Wells, *Outline of History*, pp. 385–6.
24. Shoghi Effendi, *World Order*, p. 163. (Emphasis in the original.)
25. Shoghi Effendi, *Bahá'í Administration*, p. 19.
26. Bahá'u'lláh, quoted in Balyuzi, *'Abdu'l-Bahá*, p. 27.

27. 'Abdu'l-Bahá, *Paris Talks*, pp. 83–4.
28. ibid. pp. 72–3.
29. 'Abdu'l-Bahá, *Promulgation*, p. 299.
30. Ives, *Portals to Freedom*, pp. 242–3.
31. 'Abdu'l-Bahá, *Selections*, p. 115.

Appendix A

1. Genesis 22:2.
2. Genesis 22:12.
3. Declaration of Independence of the Thirteen Colonies, in Congress, July 4, 1776. (Emphasis added.)
4. Constitution of the United States of America.
5. Alexander Hamilton, 'The Farmer Refuted', in Syrett (ed.), *Papers of Alexander Hamilton.*
6. Paine, *Age of Reason.*
7. Washington, Letter to the Ministers, Elders, Deacons, and Members of the Reformed German Congregation of New York, 27 November 1783.
8. Letter of Thomas Jefferson to Mrs Samuel H. Smith, 6 August 1816.
9. Letter of Benjamin Franklin to Ezra Stiles, 9 March 1790.
10. Letter of Thomas Jefferson to John Adams, 22 August 1813.
11. Exodus 22:24.
12. Matthew 5:44.
13. The Universal House of Justice, *Individual Rights and Freedoms*, para. 21.
14. Shoghi Effendi, *World Order*, p. 25.
15. Bahá'u'lláh, *Hidden Words*, Arabic no. 22.
16. 'Abdu'l-Bahá, quoted in the Universal House of Justice, *Individual Rights and Freedoms*, para. 17.
17. ibid. para. 48.
18. Shoghi Effendi, quoted in ibid. para. 49.
19. Shoghi Effendi, *Bahá'í Administration*, pp. 63–4.

Appendix B

1. Wilson, *On Human Nature.*
2. Marasmus is common in developing countries where there is poor access to protein-rich food sources or where unsanitary water is associated with severe infant diarrhea and the resulting inability to absorb nutrients. The term 'marasmus' is also used as roughly equivalent to 'anaclitic depression', a term coined by René Spitz to refer to children who suffer from the early loss of a mother with-

out a suitable substitute. Thus marasmus has come to be associated with parental abuse or neglect that results in a failure to thrive.

3. Herzberg, *Work and the Nature of Man*.
4. McGregor, *The Human Side of Enterprise*.
5. Meyer, *Every Employee a Manager*.
6. Deming, *Out of the Crisis*.
7. Trist, Higgins, Murray and Pollock, *Organizational Choice*.
8. Womack, Jones and Roos, *The Machine that Changed the World*.
9. Womack and Jones, *Lean Thinking*.
10. Ohno and Mito, *Just-In-Time for Today and Tomorrow*.
11. Hammer and Champy, *Reeingineering the Corporation*.
12. Covey, *The 8th Habit*, p. 5.
13. ibid.

Appendix C

1. This compilation is not intended to be complete, only helpful. Many of the quotations apply to several values or business practices.
2. Bahá'u'lláh, *Gleanings*, p. 297.
3. Bahá'u'lláh, *Tablets*, pp. 22–3.
4. ibid. pp. 57–8.
5. Bahá'u'lláh, in *Compilation*, vol. 2, p. 334, no. 2037.
6. Bahá'u'lláh, in ibid. p. 335, no. 2046.
7. Abdu'l-Bahá, *Secret of Divine Civilization*, p. 16.
8. 'Abdu'l-Bahá, in *Compilation*, vol. 1, p. 4, no. 16.
9. 'Abdu'l-Bahá, ibid. vol. 2, p. 343, no. 2068.
10. 'Abdu'l-Bahá. quoted in Shoghi Effendi, *Advent of Divine Justice*, p. 26.
11. Bahá'í International Community, *Prosperity of Humankind*, p. 24.
12. From a letter written on behalf of Shoghi Effendi, in Bahá'u'lláh, *Kitáb-i-Aqdas*, Notes, no. 56, p. 192.
13. Bahá'u'lláh, *Kitáb-i-Aqdas*, Notes, no. 56, p. 192.
14. ibid. Notes, no. 53, pp. 190–1.
15. Bahá'u'lláh, *Gleanings*, p. 250.
16. Bahá'u'llah, *Hidden Words*, Arabic no. 2.
17. Bahá'u'lláh, *Kitáb-i-Aqdas*, para. 52.
18. Bahá'í International Community, *Prosperity of Humankind*, p. 9.
19. Bahá'u'lláh, *Gleanings*, p. 81.
20. ibid. p. 175.
21. ibid. pp. 218–19.
22. ibid. p. 235.
23. Bahá'u'lláh, *Tablets*, pp. 66–7.
24. 'Abdu'l-Bahá, *Some Answered Questions*, p. 266.

25. Bahá'u'lláh, *Tablets*, pp. 92–3.
26. Bahá'u'lláh, *Kitáb-i-Aqdas*, Questions and Answers, no. 99, p. 136.
27. The Universal House of Justice, in ibid. Notes no. 52, p. 190.
28. Bahá'í International Community, *Prosperity of Humankind*, p. 15.
29. ibid. pp. 15–16.
30. ibid. p. 28. (Emphasis added.)
31. ibid. p. 15. (Emphasis added.)
32. 'Abdu'l-Bahá, *Bahá'í World Faith*, p. 217.
33. ibid. p. 218.
34. ibid. pp. 244–5.
35. 'Abdu'l-Bahá, *Foundations of World Unity*, p. 14.
36. ibid. p. 67.
37. Bahá'í International Community, *Prosperity of Humankind*, pp. 6–7.
38. ibid. pp. 7–8.
39. Bahá'u'lláh, *Hidden Words*, Persian no. 50.
40. 'Abdu'l-Bahá, *Some Answered Questions*, pp. 273–5.
41. 'Abdu'l-Bahá, *Paris Talks*, pp. 151–4.
42. 'Abdu'l-Bahá, *Foundations of World Unity*, p. 41.
43. ibid. p. 40.
44. Shoghi Effendi, *World Order*, p. 163. (Emphasis in the original.)
45. The Universal House of Justice, *Promise of World Peace*, para. 34.
46. Shoghi Effendi, *World Order*, pp. 40–1.
47. Bahá'í International Community, *Prosperity of Humankind*, p. 17.
48. 'Abdu'l-Bahá, *Paris Talks*, pp. 162–3.
49. 'Abdu'l-Bahá, *Memorials of the Faithful*, p. 53.
50. Bahá'u'lláh, *Tablets*, p. 133.
51. 'Abdu'l-Bahá, *Foundations of World Unity*, p. 43.
52. Bahá'í International Community, *Bahá'u'lláh*, p. 32.
53. 'Abdu'l-Bahá, *Foundations of World Unity*, p. 43.
54. Bahá'í International Community, *Prosperity of Humankind*, p. 12.
55. 'Abdu'l-Bahá, *Some Answered Questions*, pp. 274–5.
56. 'Abdu'l-Bahá, p. 275.
57. ibid. pp. 275–6.
58. From a letter of the Universal House of Justice to the Bahá'ís of the United States, Riḍván 1984, in *Wider Horizon*, p. 27.
59. From a letter written on behalf of Shoghi Effendi, 25 June 1954, in *Light of Divine Guidance*, p. 216.
60. Office of Social and Economic Development, 'Some Guidelines for SED Projects'.
61. ibid.
62. Office of Social and Economic Development, 'Evolution of Institutional Capacity'.

63. Bahá'í International Community, *Prosperity of Humankind*, p. 22.
64. ibid. p. 18.
65. 'Abdu'l-Bahá, *Secret of Divine Civilization*, p. 39. (Emphasis added.)
66. 'Abdu'l-Bahá, *Foundations of World Unity*, p. 44.
67. Bahá'í International Community, *Prosperity of Humankind*, p. 21.
68. ibid. p. 18.
69. 'Abdu'l-Bahá, *Paris Talks*, p. 157.
70. 'Abdu'l-Bahá, in *Bahá'í World Faith*, pp. 323–4.
71. ibid. p. 324.
72. 'Abdu'l-Bahá, *Secret of Divine Civilization*, pp. 96–7.
73. ibid. p. 84.
74. 'Abdu'l-Bahá, *Selections*, p. 214.
75. Bahá'u'lláh, *Gleanings*, pp. 182–3.
76. Bahá'u'lláh, *Kitáb-i-Íqán*, p. 228.
77. Bahá'u'lláh, *Summons*, p. 17.
78. Bahá'u'lláh, *Kitáb-i-Íqán*, p. 15.
79. Bahá'u'lláh, in *Bahai Scriptures*, pp. 6–7.
80. From a letter of the Universal House of Justice to National Spiritual Assemblies, 10 October 1994.
81. ibid.
82. From a letter of the Universal House of Justice to National Spiritual Assemblies, Naw-Rúz 1974.
83. From a letter written on behalf of Shoghi Effendi to the National Spiritual Assembly of the United States and Canada, 30 August 1930, in *Compilation*, vol. 2, p. 54, no. 1389.
84. From a letter written on behalf of Shoghi Effendi, 5 July 1947, in ibid. p. 272, no. 1857.
85. From a letter written on behalf of Shoghi Effendi to an individual, 16 March 1941, in ibid. pp. 418–19, no. 1002.
86. Shoghi Effendi, *Citadel of Faith*, pp. 126–7 .
87. Bahá'í International Community, *Sustainable Communities in an Integrating World*.
88. Bahá'í International Community, *Valuing Spirituality in Development*, pp. 17–18, 23–4. (Emphasis in the original.)
89. ibid. pp. 23–4.
90. Letter of the Universal House of Justice to the National Spiritual Assembly of the United States, 19 May 1994.
91. ibid.
92. The Universal House of Justice, *Scholarship and Related Subjects*, 20 July 1997.

Index

About the Author

For the past 30 years Lawrence M. Miller has worked to improve the performance of organizations and the skills of their leaders. He began in our prisons. He redesigned a prison system by establishing the first free economy behind prison walls in which inmates learned by earning.

He has been consulting, writing and speaking about organization and culture since 1973. After ten years with another consulting firm, he formed his own firm, the Miller Howard Consulting Group, in 1983. In 1998 he sold this firm to Towers Perrin, an international human resource firm, and became a principal of that firm. In 1999 he left to focus on his interest in serving non-profit organizations. For the past seven years he has been consulting on a *pro bono* basis with non-profit organizations. He has now re-entered the consulting business.

Mr Miller and his firm were one of the early proponents of team-based management and worked with many clients to implement *team management* from the senior executive team to include every level and every employee in the organization.

The implementation of team management led to the realization that the whole system of the organization needed to be redesigned to create alignment so all systems, structures, skills, styles and symbols supported the same goals and culture. From this realization Mr Miller developed the process of *Whole System Architecture.* Among his consulting clients have been 3M, Corning, Shell Oil Company, Merck, Metropolitan Life, Chick-fil-A, Mack Trucks, the University of Miami and Landmark Communications.

Mr Miller is the author of six books, among them *Competing in the New Capitalism: How Individuals, Teams and Company are Creating the New Currency of Wealth; American Spirit: Visions of a New Corporate Culture*; and *Barbarians to Bureaucrats: Corporate Life Cycle Strategies.* He recently completed a book entitled *The Wisdom of One: How Winning Individuals, Teams and Companies Unite Energy and Effort.* He has appeared on the *Today Show* and CNN, has made numerous appearances on FNN and CNBC, has written for the *New York Times* and been the subject of a feature story in *Industry Week* magazine. Mr Miller now lives in Annapolis, Maryland, with his wife Carole and near his grown children Layli, Natasha and Langdon.

Mr Miller can be reached at LMMiller@lmmiller.com
www.managementmeditations.com (Blog)
www.lmmiller.com (Company Site)